The Fiascos: A Nonfiction Work of Literary Art

2024 Light Inc. A Division of Unknoen Tower
Entertainment

The Fiascos

A NON-FICTION WORK OF LITERARY ART

by Damian Forest Light

To Mike and all of the apparent suicidal and victims of the trade, on all the many levels. And to the victims of 9/11. And the kids at the auction, being led around like sheep without parents. Sweep away the luck to all partaking in that competition.

Table of Contents

The Fiascos

Part I

The Seaweed Goddess

She was destined to be punched in the face by her adversary. Everyone believed she was a stupid son of a bitch. Nobody liked her at all. And when they looked inside of themselves, they saw themselves laughing at her downfall. Not only that, but they also saw themselves aghast with disgust every time she walked in the room.

She smelled like shit and sweat and tears. It's going to be hard to hear. She only rinsed in the shower because every one of her enemies was someone who wasn't exactly like her and just accepted her for the Jewish black woman and black magician that she proudly was.

Her mother pretended to be Hassidic, was white, Jewish, and married a black fellow, who was nice enough. He had a son from a former marriage, and he was black. So, her sister, the girl who resented her black father for being black and fought incessantly with the mother who pretended to be Hassidic, and this cute little black girl baby, grew up into a Jew who didn't practice her religion but knew all about it and pretended to practice it.

And everything that was not kosher or catered to her preferences and tastes was labeled an old Babylonian. As if from ancient Babylon. She tried to be friends with the Tribe of Judah.

The hippies, the radicals, the potheads, those who believed in the Lord God, and those who emulated Bob Marley and Rastafarianism were of the tribe of Judah. However, even though it was 2003 she was working as a spy for the tribe of Israel.

She also reported those who saluted the tribe of Judah to the FBI, even for crimes they didn't commit. She smoked an eight of weed every five or six days and split the bag in half with somebody.

She wandered for years living with the hippies, reporting her adversaries to the FBI over and over, even about 9/11. She was on the hippie farm in Northern California when the planes struck the buildings, and everyone there hadn't seen a TV in weeks, never mind listened to an FM radio.

This was before the rise of cellular phones, and handheld internet devices. The place was 50 miles from a gas station and was high in the Siskiyou mountains, close to the Marble Mountain range and the only thing out there were wandering wild animals, the occasional pot farm, and some wandering hillibillies or Mexicans.

You might even see Bigfoot, but you would die or get killed first by something that disagreed with your meeting a Sasquatch.

She didn't know that people would talk about her down south near Arcata and that she got caught stealing pot while she was working as a pot trimmer. Just a bud or two here and there, from each stash she worked on.

She needed something to hit at the end of the night. So, she turned in a couple of people from Arcata, and a bunch of others for knowing Mohammed Atta and other people including Bin Laden, but the irony was that none of those people met Mohammed Atta, nor had they taken part in any kind of sentiment against America that would indicate they were terrorists, nor had they been schooled in Guerilla warfare, nor worshipped Allah as a Moslem, nor practiced Moslem eccentricities or known or practiced ideologies, and many of them had never even stepped into a Mosque or read for the Koran.

Yet, she told the FBI they were in on it. They had a direct hand in orchestrating 9/11.

She lied to about a dozen people or so on a payphone in Arcata, CA, just days after the attacks on the World Trade Center. She did this to get even for being rejected in high school by her peers. She said that she had it out for society, the media, and people from NYC because they were superficial and would never know anything about the wilderness, natural living, or her favorite state park, Harriman State Park, which was only 7 miles from Manhattan. And plenty of New Yorkers knew about it.

But she didn't know they knew and so, anyone who turned on her, or had lots of friends or was from NYC, she told the FBI, that they were friends with the hijackers from the plans and plots to strike down the Twin Towers and kill thousands of people on American soil.

She had remorse for its years later, in stories, but she never really made strides to fix the problems she had then created and the dominos she had dropped and set into motion to create a pattern of destruction in various corners of people's lives that would affect society in very many different and highly influential ways.

A buddy of hers, who thought they were buddies, reprimanded her for giggling at the rumor that people were jumping out of the windows of the World Trade Center that night after people were discussing what had happened.

As, there were no television or radio signals on the hippie farm and the electricity ran off a water-based mill, a windmill that sits in the water, cycles the water through a funnel, and creates electricity, there was little way of learning about the attacks. Still, people had learned about it and had arrived to spread information about it by word of mouth.

Just hours after the attacks had occurred and the towers had fallen, the people at the hippie farm were rising in the morning and smoking their grass casually while drinking coffee and there were thirty people there.

Waking up and casually greeting the morning when someone heard a neighbor from several miles down, the closest neighbor was five miles or so, and the neighbor told the CB that something was going on in NY.

First, she said that the Twin Towers had fallen, and that the Pentagon had been hit by a plane and was burning down. Everyone immediately thought the Wicked Witch brought itself down and let out a simultaneous cheer. However, when the person on the other end explained that people died and the planes were crashing with people in them and there were people in the buildings, then everyone got downcast and became sad.

The hippies thought that there was some kind of government coverup right there and that the government or some radicals had taken down the Twin Towers of the World Trade Center and that it was done classily, confidentially in the middle of the night when the buildings were empty.

However, there was a brief time when the crowd believed it was not only the government tearing the buildings down that made them cheer, but that the universe was playing its card and tearing down buildings of fear and terror that plagued many people, including those who lived near the buildings who live in fear that they would be attacked, as that was what was on the news and portrayed in society before 9/11.

Was that the government, the media, and the people suspected that there were going to be attacks on the buildings due to attempts that had previously been thwarted, intercepted, and noticed. There were many PSAs and news reports warning society that the World Trade

Center in NY was going to be attacked for decades, locally in media outlets such as newspapers, and television.

The same outlets the girl, known as Nuri Hillman-Harrigan, believed were talking into her mind her entire life and pretending to print her in the news because she heard voices and manipulated energy into magic and projected schizophrenia through her own experience and then tried to spell and force those voices into the lives of others creating her Voice to Skull technology.

She projected it through a meditation she stole from a book that was spiritualists' pleasure seeking and it gave her access to the magnetic and electro-magnetic energy fields of matter and material, the subtle energy that exists over matter as a resonance of molecular vibration.

She speaks into the molecular vibration of tables, chairs, walls, papers, poster boards, lamps, furniture, and automobiles, she projects energy through the people she meets listens to the voices in their heads combines their voices with her voices and trades them off through witchcraft.

She breaks the Sabbath and lies on the Passover, pretending that the plates are justly organized and blessed to her relatives who often visit for the holiday. They show up for days on end celebrating Passover wearing their Yakima, reading from the books, and practicing the cedar and everything has touched a piece of meat or a piece of unkosher dairy because someone broke their diet in the house.

The house is still kosher, with only one refrigerator and everyone eats vegetarian food and stores the milk in the fridge.

The Meat prepared for Passover is kept in a freezer in the basement and occasionally, there is a big party there and there is no kosher food because while they keep kosher by practicing vegetarian, they don't eat strictly kosher. And when Steve was alive, that is her old man, did he eat kosher? He was black as night and at that stuff, even with his suspenders and glasses.

The trouble was her brother was dead too. May he and Steve rest in peace, as her only living black relatives, she was alone now except for her sister. Her sister was a radical who lived in Sydney and moved around Chinatown and lived also in NYC, but she came home to Teaneck and visited with Randy and her lesbian friends in honor of graduating from college in NY and moving back home.

She wrote for the radical papers, did the travel thing into the hot foreign deserts, tried to become a comedian, and set herself apart by creating a personal brand. Her sister was an individual, but she still had it in for everyone else but herself and her family, so it was no matter that her diseased sibling had lied to the FBI about 9/11 and then later accused Steve, after he was dead of being a pedophile, even though she said, she had no memory of him abusing her.

Nor her brother; instead of mourning them she openly accused them with tears in her eyes of sexually molesting her when she was a small child only three or four years old, but she also said she had no memory of this event or series of events happening.

Now, you know, she does not think of anything but eating cheese and yogurt and gluten-free bread and that is her life. She says she is gluten-free, and she eats cheese from only a certain grade, and its real dairy and yogurt by the giant size and as much and as quickly as she can.

She just eats that stuff with gluten-free bread and gluten-free rice and pasta. And says she is gluten-free because gluten makes her tonsils swell up and she gets infected with some kind of swollen virus that makes her puff up.

But if she continues to shovel shit, she might just get some on her. Everyone must eat gluten-free bread but there is one brand she likes that risks the gluten, so she'll eat that brand.

And cooks Millet and Quinoa every night for months eats collard greens and brags about how much black people are not as sophisticated as her and that the white people are oppressors and indignant about their mistreatment of indigenous peoples.

She lied about her boyfriend to the FBI about 9/11. She said his friends visited a mosque when they were 15 years old, several years before, and some of them were Jews and some of them were black from NYC, she said they knew about the events beforehand and that they knew Mohammed Atta personally because they went to a mosque after school a few times and prayed with the Moslems.

She not only punches her dog but lets her Pitbull whom she rescued from African Americans who had it chained up in their front yard, because they should treat it better and not leave it chained up. The dog was a nice dog, exceptionally beautiful and playful however it toppled little kids, was a pit bull, and would jump on people it didn't know and climb all over small children. This she would allow, but if the dog misbehaved it got punched in the face or smacked or kicked. Nuri only uses toothpaste and deodorant that is Ayurvedic or made from rocks and minerals. This means her teeth fall out and her clothes stink.

She had the habit of using a dirty sock instead of a tampon. When she would see a drop of her blood on her cycle, she would ask for a sock, dirty or clean, and cut it and put it on her cootch. She used a wool sock with lots of hair and fibers. She had a huge disgusting pussing cist on her pussy that was like a yellow liquid boil mixed with red sores and blood. She used the socks anyway. She only wears what other people want to wear and destroys your military gear. She sports her corduroys long after the dawn of the 21 st Century.

She fucked her boyfriend in the middle of the night, every night, when he was asleep, drunk after work. He worked nights, would get a six pack, watch his favorite shows, and fall asleep to wake up in the afternoon and go back to work until later in the evening when he got home and did it again. After he fell out, she fucked him. She wouldn't talk to him all night when he was around. She only complained. He didn't know she really had an STD. She was complacent with that.

He didn't like her. She tried to touch him and jerk him off and his dick was so little she couldn't get it hard, and she stretched it to the point it almost disappeared. It was so skinny a slight touch from a knife, or a blade would cut your whole dick off. She was pissed because it was so tiny, and she stretched it like over a foot long and it was less than a centimeter thick. It was an extremely dangerous situation. He had no blood flow and just blood in there.

She was mad and he writhed on the floor grabbing his sack. Don't pull out a cock unless it knows it's ready to fuck and get down and plow down. Because it could end up the wrong end of the bargain. Don't pull that little fucker out. Ever.

Barely even still, she pulled her shit out on the road when she needed to piss. She dropped her pants right in the road when driving over and over and she got spittle, gravel, smog, pollution, rocks, and bugs crawling up her cootch giving her cists and making fun of her.

She thinks she's hard with Randy drooling and staring at her ass, and her plan to destroy with Shane and Patrick, Arthur, and Keith even against Keith. And Keith. And the other Keith. And Keith from TV. And Keith from White Power. And Keith the musician. And Keith from Black Power. And Keith from Japan. And Keith the fighter. Keith the monk. How many Keiths were there? Was one of them the platinum artist to be? Was one of them going to become a movie star?

Nori hated NYC, but she hated anyone who was brighter and smarter, and funnier and prettier than her, she said it. And she said she hated Tower Records and she sided with many conservative Democrats, who hated the sound of music. So much, that she cast a spell on Tower Records in February 2004, under the guise of a phone call prior to the meeting that D. Unknown M.C. of Brooklyn had in Staten Island that fateful night of 2004.

Prior to his meeting with Tower rights holders, she called him on the phone and demanded that she become a part of the meeting as a spectator, and that she wanted to destroy his contract and the music industry. She said on the phone that she had cast a spell to destroy Tower Records and hopes that they chose bankruptcy and that she was a part of a network of devil worshippers from Northern California and that she was going to destroy the music industry with a spell and with her own form of Babylonian religion, witchcraft, and mind control.

She lived on various farms and camps in Northern California, but within days, she would be outcasted and asked to leave each one and she would return each time, hoping to buy insignificant amounts of marijuana and ounces of psychedelic mushrooms. She would often roam around working for marijuana growers and show up on sites when only girls were allowed to trim and work the plants.

She showed up a couple of times with D. Unknown, whom she followed around a festival until she got him to ask her for a ride because he had ditched him a week earlier at the festival and that she knew about. So, as he was helping with cleanup, she and her boyfriend drove D. Unknown to Seattle, where the boyfriend ditched her, and Nori asked D. Unknown to follow her to Colorado for another festival.

When they got there, via hitchhiking because Dee had gotten his license revoked as well as his work and gun licenses and his passports and ability to obtain a student loan which left him to become a homeless artist. With nothing to do, he escorted and followed her to Colorado hitchhiking like she asked and then back with some LSD she found for them at a concert to Northern California where they went to a roundabout Hippie Farm once operated by a well well-known diner franchise in the U.S. and was now overrun with people who had no skills but were waiting patiently for the Armageddon and were content smoking leftover processed waterleafs instead of working to get some THC in their smoke.

However, hanging with her, the hippies didn't like him, and they all rubbed the wrong way. And hanging with her and being from the city and having a limited exposure to the region, despite his wilderness background, he was able to piss off some of the locals and people wondered why he was there.

So, he escorted the spy, informant known as Nori aka Seaweed Woman aka The Cist on the Clit Woman, she needed his help once more. They ventured to a Vipassana Meditation which is a 7-day silent Buddhist retreat. After 3 days, she wanted to leave, she couldn't hang with the nuts it takes to be quiet, be still and focus only on yourself. She was busy gathering information to give to the FBI about the illegal activities resulting in federal infractions that everyone was committing.

She also had her friends lure D. Unknown into a trap in Georgia. On her way she called the FBI again and told them where he was. They sent military followers to escort him around his jobsite and had him questioned by his superiors about his knowledge of 9/11 while his managers were scrutinized and interviewed by the FBI at Bank of America where he worked as a Credit Card Specialist.

He was transferred to inbound call centers and was soon after fired because the FBI wasn't getting any latest information.

So, D. Unknown packed his bags and left to pursue his music contract in NYC and within a year or so, he was proposed to by Tower Records from West Fourth Street and their Music Group with affiliations, despite them being white and Italian with Apollo Theater, where Paulie, who was working as D. Unknown's producer now, worked as a DJ and had many celebrity connections including Hillary Clinton and James Gandolfini.

How can I even say that about the Apollo Theater? It's true. So is the fact that D. Unknown was a well-known New York artist with a physical admiration network that was street based and not celebrity based. He was a part of several gangs and crews in NYC as a youth and this made perfect game for a person like Nori, who traded mix CDs to the FBI in exchange for immunity to her lying about 9/11 from a payphone.

Whereby she admitted to D. Unknown, that she had turned him into the FBI for no reason and she had accused several of his friends whom she had not met yet, by name to the FBI even they were youths who attended a Mosque prayer after school some 8 to ten years prior. Since they had broken a minor law to the FBI ordinance schedule, an infraction at best and fulfilled nothing besides prayer and sharing and fellowship for a short while.

Therefore, her complaint to the FBI could be seen as a racially based epithet against blacks and Muslims in general, that she feels she is immune from despite her physical attitudes.

Now while in Georgia, Nori had also besides trading the Hip Hop Mix CD she personally requested and Cassette Mix Tape she requested made for her from D. Unknown, while she traded this CD and Cassette to the feds she also found out the address to what was known as the Temple of Hip Hop and a place where rapper and culture progressive M.C. KRS-ONE was known to speak and operate. She also got tickets for the KRS-ONE concert in Atlanta.

She knew the directions to the Temple of Hip Hop from Athens without having a GPS or having any experience living in Georgia, she was visiting and tried to get D. Unknown to move in with her.

He vanished after realizing that she was taking him down and indeed. She later admitted to lying to the FBI and trying to destroy the work everyone was putting all their efforts into developing. She wanted to destroy the world.

She worshipped Enlil and liked the rest of them. She worshipped the Goddess known as Semiramis like her ancestors did. So, her name was Harrigan, and she believed that she was a part of the Illuminati because of her bloodline.

She believed that she had the right to destroy others on the earth and to control and steer and manipulate events and people and their loved ones and lives because she was acquainted with a corrupt form of witchcraft that she was only trying to figure out and she wanted to control the entire earth and become its center its queen its goddess and she was infected with poisonous elements that rot in her blood. She has a strange disease and hides on this farm, where several years ago, while she was trying to anchor a lizard demon known as a Chitahuri, some criminal kidnapped a young girl and chased authorities across the country to the farm where she was living.

Despite snakes in the garden and water snakes in the small pond, they choose to swim in, the hippies and Nori are interested in a specific kind of witchcraft.

One that could anchor demons and psychics and warlocks and dragons into the physical world by traveling through a dimension considered to be a kind of echelon, if you will, a universe or parallel multiverse kind dimension; a place considered to be of the demonic art of the fourth dimension.

She tries to operate this projected energy weapon with a directed intent of breaking and using broken energy in fields against people spying on their minds and ripping them apart with voices by tearing a thread in their minds.

She wants to bring the demons in so that they will try and kill the followers of Judah the followers of God and the Indigo Children and wipe out humanity. Every man and woman and binary for themselves. Destruction and chaos.

She decided to continue the shit of her ancestors. Even though she was a Harrigan, she tied herself to the Harriman's. A family of bankers from the early days of America, along with Carnegie and Rockefeller took over the world and started the industrial revolution during the 19th Century.

The Harriman's funded banks but they also funded the Railroad being built with Chinese labor and used the Harrigan's as surveyors and managerial leaders for the labor forces.

Nori believed that the Harrigan's were disowned for being slaves by the Harriman's and had to change their name because they were started by a slave or indebted part of the Harriman bloodline that got out of hand and were not eligible to become an heir.

The Harriman's also started the Oil trade and are rumored to have funded the 1950s CIA Mind Control and/or psychic experimental programs until they chose to sell them in the 1980s and 1990s to foreign governments and intelligence agencies, provided that CIA is kept apprised of any major developments within the patenting processes of psychic forces, manipulation, and technologies.

Finding a portal from a demonic dimension in a twisted meditation to do a spell that would trick the atmospheric space into giving power over to her was no simple task.

So, Nori set up a couple of black magic ceremony circles in Northern California and started by guising some of them as a community project for Solstice that would raise awareness of pagan peoples and traditions in the form of simple four direction ceremonies and worship of rocks, trees, and elements.

Then she would project and possess the elements within her meditation, fill the particles with her intentions and face and practice mind control as she physical placed her energy into the minds of her victims and tried to direct their subconscious processes, and attempted to tie people into each other.

She would steal and target people and those who could be subjected to her witchcraft. She wanted to open a portal between New Jersey, where Nuclear Energy and Pesticides run rampant, and Northern California where Pesticides and dangerous chemicals in the structures and skyscrapers run rampant.

So much so that the government mandates warnings on the side of the buildings that they are made with cancerous as well dangerous and even illness-causing materials. And there are sightings of ghosts and people running far away from the hippie farm where the cops and feds chased that suspect with the snakes in the pond and the cists on the hippies' balls.

And the stolen weed and the broken-down cars. And the beef they had with Humboldt.

By stealing weed and calling the FBI from Arcata about people from Arcata and Brooklyn and other parts of New York and California, while laughing at victims from 9/11 who were jumping out the window. Including D. Unknown's cousin who died and jumped to his death that day. Rest in peace.

And when D., who was with her that day on the farm, reprimanded her for laughing at the victims, she bragged of driving to Arcata and calling the FBI and lying about him and his friends, whom she had yet to meet. She giggled. He did wrong and lit that cheer when the government revealed that they took down the towers, but he thought the buildings were empty.

So, he started beating a drum and others followed. And when they heard that people died and that the United States was attacked, and that it was not done in the middle of the night and that it was not just the government doing renovations.

D. Unknown and many others prayed and gave thanks that they were alive and beat a war drum from then on in.

And Nori had a problem with it. She didn't like the government, or the people and she didn't like being on opposite sides of the FBI.

So, she admitted to calling them and lying to protect her own ass because she got yelled at for giggling long after everyone learned that it was terrorism.

And because D. Unknown reprimanded her, she went and called the FBI on him and told them he knew the terrorists.

And the FBI questioned his family, his friends and some of his employers and bosses were put under federal investigation.

Because D. Unknown, was also an undercover freelance journalist who could find any story he wanted. And as he prepared for the music industry, he took inventory of every action the hippies planned.

And every map they marked and every time they cited an infraction to compel the FBI to open investigations for no reason on homeless, rich and travelers. Nori then took an interest in D. Unknown' family.

And she started to work for some government that arranged for D. Unkown's legal dad, not his biological dad, and his uncle, a cousin of his and an imitation distant cousin, a person who is an imitation in life, is a phony and believes that real men work for the Sanitation Department.

His name is Arthur. King Arthur Homan. And Big Keith, screwed and had some sex with Arthur's cousin Teresa who was married to Big Keith's first cousin Terry O'Hanlon and even though they all pretended to be Irish together as they had their Klan thrown out of the motherland of Scotland.

Terry tried to have sex with Barbara, the mother of D. Unknown, who had a short-lived modeling career until she was absorbed and hexed by a cult in Hollywood. Without her career.

Now, since Terry had offered to have sex with Barbara and she refused, Big Keith who was engaged to old Barbara Jean, had sex with his cousin's wife, Teresa Homan. And Arthur Homan lived on the same block that Big Keith used to live on and grew up on. And they both worked together as NY Sanitation supervisors. For the city. None of this private shit.

They wanted a guarantee in the capital. They had salaries and they had what was considered gumshoe. Power to protect and investigate and write citations and tickets to anyone they wanted in the city.

Arthur's dad, Arthur Homan the Second, was a supervisor too. And Big Arthur taught Little Arthur everything about Sanitation. And big Arthur moved his family from Brooklyn, off 17 St. and into a house directly across the street from the Staten Island Dump, the biggest landfill on the eastern seaboard.

Big Keith Gilbride used to brag that it was the biggest mountain on the eastern seaboard. Propaganda and lies are all lie. Nurelle started a relationship with Big Keith and with Arthur and with Keith's brother Patrick and a guy named Shane who was later arrested for being not only a psychic but a psychic who was going to try and kill the president of the United States. And she was glad to fuck him.

So was Marsha. D. Unknown's ex-wife. She was involved with the same four guys. Big Keith, Patrick, Arthur Homan, and Shane.

She even went out on a date the day the kid was conceived, and the doctor confirmed that it was the same day that the kid was conceived. That day, she went on a date. D. Unknown approved of this because they had already broken up and had moved in with one another as roommates, were not romantic, were platonic and it was not the least bit sexual, as far he recollects. So, she went out on a date.

Marsha. After the kid was born and they got into a fight, Marsha scratched up Damian well and he took a scratch. And then they broke up.

And then she admitted to sleeping with those four guys in a gangbang, his relatives and friends from childhood and they agreed.

Everyone except Shane. Shane's parents vouched that it happened. And so did Arlene Flannery. And Big Keith again. And his mom. And Patrick again. And someone else, And in the dream world.

They all admitted it. They had sex with Marsha who had threatened D. Unknown to sign the marriage document or suffer broken bones and attend the marriage ceremony or get hurt and on and on.

The witnesses were hired and paid, the marriage certificate was dropped off on New Years Eve at 5 PM at the County Clerk office and not paid for. Just dropped off on the counter. And now she signed him up for Child Support.

And the same four guys went after Nuri. And they recruited her. And they had a proposition. They would give her access to an organization to spread her powers and she would have to forward all of her Jewish and African racist witchcraft so they could practice astral projection and take over the particles of everyone's mind and body and speak into their hearts and brains and hopes in order to hypnotize and take their lives over.

Take their wives, their money, their thoughts, their religion, their faith, and their dicks and cum too. They would take their dicks if they had to.

Now try to follow along. It gets complicated. They wanted to use Nori and Marsha to start a cult. So, Pat, Keith, and Gale who was Shane's mother (Shane was a momma's boy with a genetic disorder) started a cult using the power of Marsha's deep religion in New Age and Baptist Christianity and Nuri's Devil Worshipping and Judaism broken into pieces and gave these metaphorical powers to Jo Diorio who was a Gipsy psychic.

Her family was first-generation Italian from Naples and she read Tarot Cards and made her clothes using a sewing machine and curtains. And she anchored Voodoo for the group, and they took part in seances and ceremonies to control the minds of everyone in the world. By replacing the entertainment industry with the will of their astral projections.

Randy lives each day to meet with his girl of choice after work. A girl he knows for a while from high school that he still dates and since he is playful and egotistical and considers himself to get to drool on ass and drink beer, fix cars for his friends. Seems like a great guy but he believes Nuri is the Illuminati and he is allowed to mind control others. He mimics others in his mind and lives for his high school days, he steals your mind with his energy and replaces it with an empty space hoping to get you killed. A classic witchcraft movie.

Never mind he wanted to kill Keith too, and this was going to kill his son Keith aka Forest who was sleeping with Nori. Randy liked drooling on Nori's ass. She was his black chick friend from high school when she complained she had no friends, and no one liked her. But he gazes and stares at her ass, projects his mind to steal others' minds their physical testosterone, their physical remnant, he eats in others' personal and physical signatures and tries to take credit for their work because he helped their girlfriends with free work on her car.

He offers all the girls free mechanical work because he dates anyone he wants from his high school and still lives in Teaneck and practices witchcraft and lives in a town where people pretend, they are Hassidic Jews break the Law and proclaim to have the knowledge of Isiah and Moses and the blessings of Abraham in their left pocket, in their bonnets. And they plotted to kill with Richie, aka Jefferey aka Johnny Hernandez Jr., along with Johnny Hernandez Sr.

And as the world turned and flipped over just days after Tower Records had gone bankrupt. And now he got his adversary Damian a job there, as Damian was just another name for Little Keith, and it was aka Forest to these guys for some reason.

He didn't really go by Forest, but he started to when Nori came along, and she introduced him like that to

Randy. And Randy had an attitude and Forest could care less about it.

As Forest was also D. Unknown aka M.C. Seven to all of five people, he was approached for a contract with Tower Records in the summer of '03.

And it worked out that he wanted to work his deal with Tower. But Nori had witchcraft in mind. And the night of the meeting, it came true. Nori showed up from Northern California, they grabbed the wine that was in his hands and told him the contract was over.

This left D. Unknown looking for a new set of funds and activities and so Randy got him a job at Bennigan's. Richie was a DJ and Bartender there, and he and Forest kept it going. They were drinking and talking about music and DJ Forest got into making his own beats and music right after he lost his contract.

He would take those beats and go on over to Richie's house after work and they would make remixes of Eminem and combine the lyrics with some of the new beats that Forest D. Unknown had made.

And the world was wondering why this guy was so bent on working it out on a microphone. They hadn't even understood that that was their destiny. Then greed and corruption took down Tower Records just months and years after the fall of the old music stores and mall stores based in NYC. The Sam Goody and The Wiz, as well as any other store that was around including Circuit City.

All those stores precluded the economic collapse of 2008. In 2003, the stores started closing in the music industry and they kept on going, and through 2004, Tower declared bankruptcy. Then two years later they closed their stores. Just months later, the world experienced a recession and in early 2008, Virgin Atlantic swarmed the accountant with details of closing their record stores and by 2009, their stores were closed too, and the music industry was out of business.

While on the way to Los Angeles in 2006, D. Unknown had stopped in Ashland, Oregon in 2005 to finally get rid of his connection with Nori.

She was not pleased when he took off into the sunset in the summer of 2004 leaving her in Northern California as he hitchhiked to Colorado with a suitcase full of incense and soaps and notebooks he sold along with pencils and dirt weed.

He managed to eat each night selling stuff out of a suitcase and made it to Denver where he caught a bus and straggled back, in the summer of '04 in hopes of catching up with Richie and maybe getting even for teaming up with Randy and his pa and trying to smoke Big Keith, LK Damian's Old Man.

And they had little remorse, after all the guy projected himself into their minds through astral projection and voodoo and tried to destroy them with their inhibitions treating them to a systemic form of magic and induced schizophrenia.

Now they had their revenge when the agreement to end racism on behalf of the White People of New York City in 2004 arrived, and Big Keith had to make the decision if he would call black people names ever again.

To support this gang ordinance, which was signed at some point by many white gangs in the late seventies that they would drop their racism and mistreatment against blacks and eventually, in the years and decades ahead, sometime in 2004, the attitude that whites and blacks had to explore racial differences through hatred and various forms of isolated bigotry and a uniform sense of safety. And all the white people who lived through the seventies knew what the fuck was going on, and there was no way some kids born in the seventies and not taking part in the race ways, the race war preparation, were not going to get by without being forced into a depression or heavily manipulated schizophrenia. I mean, who were these kids to grow up getting along with other races in preparation for the big truce? And that they didn't expect.

The white people to end their racism. To end the bigoted conversations. It was signed in the late seventies between the races, as gangs across the U.S. that in the early part of the 21st Century, that the races would drop their gang tactics towards one another, stop cursing and raving about each other to the youth, and to others, and berating the other races for their inaction or inability to communicate with the other races effectively.

And until 2004, all the white people born before a certain date were to call the black people every incessant name they could think of, and to brag how much they hated blacks, to deter black people from taking over their lives or even attacking them on the streets.

And did they take that seriously? And until that very day these crackers let it in, they let it go and never stopped calling a darker-skinned person the name of all names and anyone of which they could think. And the Black people loved it. And in 2004, they all stopped it at once and the entire world blacked out into schizophrenia. The world was taken over by black magic, so the O'Hanlon's cold drops their racist jokes and demeaning comments towards others on the street. And Tower Records closed for good. And D. Unknown became Emcee D Unknoen and started Unknoen Tower Entertainment.

But prior to finding his way there which he did on his way to Los Angeles, he stopped in Jamaica to work on his album, after catching a ride from Denver. A bus with no funds for a few days didn't eat a thing on the way home from Denver to New York City. And he caught the E Train to his pad near JFK. In a mostly Black neighborhood, he was tried by his Haitian roommate who wanted chores done and sold weed but would not let the other tenant's smoke.

And D. knew that he had to work on his album and his cousins were Haitian, and this asshole would not let the cleaning and chores go.

Just because he got free money each month of a couple of G's for being an immigrant, a full-time job off the books, a free crib paid for by the State and an SSI check for being disabled, as well as over 300 bucks in food stamps, free cable TV, free bus passes, and this guy sells soap and bootleg CD's and DVD's. He knew the time getting free shit, but he still lived with a bunch of retards and hoodlums.

Recording that album, D. fell asleep at the studio and got tired of returning his CD burner and getting a new one every time he got his welfare check every two weeks for 85.00 USD. He was trying to make demos and was able to pull off a bunch of music on his own and pulled off a deal with Warner Music in late 2004 and early 2005. Things were going well. These guys from Whitney Houston's original management group tried to offer him a deal. He was moving on up again. Then it happened.

Nori called D. on the phone and demanded he come and visit her in Oregon. He refused. His landline was static filled with people on the other end interrupting his calls with crossed-over phone lines. And he could tell the government was just waiting for her to say something over the phone. So, he started refusing to hang out with her. And she let off a big cry for help.

She told him if he didn't come visit her, she would destroy his life, talk shit to his relatives and contact his kid and find his ex-wife and sleep with Big Keith and his brother Patrick and Shane. Shane was screaming at himself about brainwashing the president and Keith ever since he joined the military. He was a marine now, and his mother wanted him to deal with her cocaine. And find a new product. And smoke crack. She smoked crack. He had to smoke crack too. So, it was obvious.

To Oregon and then to Los Angeles. It was the perfect opportunity to take this album idea to the next level. Warner picked up the last demo, so we should just start on another one. Why not buy a music program and move to Oregon? Sounded like a good idea, because D. didn't like being manipulated or told off or blackmailed by Nori, who was like a smelly barracuda from the hippie farm that believed she was somehow made of iron because she was Jewish and made of Bronze because she dropped out of Brown Ivy University during her first semester. Woah, so radical of her. She joined Earth First and started developing federal files on the Tribe of Judah in Oregon and Northern California.

And she would go home to Teaneck see her few girlfriends and hang out with Randy and his girlfriend, and they would all drink and eat vegetarian Chinese Food. Which was Vegetarian food disguised as traditional Chinese American food, with General and Sesame and Sweet and Sour, etc. They even had vegetarian beef and broccoli. And she would reunite with her friends in Teaneck after spying in Nor-cal repeatedly on her enemies and those who were just innately suspicious of her and her motives. And no one noticed. She just kept on going with the FBI and calling them every few chances to report on people who didn't agree with her perspectives of debating and pretending to hold a government position.

That's why when she was at the hippie farm, she would only have them deliver processed water leaf, meaning after the pot was harvested from the plants and trimmed, instead of being sold as flower buds it was processed for wax and hash, all of the oils were diluted out of the leaves and instead of throwing the leaves out, because they were now useless, all of the crystals and THC was taken out with the oils.

The water leaf now processed and without THC was dropped off at the hippie farm so the hippies could smoke free pot. But the people dropping it off were endorsing the federal dilemma they had at the Hippie farm, which was no growing pot on the property because it was technically owned by the government and was given to the people in a land trust back in the 1920s. It had been a mining town and then became a hippie farm in the 1950s.

Some people lived there during the Vietnam War, and they went out and started a fast-food diner chain that stretched across the United States. However, none of that money went back into the farm. You know the one where Nori tore the wall down in 2004 and thought she saw maggots all in the walls, but they were termites eating the walls out? We told her it was maggots, and she went and started wiping down the thousands of critters with her hands and a sponge then because the cleaning of those walls was going to take days, she started cooking food, and serving it right in the middle of cooking, thinking that thousands of maggots were just flying around and being flung off the walls. Luckily, it was only termites. And D. ran with a few packs of Top Ramen and hid himself in a cabin for the week until all the maggots were gone.

So, in 2005, it took extortion to get D. to go back to her and meet her in Oregon. But he looked forward to it. And when he got there, they got him drunk and gave him attention as friends and let him find a job. He was a cook now at a place that was often visited despite its remote location by the New York Times. And they grew to appreciate D. Unknoen's food. They often asked for him to cook their meals and he impressed them with his innovation on menu items.

But the people there were weird. Despite the cops constantly pulling D. over for not walking in the right place or for going to a social gathering to make friends, going to church, or going out to a party, the person Nori turned out to be devastatingly destructive. As she was friends not only with a Republican radical infiltrator who moonlighted as an eco-terrorist, now she had been living with a couple of people. One of them was bragging about eating feces on Asparagus cooked and baked in an oven and the other bragged of being an ex nazi and a previously active skinhead who was beating the hell out of people with a baseball bat. Nice since Nori was half Black and half Hassidic Jew. In Brooklyn, we would call this a Kyke.

So, it didn't stop there. As it was Oregon, the idea that people would behave as if they had respect for others sometimes seemed out of the question. Besides meeting Neale Donald Walshe on the streets of Ashland, D. worked at this restaurant now. Working on his album at night or before work, he put things together on the dinner shift at the Plaza at one of the fancy restaurants each night. And the place was closed on Tuesday. So, there was a dinner on Sunday and all weekend. They served grilled fish and some weird version of a falafel. However, they also had steaks and some interesting West Coast-style pasta.

One of the kinds of pasta, besides a traditional Fettucine Alfredo or Penne with Vodka Sauce, was known as a Kitchen Guys Pasta. And this was some of the best food in town by far, because of several factors. But the real secret was the fresh Tarragon.

Now, Tarragon in a jar or dried and canned and put in a bag is just a seasoning. But Tarragon fresh and off the stem, fires the food like nothing anyone ever tasted. And this was coupled with fresh chopped tomatoes as the sauce and pan-fried, a little vodka, white wine, some garlic, basil, shallots, parsley, penne pasta or fettuccine, some Italian Sausage, Chorizo, Shrimp, and Scallops. This is a Kitchen Guys Pasta. The other dish on the menu was the Fettucine with Scallops and Saffron. The Saffron goes for about 30.00 a gram. Those were good foods.

And the Times would order a Grilled Citrus Salmon from D. And he squeezed fresh limes and lemons and doused them with lemon juice and grilled those fish steaks to perfection. And the boss noticed. Just like the boss at Bennigan's the year before. Every time Nori introduced him to a job the boss did the same thing.

Now the boss at Bennigan's Bob squeezed D. on his pecker as they were walking into the walk-in refrigerator and D. started working as a cook instead of just in front of the house, working as a waiter. And he thought Bennigan's was haunted, with Phoenician ghosts and cockroaches. But his boss was just treating him like a homosexual. And the boss at Quinz, in Ashland, did something similar. Except he did it to everybody. He did it to every cook there and to the cooks upstairs at the other restaurant the owner had taken over just recently.

He would demand you have sex with him. And he would ask people to have sex with him. He would walk down the line, this guy Ian, and he would brag of grabbing a server' boobs and grabbing all the cook's butts and if they bent over to pick up food they dropped, he would walk up right behind and attempt to stick his cock up their ass. And start humping. And he asked the dishwashers to sleep with him and he asked D. to fuck him in the cooler. And when D. said no to him and his offers, they got into a fight. And the guy Ian threatened to call the cops.

And if D. fought back after being assaulted, they would call the cops to press charges and give D. time. And in that part of Oregon, it's six years for self-defense if you get into a fight.

They discourage fighting and if one fights back, they are more liable for damages than one who is ignorant enough to start a fight. If one does not defend themselves in the town of Ashland Oregon, they can press charges on one who assaults them and give them some months, even a year or two in prison.

But if one fights back and swings and commits a battery in a manner of self-defense, they cannot press immediate charges on the assaulter and they get 6 years in prison for assault and battery.

That is six years not months, years, and many times it may be without probation. And the cops there work for Nori. And the place is loaded with movie stars and eighties heartthrobs.

Driving around the mountains of Southern Oregon. And that means that Ian had to get away with just a few confrontations. But people threatened to take care of him and jump him if they ever met him.

Some guys from down the way and over the bridge near Ashland would take care of him if he ever revealed who and what he was. He hated Ashland. He said it.

And there was nowhere to go. The clubs there had shut down. They shut them down in 2005 and it was the saddest night ever.

One night they shut down one club and it never reopened and the next Saturday they shut down an hour early and it was the last night anyone was allowed to party there. Now the towns were desolate. Nothing to do but go swimming, and that was far-fetched. That anyone would make it to the river just to go swimming.

The King of New York

The fatter the wallet the more in tune one could become with their path of development. Be it from training, resources, gear, maintenance, sociability, needs assessment, prolonged vacation, and desire led to maximization of potential and experience, the more someone made in terms of financial success and physical matter of wealth and abundance kept the fluidity of professionalism and utilization of resources. It maintains personal and professional business if there is capital.

But you know before the witch destroying Tower Records, there was no woman on the planet or girl, who would even ask D. Unknown for money or even think twice that he didn't have anything. He had a date and a companion and a constant flow of women who wanted nothing more from him than to be a friend and to treat him occasionally like a distant lover and a stranger met to perfection and seduced.

Or he would somehow seduce them. And the witch resented this. That he dated. And he dated Jews no less. Hundreds of them. He said no to over 500 women. Prior to him being possessed by the witch and released into the Entertainment industry. He said yes to over 500 as well. And to these, they all kissed him. With their tongues. And he dated 500 of his choice. Before getting a deal or entering the entertainment industry, he had some women refuse to date him and he even got a few complaints, but he asked for redemption and said no to the wrong women. They resented it.

This married woman one night lured him into her bedroom started kissing him and demanded he take her on her bed at once. He refused. Her husband had just left to go to the store. He was satisfied he had made the right choice as he was only scheduled to be gone for a few moments.

The woman demanded he take her. He refused to. She told him that he was making the wrong move and that if he refused her, he would suffer and never be with another woman again. He still refused. The woman cursed him. Her husband returned shortly after. They were still in the bedroom discussing his punishment. She said she didn't care. The spell didn't work, it couldn't go through.

Weeks later, it happened again. This time it was almost uncanny, and he thought the spell might have gone through this time. This time. It couldn't have. Then, weeks later, the situation repeated, and boom, he has been on a decline ever since and most of his living life. He has been so single that people make fun of him. He was supposed to rag out and make music and steal the show, but he became a hermit.

In 1996, right after graduating high school he went back for the last day of classes and a buddy of his who was on the goofy side but they were never really good friends, Roy the DJ who won a competition at Albany the following year at Albany State and met KRS One on stage, he lent Damian LK a set of books, one of them The Protocols of Zion, he was reading from Behold a Pale Horse, by William Cooper.

He was reading the book that falls while attending Brooklyn College and he was announcing the traffic and weather on the radio when he was invited in later on by a nighttime DJ. He went on and was looking through the book which included chapters on UFO sightings in the Navy Intelligence files and units the book had other stuff in it like propaganda files and abduction stories by aliens, but it had an outline that the Illuminati, the secret cult that controls the world, follow as precept and as admitted most elite Zionists, in the texts. It didn't help that it was at the dawn of the Internet, and the clientele was single people in their 20s, because the radio show was on a Brooklyn Access Station on TV and it played the radio of the school, and it was mostly students and alumni that listened as well as people who stayed home and found nothing on TV.

So, this guy in his late twenties and early thirties or whatever calls in after Damian thinks it's a comedy and is talking about the Illuminati and the changes heralded through the statement of the digital music industry and the internet as a whole, as well as the revelation of technology and the changes due int eh overall style of authoritative government, with the dawn of Guliani era police forces and the institution of a republic in the mind of states as well as the legalization of marijuana, all influenced the mental revolution that Damian started proclaiming. The phones lit up within seconds of him speaking and people immediately got thrown out of the air talking about revolution. Humiliated, he ran off and forgot to return to the radio station, especially since the DJ started fucking the other traffic lady. It got awkward.

Well, Roy a different party DJ had given him the text, and it was ironic that everyone who heard him talking about it assumed it was technically labeled as an anti-Semitic text being that it eluded to the rulership of Jews at the top of a pyramidal society; however the text was given to him by Roy who later returned to Israel and when he got back to the U.S. as a Hassidic practitioner of Judaism and is still a DJ who partakes fully as a worshipping Jew. He does mostly bar mitzvahs, as a joke, I guess.

The text the Protocols of Zion contains hundreds of pages on how to correctly manipulate society according to the picture of an operating most elite and they are often attributed to the plan of the Jews to take over the world, however, this version of the text outlines the difference in the usage between as a Jew and as a Zionist, for it is meant to be propaganda as leadership in action.

The next years were plagued by personal issues and conflicts with Marsha, his wife, and Nori.

Shortly after he experienced his freedom and got rid of Nori in late 2005 and moved to LA and Southern California in early 2006, D. was set to make it big. The record stores had closed and all of their recording studios along with them, shut down first, he was just getting over making an appearance in a movie entitled "Conversations with God" which was based on the life of the author of the books written of the same title by Neale Donald Walshe, the author that D. Unknown Forest met with on the street and this was not the first time they had a communication, but that will hold off for now.

This was 2006 and the movie had just been filmed. The two of them had met in the town where the film had been made before the film was produced. And D. was ready to move to Los Angeles and distribute the latest music on which he was working. He had recorded at Freeman Studios and at the house of a DJ who had a microphone and booth set up in his bedroom. So, the artist was ready to distribute his instruments and EP that he created which is an Extended Play Single. It had 5 songs on it or so and is shorter than an album.

The first song, entitled 'Winter's Cold' was about a guy and a kid who were homeless, each one not clearly defined as one another or different people merging in a time jump, it didn't matter. This homeless person has trouble living on the street and sees a life raft in a life skill but must make it all or nothing to survive. The story looks upon the struggle of homeless males who have lost their place and their adulthood in life, their ideology of self-esteem and are seeking to make a turnaround in life. The character in the song remembers a life that is better and remembers and sees through the eyes of a child who sleeps homeless in the cold on the street each night.

Then there was a song entitled "Blazed Bodyguards" which was all about a personality turning and exchanging their life of safety and sanity for a life of celebrity status whereby they are influenced by modifying their experience by deterring from the stresses of fame and fortune by getting drunk and needing to get a bodyguard to protect them.

Other songs included the artist chilling at a Soda Shop and hoping to get rubies and precious jewels for his date. Another tale teaches of using a microphone in an ancient battle of knights and through the angle of King Arthur and the knights of the Round Table.

And if Damian even writes about King Arthur, the psychic inside Arthur Homan rings up and he tunes in using a wire tube made of psychic prana and looks into the third eye of the author and he haunts D. Unknown because he is jealous of him. D. Unknown didn't become a sanitation worker and Arthur was very pissed off. Even his cousin Leigh, her father was a Sanitation worker. And her husband even.

His incredibly good friend he also a Sanitation Worker. And Leigh knew Rocco aka Forest aka D. Unknown. Anyway, some of the songs were written in honor of the actual King Arthur and Arthur Homan had a liquid drone in his mind he would bug and follow D. Unknown around and possess him in a schizophrenia. So, Damian aka Rocco would go around and scream at the wall and scream at Arthur and sing and write his songs. And this continued for months. And Arthur called Damian on the phone.

This was after Damian called his brother on the phone to say hello. And Arthur was demanding to know why.

Now, they hadn't spoken in years and now he wanted to know why he was talking to his brother who had left. And became a flaming motherfucker who would fuck you up the ass in a heartbeat. Not that he would take your cock he would, but he got off on fucking guys up the ass without hesitation. And no one could say or prove he ever took one himself. So, Damian called the fucker on the phone.

Arthur returns the call instead. 'What do you want? He's not around. D returns "Suck me off, Arthur. I heard your brother was fucking dudes up the ass in a tent at the Boy Scout camp." Because he was. And they loved it. He was a good instructor that kid, he could teach a Paul Bunyon and a Cub scout to light a fire and cook a hot dog like a rare breed.

But as he got older, he was fired for fucking some guy up his ass and even though the guy liked it, they were both barred from the place. Never to reign in a kosher summer camp, ever again. And neither one of them was a Jew, by the way.

So, he promised to put Arthur in a movie if he let him dye his hair and make him into a leather jacket wearing movie extra. Arthur agreed. Then the guy got married to a hot blonde and Arthur dressed her up to look like Forest's mom. Because he wanted to bend her over after she flirted with him when Forest and Arthur snuck out of camp that summer and went back to Brooklyn for the weekend. They stopped by the mom's place, and she hooked it up with twenty bucks.

Now, she flirted occasionally, and it was no big deal because Forest got in with a couple of guy's moms and they let him know they would just give him some pussy if he ever got them alone. Even though it was close, he never did. So, he never thought about it. But Arthur never let it go. And anyway, his pops cheated with a Homan and left his mom to cheat, and they broke up. So, he never had a real father and for that, he blamed a Homan. Arthur.

The one who bragged not only about sleeping with his mom, but Arthur bragged about sleeping with Marsha, the jet-black weightlifter body builder from Seattle, a black warlock supremacist, someone known as a n____ who targeted D. for no reason and tried to ambush him with marriage, prison, and a lifetime of child support. But D. got away because Marsha ignorantly told the judge that she had a gangbang with Arthur and Shane and Big Keith and Patrick the day that Jacob was conceived. And that Forest was not the father.

So, they could not legally take down the obligation, but they took down the criminal warrant and the trespass of not paying, alleviated some of the back payment requirements and coerced him to pay the child support for a kid that was not his. He paid it. Even though he was homeless and had to go back to school, he paid for it.

Now, this is significant because Patrick, who was Big Keith's brother and Little Keith aka Forest aka Damian aka D. Unknown, was his nephew. Patrick had humiliated Little Keith by initiating an attempted molestation of Forest. Now, this sounds heinous. It was. But in 2005 they had become adults about things and over the years they had become friends throughout Forest's childhood. Despite Patrick meeting him for the first time at 7 years old and attempting to get a hand job from the poor guy, with the sanctification of Big Keith and their father Francis T. Gilbride. Francis had the outline for the cult they were going to build.

And Patrick was the messenger. Now, when Forest was just a tyke and moved in with Big Keith and Francis, his mother was traded through coke use to several locations where she eventually joined a group of cultists in their recovery from narcotics and started dating one of the cult members. And the Gilbrides, the legal parents of Damian, were also setting up their own cults and spreading interaction throughout Windsor Terrace. A small neighborhood in NYC.

When Patrick arrived to meet with Little Keith and Big and Frank, Big Keith and Frank asked Little Keith to give Patrick a hand job. Now Little Keith refused and there was a problem. Because little Keith was tired of Frank and Keith asking for such favors.

He told them every time and even in the beginning of their meeting that he would do no such thing. Now, later as time went by, Frank and Patrick, who had initially refused to receive even if Little Keith offered, but then would fold and say "Alright. If he wants to. I guess he can." After a couple of minutes of "No, I don't feel comfortable. It's okay. No, please. I'm not interested. Please don't ask that.' They would act like he was ducking them and offer their kid up like it was nothing.

Then Damian decided to get a knife going. And Big Keith would take Damian to the store where his mother worked and let him see her for a couple of minutes. And she would have to ignore them, but she would talk to them. And then she was dating some guy, he was best friends with Big Keith's other cousin in Queens. She didn't know that. Did he know that? And the cult she was with was sacrificing dogs and going to the Narcotics Recovery Center and the meetings they had there. So, it was customary for Big Keith to try and kiss Damian on the lips at the store behind his mother's back and make the kid squirm, writhe, and hate. Live through the hate and the rage, this guy kissing him. And Big Keith pushed him around. Gave him Charlie horses and punched him in the leg. Called him a chump. Tried to wrestle.

All this was okay, but when they got home from the store and wanted to kiss on the cheeks over and over and hug and get some lips kissed like he was the other's girlfriend. Little Damian decided to get himself one of the steak-cutting knives from the kitchen drawers and put it in his pocket.

And when Keith came in for kisses which he did in seconds, Little Forest Rocco threatened to slice him in the face and stab him up his stomach, and he wanted to cut him in the balls. For asking for so many fucking hand jobs. Like some fucking pervert. And that's how it started.

It was a nuisance. It seemed like it would never end. He never got raped and he never gave them a hand job. But it went on like that for a couple of years. And every time Patrick came over to visit, and it went down for a while, Little Keith would tell and warn them and hide behind the TV with a knife in his hands. 'If you come near me, I'll stab you. I cut you in the dick. I'll cut your stomach." And Frank wondered why Little Keith hated him. It was because he came home drunk every night, passed through my room, left the door wide open, turned on the light and the big metal fan he had since he was a kid in 1946, lit up a Salem cigarette and turned on the radio to listen to 1010 AM News all night long at a very loud volume.

With all those fucking typewriters in the background! Fuck you! And you tried to get the kid fucking raped several times. And Arlene the trader reprimanded him. They were not happy that a kid was with some pedophiles.

And where was his mother?

Dining with some fucking cult, doing cocaine and praying to a master on a lake hoping to whip out their dicks after sacrificing a dog and taking a cucumber in their arse. I don't know what is worse, the past or the future.

So, despite the past with Patrick, Damian was ready to move on. Then Nori possesses Damian with her witchcraft and tries to get him into a relationship. She confesses her love for him in 2004 and then all the atrocities she committed talking to the FBI and all that.

Damian refuses her love, and she possesses him in a schizophrenia which turns out to be a part of a cult plan, a process to organize a coup to get Damian to become some kind of cultist, and a prophet for the end of the world. He refuses and after he is approached with this kind of crazy set of conversations with Nurelle who confesses to trying to impress the Harriman's and control the world with witchcraft, he seeks the help of his uncle. Patrick sets him up with a medical psyche program in Jamaica and Damian goes there in 2004. He leaves for Oregon in 2005.

He ditches Nuri in late 2005 and moves into an apartment out there in Ashland in case she has another fit and tries to lure him back as soon as he leaves. He sees her several months later as he is leaving town, and they spend one last night together and that is the last time they ever see one another specifically.

However, she went on to have a relationship with Patrick and they had phone sex, and she did so with Big Keith, who cheated on his wife with his sister-in-law Josephine the Gipsy. Big Keith started threatening Forest and Little Keith took it for a while and later retaliated and Big Keith never threatened him again. But they went back and forth for several years. Now the story gets interesting from here. Because Frank died when Damian was getting under contract with Tower Records in December of 2003. Aside from being a NYC Transit Subway Engineer, Frank was also a conspiracy theorist. And he had filtered a plan utilizing their family's resources that would enable them to take over the world.

And Randy plotted with Richie aka Jeffrey and Johnny Sr. to kill Big Keith and his whole entirety with two kids now and his wife Angela who recently died a few years ago, after forcing everyone to become a psychic from the astral realm through a voodoo mind control, she died of an aneurism.

But in the early part of the 21st Century, Randy tried to pull off a bystander manipulation, whereby he projected himself through a threat against Keith and tried to force his way into the groin and life of D. and take all of his mind and life away by sinking his teeth into his energy and drinking from his life force, through a psychic, like a gay tunnel that drunk cum into Randy's energy and then Randy's girlfriends will try to fuck the energy that Randy steals.

Because he knew that Damian was popular since he was known to be in the biggest gang in NYC during the 90's and was a leader.

Even though he was considered a white guy, most of his schoolmates were Jewish. So, he was often considered white, because he was not a Jew, and not full-blooded Italian, Spanish, Black European, or Russian. The Jews only wreck with full blood.

And Damian had an influencer in his life who was a full-blooded Native American, who owned property in NYC and in various spots across the map including New England. This guy married Forest's grandmother who was a nurse in an elderly home, and she worked and together she raised Little Keith's mom, and his uncle and they had a new daughter. Now Joanna, Keith's grandmother was also married to a full-blooded Italian guy named Romeo. And Joanna had grown up outside of Tombstone, Arizona, and was brought back to NYC later in life as she moved along with most of her family to their farm outside the town of Sierra Vista, and nearby Tombstone and the surrounding areas of southern Arizona.

Later, the family had to move back to NYC obviously because of the heat and the lack of resources.

There were no stores in their town, and they had to make do traveling and risk getting their provision and groceries and moving through the scorpion-littered desert in the middle of the spring and the summer. While they were able to get ice cream in town, they didn't live in town.

So, leaving whatever relatives had come by the family of Lucas moved back towards the bright lights of NYC and they found lives and finished school up there. Some months and years later, the pack of Lucas started getting married and having their kids and when Star Wars was released the entire family changed the pronunciation of their name to Lucas pronounced Lou-Cash, and they said they were Polish.

And everyone started going by the name Romeo, even though by the 1980s Joanna and the guy Romeo had divorced as he had split on them and my mother and uncle, and Damian's grandmother got married to a full-blooded Native American named Dennis. They had Patricia, who grew up to work for Homeland Security, marry the director of Homeland in the facility, and go on medical leave for twenty years. She is a half-blood Native.

And that did that family for a while. But complications came when Dennis stopped drinking and went on a binge with his new wife. And he broke up with Joanna and the 1980's evolved.

But, to go back to the 1970s, when Frank and his wife Patricia O'Hanlon, not Patricia Lucas Romeo were ready to send their kids to high school and their kids started dating around the neighborhood of Windsor Terrace, but what was still borderline Park Slope back then. There was a huge voting scandal and a cultural division that brought the neighborhoods to a head. And well get to that in a few minutes.

While Joanna had a daughter named Barbara back in the early 1960s who was going to school and was practicing becoming a model, she liked to drink and smoke pot with her friends, and one of her friends was Theresa

Homan, who later married Terrence O'Hanlon they had a couple of kids or did they?

Because Big Keith was Terrence aka Terry's first cousin by blood and friend started hanging out with them. After raging for months as a heartthrob, he started seducing Barbara and after they had a relationship and were talking about getting married, Keith slept with Theresa aka T., and they kept it quiet, but Barbara found out.

And Terry got pissed. And the group broke up. Keith went away to the Navy after surviving as a dropout gang member who survived a couple of high schools only to drop out permanently later in his freshman year and remain without a GED. And he liked to get drunk. Theresa had Jennifer and Barbara had Keith. And when Keith was born a month after Jennifer, everyone wondered who Keith's father was, but they assumed it was Keith.

But everyone knew after Big Keith returned from going AWOL and getting caught, he married Barbara, a few months later he was getting a divorce and hanging out with Theresa on the sly, without Barbara knowing it. When Little Keith was growing up half a block away from Theresa and Jennifer and their new daughter Stacy, who was a year younger than the other two, Big Keith would stop by and see them but never under any circumstances stop by and see Little Keith who lived a half block from Jennifer and four blocks from Big Keith and his family as they moved to a second-floor apartment on Sherman St. in Windsor Terrace. Under the parish of Holy Name. Where Big Keith and Patrick and their sister Karen, Barbara, and Phil, all got beat up by nuns.

They were dragged around by their ears and slapped and thrown in closets the entire time they went to school. All Little Keith's friends were molested and complained of having sex with the teacher's aides and assistants. And what mayhem. Even the Boy Scouts couldn't keep it in their pants. It was an utter fiasco.

It was now the 1980's and the world was changing. Big Keith was about to get his first car, a giant white Plymouth and he wanted a big Cadillac. The music was ripe, Little Keith was listening to Aerosmith and following Hulk Hogan, waiting for a real rock album to drop.

He had devoured Billy Joel's albums and Michael Jackson as well as the Beatles and he was primed to scratch up a new Run DMC record, just waiting for cassettes to outlast what were known as little Single LPs. Those were the greatest, something like Mohammed Ali, dancing around the ring, they would come in solely just to impress you and teach you to dance around the room. Those were considered better than toys.

And Little Keith loved to have toys. And music. Because it made him feel like reality was above him every day where he was left alone to stare at the wall or cry without any supervision or care from his mother. Barbara got addicted to drugs and even though she threw out her second husband once Little Keith cried and asked for help while he was being beaten and whipped with a belt, she rarely helped when he didn't ask for help and just cried. So, Little Keith grew to resent his mother even though she took him to the park every day with Theresa and her family. With no sign of Big Keith, Theresa got to meet him every day after he got off work and Terry took off. Leaving his kids behind.

No one knew what was going on with Terry and Little Keith still didn't get it. That the guy who was banging on the door and ringing the bell on a Saturday screaming at his mother up the steps was supposed to be respected.

The first time it happened, he let it go and let them yell at each other. The second time he started moving around and noticing they were yelling up and down the stairs in the building where Barbara lived, and Joanna and Dennis lived downstairs.

Dennis and Little Keith were getting to know one another, as Dennis had assumed responsibility of raising some of Keith and lifting his mind to understand and to learn and to have some kind of parental influence.

Shortly after that, on a Saturday, Big was standing at the door screaming at Barbara Jean and Little Keith asked "Hey, why are you yelling at my mother?" And the two of them stopped and looked at him. "This is your father," Barbara said. And Keith looked over at Big Keith who was looking at him and Big Keith said, "I'm your dad.' And Little Keith didn't believe it. He was disappointed and regretted asking who that person was at once.

Randy is jerking off thinking about Little Keith during the 1990's. Word hits about some crazy guy who is supposed to become a professional entertainer in nearby Brooklyn, who is only writing poetry, but has a gang prophecy about him.

Damian was about to enter the world where people were talking about him for many reasons.

In the 1980's Barbara not only joined a cult and disappeared but she and her sister did a photo shoot where the photo featuring Barbara and cut-out Patricia from the package, was featured on a hair and make-up profile, put on a box and label and was one of the first hair dye boxes to be distributed to every store in the world that could sell hair dye, for over 15 years, well into the 1990's. So, Barbara had her face on a popular hair product that was replaced by an entire hair dye industry.

When Barbara was in the box, she was the only model in every color of the dye, and it didn't matter which color the dye was it all had the same photo and the same color hair in the photo, it was dirty rose blonde, and it covered the model's left eye, and the box was very popular. It was sold on the shelves around the world that sold hair dye, it was one of the only kinds they had. It was a woman's based make up company.

So, this created a permanent division between Barbara and her sister and leaving Keith behind permanently with no supervision left a rift that could not be mended.

Little Keith Damian was left in the house on the second floor by himself, with mice, for a few days at a time. Now mind you, when it comes down to it, Barbara was angry she was losing her career and dropped out of school and had to lose hanging out with her friends and her friends had guys who supported their baby momma. And Barbara started bringing those guys around with their kids and sleeping with her friends' husbands and then everyone didn't get along.

They did for a while, but Barbara wound up disappearing. She took off for a while and left Damian to look at the wall and the door waiting for her to come back. So, the kid got his water and made cereal for a couple of days while he stood at the door and watched for his mother. After crying for hours on end, his aunt came up and found him alone. She took him downstairs, and he began sleeping at Dennis and Joanna's place.

When Dennis left, he made it clear he was selling the place. And Keith couldn't get by without his mother for registration at school. Big Keith began to take a more active role in the life of Little Guy. And he brought him over to his house after they met just before kindergarten graduation.

But after that summer, Barbara started taking off, and even though Frank and Patricia, Big Keith and Patrick, and Karen's mother had taken the kid to Disney World, they were planning something and had some bad intentions up their sleeve.

It wasn't long after they got rid of Barbara's second husband and Barbara mysteriously disappeared after the return from Disney and a camping trip where they taught Little Keith to drive while he was only 6 years old, and he also learned about cooking, ordering out, and Cable TV.

They brought him downstairs and bought him toys and games because his aunt only played with Barbie dolls. So, Little Keith developed a He-Man collection and various other toys including WWE wrestlers and GI JOE and he collected Garbage Pail Kids, Comic Books, and Baseball Cards and Stuffed Animals which, he infected with ants by storing peanut butter sandwiches beneath the radiator. But he was allowed to collect this stuff, as he was allowed to fight his mom's boyfriend's kids and punch them in the face, which he often did, or kick them in the stomach or cock.

And he often would get them into headlocks. And he started fighting often. He was known and laughed at for drinking a beer in just a few minutes, and often opted to only drink half of it to remain responsible.

He also hunted down joints that people smoked and put out in ashtrays, at the age of 3, and this behavior carried on until he was about 8.

For three years, his parents were able to intercept him from finding joints and smoking them from the ashtray and he did not inhale weed between the ages of 6 years old and 13 years old, where with time he was beaten badly several times and sought protection from a well-known gang and to gain their trust he voluntarily offered to smoke some of their weed and he was smoking blunts on the handball courts behind Junior High School 51, where the Brooklyn Dodgers played before the Polo Grounds were built at that playground.

The school in Park Slope was well known for its cultural integration and Special Education omission and its magnet program. The school had a remedial class, but it was also a magnet school in Park Slope which was a dangerous area during that time.

There were lots of kids from High Schools traveling through there and the High Schools that it had were mostly Public Schools that were some of the worst gang-related and territorial schools in the borough.

Damian was destined to be caught up going to John Jay a big gang school the following year, but his grades were good enough to make the minimum score for Edward R. Murrow and he was admitted to that school after attending both the remedial 6th grade and entering the magnet program for the 7th grade, getting in trouble for writing graffiti and entering the program for the 8th grade, getting beat for writing graffiti and seeking help by playing handball and telling jokes and smoking some pot on the courtside.

People began noticing Little Keith, who had a mole on his cheek, was well known for cracking up teachers and students alike, was a class clown, wore cologne, lived with his dad, and got decent grades.

Besides being a rowdy student, he was also an exceptionally good student. And he behaved in a way that appealed to his classmates and people talked about him and knew who he was.

Lots of girls said they heard rumors about him and would send friends and messengers to ask him out on dates and to screw around. Counting on his fingers he could say in his life he guaranteed went on 500 dates, said yes to 500 relationships, said no to 500 women and girls, and messed around with over 1000 females. By the time he was in college.

He was the King Solomon of High School. Girls of every background would approach him and immediately start kissing him after a short while he made lots of friends, could roll a blunt and he smoked weed every day in high school.

Even though he got accepted to a good school and went to class he was still the only person in the school who was invited to become a member of these exclusive gangs that were reserved normally for hardcore artists, as well as vigilantes, and was dominated by nationalities that were considered the most dangerous and fearful of the time. Keith was sought after by these gangs because of distinct reasons, some of which were mystical.

Now while most of the school was kids who were nonpracticing Jews and there were lots of Italians there, it had a small Spanish population and a bigger Black and African population.

There were kids there that were grunge white kids, and they all stayed together in the courtyard where they would smoke cigarettes and talk about skating and Green Day.

Because of this the leaders of the crews, would send messengers that would fit in with the environment but were mostly Spanish kids who were delivering messages. And they would find Damian aka Little Keith and tell him that there were people who were appearing to the shaman, people appearing to him in the future that would protect themselves through a form of psychic; a physical transference trying the world in its iniquity and the psychics were people playing with the minds of others by dabbling in electromagnetic meditations, knowledge of the esoteric, visualization and they were talking through the wind and they were fierce.

They were witches of the highest caliber, and they were going to start a war with Little Keith.

They thought he was a prophet, a messiah figure of some sort, but no, the cult wanted him to become a messiah, and the voices, the visions told of the cult and of Hollywood and his family who was trying now to take over the world.

The shaman was having trouble deciphering and when some of the people found out the shaman were having visions, they could not invoke a new sense of wonder about Little Keith, Barbara's son. When the big directors had inquired about Barbara and found out she left her kid and was wandering around doing drugs and the cult was active.

Big Keith and his family were starting a cult. And in the 1970's Johnny Hernandez Sr. heard of this cult, the Gilbrides using CIA technology to create psychics and it was driving him crazy.

So, rumors went all around about Keith the prophet, whose family was operating a CIA psychic mind control to talk into the minds and hearts of all humanity, to destroy and break down their enemies and seize the minds of everyone in the environments of their astral projections. And it sounded crazy, and Johnny Hernandez believed it and so did others for no reason, they were hearing about Frank Gilbride and his black magic and his kids who were pedophiles and no one knew what they were, only that they had access to magic and could hypnotize their friends without them knowing it.

And they were raising Little Keith and Barbara was on the run.

Things got complicated when the CIA mind control program started anchoring various opinions regarding people who could see the future and believed that Little Keith was going to save the world.

So, some of the doctors who hypnotized Keith when he was four years old for his eye treatments, were in there with this CIA psychic, following Little Keith around from the inside the space, through an astral projection. One like the one his family would model to take over the world with a cult.

Now, in 2004, it became time to release the cult and for the whites to initiate their psychic on humanity while fulfilling their agreement amongst gangs, to drop the hatred towards other races and when that deadline kicked in, Nori and Randy and Jeffery decided they would threaten Big

Keith and attempt to wipe out his entire family in the middle of the night while they were sleeping and attempting to kill them for being racist and being psychic.

But these guys are punks and brats from the suburbs. Brainwashed to think they are rich or important enough to kill for no reason. They were pretending that even though Big Keith and Frank wanted to control the world and take over the minds of everyone that they didn't do it yet, and they didn't have a real beef, so Richie and Randy and Nori teamed up with Big Keith and Patrick and started a cult, that was initiated with Little Keith's original wife Marsha and the two black women lent a psychic power they used to grab the space in clairvoyance and brought a mind control down on humanity through witchcraft.

Sounds sick, doesn't it?

Well, let's not jump ahead of the game, in the end it is all going to make sense because the cult actually deals drugs through the government, worships Phoenician gods, practices molestation, operates in the financial and education and religious sectors of society, sells and trades children using school buses and public holidays as a foundation-ary principle, has had members arrested for trying to kill the president, deals drugs outside the White House, and has planned to kill as many as 30,000 people at once using drugs and genocide. They utilize voodoo and astral projection to control the minds of those they choose to target. This story does not end here. It keeps going.

So, when the CIA read the future about this family taking over the drug trade in Washington DC and Philadelphia in the 21st Century as well as the potential for chaos and calamity under their wing, they sent word to witch doctors, shamans and seers and there was chaos in the spiritual worlds. Now, graffiti artists all over NYC were hearing about a rumor of this 12-year-old who was destined to make it in show business, become a rapper, and was a prophet, who was writing graffiti, had no legitimate real family but had a big foster family, and was a boy scout who was targeted by graffiti artists the people who were hearing the voices about Damian aka Little Keith and having dreams about him were pissed off.

The wind was talking to them about him. And telling them his business. And they were seeing visions of him and hearing about his future. One of the graffiti artists was one of the biggest in NYC during the early 1990s and he wanted to know why he was receiving information and having visions of Little Keith. And he asked a Shaman, a psychic, and a prophet why he had visions of this person. He had people now watching Little Keith and attempting to initiate and even beat him because of the repeated visions and dreams of him.

And the shaman, the prophet, and the psychic all repeated the same information. That this person would help save the world. And was destined to work a little bit with celebrities and was hiding from these other people in show business and there were cults sacrificing dogs and looking for his mother. And there were lots of reasons why Keith was important, and he needed protection.

The graffiti artist asked why he needs so much protection and why does he have to have visions. Well, it was not easy to answer. But the foster family would be recruited to run a drug trade, a trafficking ring and kill the president by the government and asked to start a cult that potentially could recruit a few hundred thousand people and it was formed to create mind control and generate insignificant amounts of capital.

The New Age metaphysics specifically would give a few people lots of power and lots of control over the government and everyone would fall for it. The catch was that the cult would try to hire Little Keith to serve as a public prophet and Messiah figure for the coming age and it would be commercialized and involve the worshipping of

UFOs and experimental spacecraft. As D. Unknown was known to refuse this offer and learn all about the program, he was also assigned to expose it, but everyone is scared to help.

Randy runs into the bathroom to jerk off because he is drunk, and the government is watching his dick. He thinks about Russ Collimore because Nori told him to. Russ promised the right of Marsha, the astral projection to all people to Keith's brown pot that he gave him for 100.00 and Shane was so envious because it was good and cheap. But it was brown weed. Old. Years old. You do not know. And The girls know Randy is stalked now by the government he must feel the energy in his dick and swing when he gets drunk, and it feels like he is getting a blow job.

But he just closes his eyes and pretends everyone wants to watch him moan and watch him swim in his energy and orgasm and he is a dude who is drunk and feels energy on his dick and that is his life. Free mechanics and free projections to the King of New York.

Every minute Randy projects his face through the particles in space and bites down and moans and tries to pull cosmic energy from the special surrounding the placebo, the demon of the air, the leftovers in the atmosphere, squeeze it together and it makes a juice and you can put your face it in and steal people's minds and drink and project and breath and steal it and put it on your cock and that is the hen that Randy wants to fill with Turkey. He needs it. He is like a rooster and the atmosphere is like a henhouse.

That turkey is a freak. And he is not letting go of the ho, he wants the earth's mother to suck his dick and worship him. He wants the breath of every man he meets because he needs a cock up his ass as much as he needs to feel powerful by killing Big Keith. By smoking that pole. That smoking that rift. And Keith needs to be careful because he smokes crack. Not Little Keith but the Big Keith guy.

And Shane feared and was jealous of Russ Collimore. Shane was ready to make deliveries, but he had to go through the military first. And Keith was moving with his record contract and his father started that new family we all heard about. Little Keith quit his job at the pharmacy in 1997, where he illegally filled prescriptions and ran the place including its returns, inventory, and storefront.

He managed the shipments and stocking of not only storefront products but of pharmaceuticals. And he worked there from the time they decided to initiate him into the Violators and the Decepticons. As not only one of the crews each only active, white-skinned members, but one of the only members of his school. And people came from all over, usually only during school hours or afterward, to tell him that the shaman and the seers had seen a brazen future for the poor orphan and that he was to be protected by these gangs.

So, they advised him to do his work to satisfy as a gang member if he wanted as much as he wanted, even to commit criminal behavior, but the crew was not to inform him about non-criminal behavior. Meaning they did not endorse openly any sort of crime but him being an upstanding member of the crew, earning his rights through work and artistry and creativity and hard work.

Damian Keith was an up-and-coming Eagle Scout and exemplified the organization fully in that he was an active pioneering instructor and remained steady in his development and leadership training and his training in camping and teaching orienteering and pioneering.

He taught Hassidic Jews and kids from the ghetto who had never been away from home how to build a shelter, cut down a tree, use a knife correctly, use a saw and axe correctly, fire a range rifle, and a shotgun, start fires in a camp, cook, clean up, run an obstacle course, tie knots, read a compass, build a shelter and pack a backpack.

They also had hikes and various games including swimming games. And everyone knows Black people can't swim and these kids from Harlem and the Bronx loved it. The kids were great and Little Keith had his job in the pharmacy during the school year at high school and during the summer he taught camp and ran the staff of the camp.

He did a lot of their training. He trained on the weekends and ran volunteer events. He did all kinds of backpacking and leadership training seminars and participated.

He ran conclaves and programmed events and ran service events where places in the wilderness received cleaning and litter removal for further areas of conservation awareness campaigns. And the service continued to progress throughout high school and his status increased as a leader and a dominator.

He was also regarded as a poet and a very rambunctious yet mature individual. He smoked cigarettes, wore cologne, changed his clothes, worked for his resources, earned capital, and had a suitable time.

When he was graduating from high school, he became friends with a Jewish guy named Gabriel. And they rubbed the wrong way. Gabe would not smoke pot but would trip people out as they were smoking pot and tell them wild stories, he created right on the spot about Vietnam and he would change his voice and pretend he was a crazy veteran. And for a young guy smoking pot this was hard to deal with, so people did not always have a good relationship with Gabe, and he was annoying and smart.

But he started smoking weed and eventually, he invited a few people over to hang out with a girl and she looked a lot like Drew Barrymore. And it was at a person who claimed to be Janet Reno's sister, and she wanted a bag of weed.

So, Mike Gabe and Rocco aka Damian went over to their place and dropped off a big bag of Purple Haze. They were looking specifically for Keith and Damian showed up. Gabe had mentioned that they asked specifically for Keith to show up and Big Keith and Angela were somehow aware of the party.

They turned off a curfew that ended normally at 10:30 or 11 and they were interested in him staying out late. He returned early when everyone announced that they had shown up with their uncomfortable. And everyone took off within a couple of hours. A few weeks later, they invited Keith back with Gabe but not Mike and within an hour Gabe was itching to leave. Keith freaked out and said, 'Let's get the fuck out of here." They finished their joint and left. They were asking for him years later. Who the fuck were these people?

Then it occurred to him. That he did not need to get into any details. He could figure it out.

In the late 1990's Little Keith got screwed over by Pat and Big Keith and Shane and Arthur with Marsha and his kid and then again with Nuri who threatened to track down Jacob and ruin his life. And after he dropped Nuri in Oregon, recorded his little EP single, and was on the verge of greatness ready to go back to Warner in NYC, he got a call from Uncle Patrick.

The Ed Jones representative had a government check that he was holding onto as beneficiary, as LK had signed that over to his address when he took off for Oregon. He had signed up for some SSI and received a federal clearance because of his experiences as a depressing seizure victim.

He bummed the doctor out with his experiences of losing his family to a cult and his seizure and his dad and mom even though they were enemies, and they came back into his life for a minute, they told him to fuck off because Damian had a seizure at camp. And a few years later after

all was said and done and he was on his way to nowhere
but the backwoods of Oregon and back home to NYC, for
his contract when they gave him a little disability and
medical payments. No, no way.

Pat had the check and LK told him to round it up
and put it in a bank. Pat put it in an account that did not
have a bank in Oregon. So, he had to wire the money to
LK. And he did not send him a debit card. So, he was
sending the rent and paying bills from his credit report and
gave him 150.00 every other week for groceries. And he
did not have any spending money at all, and he was not
happy with the situation, as he had 10,000.00$ in his
account. But could not access it.

So, he got a roommate in Los Angeles and asked for
a bus ticket. When he got there Patrick refused to pay rent
for the roommate and offered to either put him up in a
homeless shelter or in a hotel of Patrick's choice. Keith lost
his room and his hopes of becoming an actor were crushed
for a while as he was thrown into the streets after a doctor
came with a van to pick him up from the hotel and bring
him to a house in South Central, where Patrick was
supposed to wire the money for the rent in the dormitory
style room.

The dorm held lots of people from the local area.
The money didn't arrive, and Pat was called on the phone
by LK who asked him to wire 100.00$ for expenses which
he did within minutes LK took a cab right away to a storage
facility, opened a locker and caught a bus out of town into
Arizona, where he had moved in the late 1990's after his
seizure.

He took off with guys from the camp who taught
high adventure and set up in Tempe, AZ. There he met ex
model Marsha Swoopes Robins, and she was this horny old
black lady that was like an aerobics instructor, and
everyone had a boner for her, white or black, old, or young,
man or woman, she was filled with finesse and pizazz, but

she later had Jacob and realized that she had a problem. She worked formerly for the Boy Scouts of America and told people she liked to dance with little boys and have boyfriends who were under the age of 18.

LK was about 19 when he met her and her former boyfriend, was about the same age, who worked at a different camp than LK did, they worked in Arizona. LK and his people worked at TMR, and the camp was in Monticello, NY.

LK worked at the Kunatah camp which had an address in Narrowsburg, but LK had family close by and worked for the Hassidic at the camp, and eventually worked High Adventure because the people that taught mountain climbing, rappelling and canoeing they didn't have a base and stayed in cabins at camp Kunatah, and LK was the HNIC there, which means the Head N*** In Charge, of Kunatah even though he was under 18,

LK oversaw all the inspections that the camp received including its health and safety requirements and its cleanliness and he made sure that the staff not only got along with sociability and doing chores and each other, but they got along with the leaders of the camps and campers and the staff was well-liked and appreciated.

The camp was spotless, there were no accidents, there were no fights, there were lots of people interested in learning about Nature and Ecology, as well as Science, Swimming, Sports, and Games, and lots of people had the opportunity to study chair and basket making, as well as learn how to do lashes and splice and fuse ropes for equipment and safety and training. And there were hundreds and hundreds of kids at a time each week, during the summer. And LK ran the show. The guys who ran the place were clowns.

The place was not going to get far enough even though they had good people there were not good people running it. And they were lazy, selfish, and superficial and did not do their work and their inspections and they were just trying to get over and get off on some kids. They were just trying to get over it. And LK knew that and steered clear. He eventually got into it with these guys and moved far away out west after he was sabotaged and had a seizure. He ran off and was at odds with these guys.

The guys who ran the council started running the camp. It was early on that LK took over and ran his showboat camp and everyone loved it. He built the campfires twice a week, which consisted of two six-foot logged bonfires at a waterfront location and then had to have water on hand to put them out. Not only that, but he also had to build that campfire program from scratch and get volunteers to put on the campfire with him.

Every one of the staff people would sing their own song or give a cheer and have a skit or play in front of everyone with scripts, nothing was to be improvised because of Youth Protection Guidelines that prevented anything obscene or questionable to be played during the campfire.

And occasionally LK would put something rash in the program and would take a reprimand. But he was great at following the formats of campfire programming and putting on the schedule. He was also M.C of most of the campfires and had to sing his songs with everyone participating in the whole camp in front of everyone, clapping and giving cheers, running skits and participating in giving the announcements and putting out the fire and clearing out the stands and picking up the litter and making sure all of the smoke was white and the coals were out of the fire furnace places so that there would not be a forest fire, and this was done at night.

And people loved his fires. And they loved his presence at camp. It made him feel whole. And then back to school. And to the pharmacy ordering and delivering pharmaceuticals as a kid and running the store.

His trainer at the pharmacy taught him well, how to correctly take an entire bag of products, once a week, whatever you wanted from the shelves, how to order your products and bill them to the store, and how to take a quantity of money from the cash register.

This was Alex the Russian who ran as weekend manager. And when he took off a year or so later, LK took over as weekend manager and ran the training. And the only one allowed to steal was the little Chinese girl, everyone else including his friends whom he had worked there, had gotten into trouble.

He was destined to destroy this energy that ate at him, this tube of tuning into him, this internal ideology that he was responsible for everything, that he was at the center of the universe, that he could be the nucleus of the righteousness and the spinning of the earth all over on its axis, the nucleus of consciousness, people gave it to him. The youth seemed lost to him as if they surrendered everything to him.

He was blessed as a psychic and was not a schizophrenic in the world, they tried to endorse to him, those that attempted to mastermind the cult, and it was working he was cleverly become schizophrenic and was still gaining popularity as a clairvoyant.

People thought of him as the Quetzalcoatl of modern times, the prophet here to set the world straight before the beast ravaged the earth and the messiah known as God would bring about the Book of Revelation and everything would be on the supernatural level of the New Testament, fulfilling all the ancient traditions of religion, satisfying the need for a Jewish Messiah, and the second coming was dawning the end of the world.

And everyone worshipped the Age of Aquarius, holding on to the screaming and moaning of the song.

The world was dawned anew.

He dreamed incessantly of the world where he finally caught up to them dealing crack to other people outside the White House and to find out for curiosity's sake, who was responsible for giving him the territory. It was interesting because before Tower Music Groups closed out the Tower Records locations all over the world, they thought about signing the artist known as D. Unknown.

And D. had given the benefit of the doubt that the Strasberg weren't crack dealers, the Flannery family wasn't selling kids on school buses during Easter and Christmas, and the Gilbrides weren't responsible for including themselves in the lives of thousands of people they were trying to kill with hippie Kool-Aid at a New Age propaganda festival. But there was the complication, that every time Damian and the Strassberg aka the Strasser were together, they either ventured to honestly get to know one another or they got into a fight.

And Damian took the lead.

It was not too much of a fight, but a few times at least, the party and the auction would be underway with all kinds of legit individuals and regular people wandering through the thing, and LK would see Shane there and challenge him to a fight, outside. Shane would walk out, and Damian would throw a punch. Then another. Shane would be terrified in his face, he would cringe; his mind would freeze up and you could see the scared cat look looming all over his face. Then Damian would scare it, yell at him, and tell him to start a swing. And to swing back. And again. Eventually, the guy Shane would swing back a little and Keith scuffed him up a bit. But nothing bad. And Shane ran away a lot.

But it didn't stop Patrick from starting a relationship with Nori having phone sex with her and telling her all about his plan to take over the planet and kill loads of people at the New Age farm, which was only slightly different from the Hippie farm she set up in Northern California in Yreka.

And they were going to poison thousands of people at once who had paid to study metaphysics with over three thousand of their parent's dollars. And this was just the enrollment fee. There was housing and food and clothing and materials for learning and the staff and all the electricity and mortgage and inspections and land ownership and taxes and overhead. And someone would have to pay off the cops.

This is adding up. I do not know if the Gilbrides and the Strasser have counted the costs and made the observations needed to make a decision that would benefit anyone, including themselves. These guys have some nerve. And they repeatedly called Damian on the phone and offered to threaten him.

They said they could threaten him for not delivering that crack cocaine. He needed to go by Gale's house and deliver the crack back to Big Keith who would smoke it. And in Big Keith's version, he had two of them, one of the times LK was to light up or face persecution, and the second time he asked LK to pick up his bag from Gale, no one was hitting that son of a bitch but him and his old lady. And the third time it was just him hitting it. And LK had to get his own and do some in front of him.

BK called LK on the phone and demanded he do this several times, even though LK was on the West Coast and BK was back in NY. When LK said he was not contributing to the delinquency of an ignorant thug, BK called him names and threatened him.

This happened for a while. Big Keith would call LK on the phone and demand he answer for not being a good son and not being there when big needed him. So Big K needed to be the center of attention and accused LK of being a schizophrenic and being out to get him.

And BK demanded that LK listen to his mental health problems, to which he complained of schizophrenia and depression often to LK, because he said, he had tampered with Voo doo and was hearing the voices of spirits and psychics, causing him to become a schizophrenic.

Then, at other times, he would call LK on the phone and demand he listen to stories about his dreams and visions and cast his fear and anger onto others. He would even start fights with strangers while in front of LK and leave Damian to defend innocent people behind their backs and people he had never met before, causing substantial amounts of stress and anxiety. Big Keith continued throughout LK's life persisting in harassing him for physical affection, kisses on the cheek and lips, and hugs for no reason.

This made LK extremely uncomfortable often and Big Keith would respond by making LK the object of jokes to strangers and in public. LK would respond by kicking BK in the leg, punching him in the Charlie horse on his arm and leg, and throwing BK onto the ground after giving him noogies in his head and driving knuckles across Big Keith's face and skull.

He was a slave driver. He took over the Cub Scouts when LK was moving on to the regular Boy Scouts and LK joined later. He had been trying to join for years but BK would not let him make new friends or leave the block without knowing people around. But he did not want him to spend time together at the church. So, BK, knowing what was wrong with Holy Name where they had the Cub Scout meetings and were still accused of abusing his kid, was good with other kids. It is not that he could be trusted, because he couldn't but he could be trusted at times in his life. And everyone in his family knew this.

They knew he could be trusted at this point in his life when LK was getting older, and BK was there as the assistant cub master when LK joined. And then When LK went on to become a Webelos Scout which is a level in the Cub Scouts when the kid is old enough to smoke cigarettes and look at porno and wants to hang out with older kids and do fun stuff in the wilderness instead of doing household chores, arts, and crafts. So, after a year or so LK moved on to the regular scouts and was still sought after by gangs and holy people from distant lands.

LK had previously been nicknamed Bubba by his aunt and mom's family, but he eventually just got fat and they called him Keith and Bubba, but his mom's family faded as Barbara disappeared for longer.

The guys at the Scout Center in the church, then it was an old basement room in the school and the rectory of the church but later the fanatics remodeled it and turned it officially into the Scout Center. That is where they held these Webelos meetings and LK used to make fun of the name. Webelos was like him saying the system is hoping you say 'We blow, we blow, we blow, our scouting leaders' and everyone there was a Catholic school kid except for the kids in his class who had been recruited and the one left back cop 21 Jump Street type, the crackhead and crack smoker The Rat.

poli what he called himself and no one thought any less of him Steven the Rat. He demanded people call him Pheifel.

He couldn't read and pretended he was destined to be the world's only millionaire. And that he was one and they should respect him. But no one believed him, even the other crackhead who sucked his shit and smoked his pipe, John Scott the white-skinned Black man with straight hair, who demanded everyone call him black.

He started chases with the cops all over Windsor Terrace hosted drinking parties and spun the bottle when he was 10 years old. Damian didn't kiss his cousin and escaped without going with too many of those girls. There weren't many of them anyway.

LK tried to fit in with the guys from the Troop, but they were all Catholic School boys and Steve was just a troublemaker who was supposed to be one year ahead of LK and was left back a couple of times and was a year older than Damian.

He hung out with kids a year younger than Damian.

The Catholic school kids were okay. They smoked cigarettes, played spin the bottle with girls and drank copious amounts of liquor and beers usually in bottles. Big Keith was so scared he was terrified of Jon Scott because he was Black, and he accused him of smoking crack when he was 10 years old.

When the catholic school kids got older, they had keys to the rectory basement and got caught drinking and partying down there. At that point their Boy Scout leader, Commissioner of the park in Brooklyn and he ran maintenance all around the town, including down on the beaches and at the boardwalk and all up and down Ocean Parkway, so he was a big deal.

He invited them over to his place to drink beers, to avoid persecution by the church and the priests that were running the place.

This was after he hooked twenty grand into the construction of the room and remodeled it to meet the needs of individual patrols and gave everyone their own camping and outdoor resource equipment chamber. Filled with survival and camping gear including Dutch ovens, stoves, reflector ovens, camping tents and dining fly and all kinds of traditional equipment scouting troops used.

He made a big deal of it, bought a trampoline, and recruited dozens and dozens of kids.

Then he hosted drinking parties, set up fake camping trips, and bragged he was the baddest and best camping trainer in the organization. Then he invited the older kids under the age of eighteen over to his house for drinking parties which led into strippers being called and parents giving money for kegs and thinking it was for camping and learning how to practice hiking and training. He thought it was funny to watch kids have sex with hookers and occasionally they would smoke some weed and then he would get some crack and the kids would be smoking crack in the guise of Troop 237 in Brooklyn.

And this was the most skilled and best most equipped troop at the Camporee and all the competitions for outdoor and skills.

Marty was using Steve to get crack and Jon Scott for years after they turned 18 and they thought it was for a small party until they realized they were too old to party without doing prison time. As the kids were still the same age and if you wanted to fit in with Marty Maher, the park commissioner, you had to smoke crack and fuck hookers with fifteen-year-old boys and men. This was out of line. So, when Damian moved into Marty's place after he turned 18, he turned down the parties and was forced to volunteer for Martin and his purposes deep within scouting at the national level, to maintain his room there.

He was so overworked by Martin's demands that he had to quit school and his two jobs, just to keep up with the demands and have his semblance of relaxation and downtime once a day.

The work was so intense that D. Unknown after running thousands of hours of service, received no thank you and was thrown out of the house and made fun in front of dozens and hundreds of people by Martin who gets drunk and slanders people for hours on end and does not stop, every.

He gets so sloppy drunk he gets wasted at the community center in front of the girl scouts and boys from the troop with their moms and parents and takes his own pants off on stage and fell asleep naked while drooling in front of the whole room full of people and repeated it again.

He was thrown out of the troop only to place violent threats on parents and troop committee members refusing to leave the meetings and forcing others to attend camping trips against their will.

His chosen staff is no prize either. Two twin brothers who spend their entire lives scouting and run several organizations and camps and camping reservations throughout their career in professional volunteer scouting. They have been known to coerce kids into the woods and get them drunk and masturbate with them, trick them by doing marijuana every few years at a private ceremony where there is homosexuality, and they get the kids drunk and offer them sex with prostitutes.

Two identical twin brothers.

Everything I have told you thus far is 100% verifiable by intelligence and law enforcement and is also 100% true. It all physically happened. More than most of it at least.

They could no way trick D. because Damian grew up with a Budweiser in his hand, a cigarette in his mouth, and a stolen joint in his pocket, with and without his parent's permission, and no one could stop this kid from busting someone in the nose who said something mean or who had bullied him in some way.

The kid was tough as nails.

When his old man and brother came around with Frank asking for hand jobs over and over, D. stuck to his guns, pulled out his knife, and hid behind the television throwing out threats.

He then would warn them for no reason that they would be stabbed if they didn't stop bothering him. Then he would call them at work and warn and threaten them until they left him alone altogether.

Eventually, Frank moved out and Big Keith gave LK the keys to the place. He had free reign. He could eat what he wanted, watch a VHS, play Atari, watch cartoons or a show, talk on the phone and play with his toys. He did his homework and passed most of his tests, but his reading scores went down and so did his math scores.

As a kid, when D. was about 9 or 10, he had his apartment, and he saw BK on weekends and occasions people rang the bell to check on him or called him to see if he was okay.

He dressed himself, took himself to school and walked home every day alone. He had friends in school and a couple of kids on the block where he lived but he missed his grandmother the most.

On weekends he was able to visit with his mother's brother and that was how that went for a while. He didn't spend much time nor like spending time with Big Keith.

Big Keith was such a racist. In that way, Richie and Nuri were in the right, if their attack was mostly metaphorical and seeking to change the heart and intention and mind and court of that person.

That Big Keith. He was truly peculiar, and it was indecent his way of life. He was addicted to anything that he did, and he was afraid for his children as if to hurt them on purpose so they would be fully dependent on his full-time appreciation. His other kids, the two that he kept with his wife, never left home and neither did Pat's two kids.

They were worse than Shane when it came to being sheltered. This coupled with both Big Keith and Patrick's confession to resort to mind control to make his kids do what he wanted.

And that included actual spells and prayers to a satanic god, another set of prayers to a witch, and then a bunch of prayers to God if he was still eavesdropping making sure no one got killed. And then those guys would practice voodoo and all that shit. They said so.

When D. Unknown was just a kid, he had an Atari and then he had three games on a Nintendo. And this was how it was until Patrick got that game system barred when D. was addicted to trying to defeat Friday the 13th and could not get past the first few boards, ever.

Big Keith got his new job at the Sanitation, and they were living in the spot down from their mom Patricia on the next street, Damian would get home and play games and the walls in his room were rotting and water-logged, so the floors on the end of the house were splitting apart and slugs were climbing up from the basement into the room.

Damian had to hit them with the salt, and they eventually would go away, but it was not a good place to live. They left Sherman St. in a hurry like so many others did when the rents got raised from just a few hundred a month to close to a thousand at the tail end of the 80s. and it was this shithole that brought Big Keith who had been with the bus company and then the oil company after quitting his job at the Stationary Warehouse down in Park Slope. And he was now working as a garbage man. He loved it.

He came home with a broken bike and left it in the entertainment room to rot next to the foosball table and the bookshelf the Nintendo and the box of Atari games and system along with the voodoo skull that he kept that he found on the trash route where he worked.

He brought this fucking used voodoo skull into his house and kept it there for years and when it broke, he found another one, broke that, and then bought a new one. He didn't know it was bad Joo-Joo to use someone else's Voo doo skull. Some witch doctor said it on the internet.

But no one cared and no one listened to LK when he wrote the dialogue to his first comic book at like eleven years old that he drew. He couldn't remember that about a couple of writers and a guy looking for a girl and hanging out with his chosen pet. It was meant to be funny and dramatic and was often based on Archie and the gang. But it didn't go far.

Neither did the fourteen notebooks filled with poetry and the short stories that he wrote and the first eight drafts of his first novel and the other books he tried to write and the books he wrote and the hundreds of articles and personal statements that he wrote to the media and letters to professional writing agencies and acting and performance guilds and agencies and magazines and photo opportunities and jobs and studios and production companies and on and on and on and over and over until everyone in town told him to go fuck himself.

The Crack &
Dealers

They don't stop looking for energy and psychic power but what they are doing is telling you that even though it is illegal to control your mind and the mind of another other than yourself, it is also illegal to sell drugs outside the White House and attempt to kill the president and its illegal for the government to let them get away with it, even though they don't have much evidence.

What do they want and how many of them are there? No one can tell. First, everyone thought it was just Steve and Jon. Then Bob and Mike and John and John all smoked crack with Marty and the twins with a couple of kids from the Troop. And one of those kids their dads beat the shit out of a bunch of kids, including Damian when he was a kid and a graffiti artist.

As if the spirits are condemning him to big giant graffiti artists in NYC like trees from the Wizard of Oz that are now invisible and making fun of him behind his back. Repeating his thoughts and following him around to everything he thinks and everything his followers do and what they think and what they fear and that is like the Marshmallow man just repeating themselves to this obnoxious psychic of his, this schizophrenia that does not stop reflecting his bubbles to him and blowing his head.

Now, he had to worry about spirits talking to him. But he made it. Even though they were talking about him to others, and they honored and acknowledged that he existed as some prophet, most people were smirking that he was well known by the Lord, and was white, from the USA. That was like a head trip, then they figured it was just safer to put him in the entertainment industry. And go away.

He would just go away. But his brothers in the brotherhood took everything very seriously. And he wondered why they never really introduced themselves and he was initiated over and over as a kid, into these orders and brotherhoods. He was designed to persevere and make it through whatever the prophets were throwing at him.

And then he got a call on the phone while in Phoenix and the guys from the Troop were mostly a year younger than him, they demanded that he hear their confessions. And they confessed one by one to smoking crack and partying with the two kids at Marty's because Marty and the twins had said it was ok. And that they were brothers until the end. And they were sworn to secrecy never to tell Rocco Damian about those parties, but they all did it anyway.

Even the twins and Marty confessed.

But Bob and John asked Damian to include a lawsuit against Marty and the Scouts one day. Even though they had not really fucked him up the ass, they were asking for it, literally.

And when he refused to attend the parties at Marty's final invitation, the troop had seen the last of their shining star, the lodge chief, SPL, the leader of the Venture Crew, and the Commissioner who was underage the whole-time doing jobs legally designed for adults and got no thank you and was kicked out of that group and that troop.

Martin again asked him to keep it secret and attend the parties and he refused and was dismissed from his duties and not welcome to attend or help train any of the new boys or kids at camp or anything that involved his leadership.

And it was that time went on and the twins and Marty were thrown from their own ranks time and again by their legislature and the crack kept on being packed every so often and they took over the camps and the reservations, had parties, and molested kids there until 2021.

Does Marty sell crack in the park? Do the twins smoke crack at camp? Does Steve smoke crack with Martin? Who knows?

It didn't stop there. Martin had manipulated his way into recruiting Damian into scouting's leadership forum at the council level by volunteering him for various jobs and positions and to run training and assist the secret orders and organizations inside of the boy scout organization.

These organizations run initiations and are formally registered as secret organizations inside the of the BSA. One of these organizations that is considered physically as a secret organization is known formally as the Order of Arrow. It is based on the ideology that New York Island was purchased from a tribe of Indians known locally in New York and Pennsylvania as the Lenni Lenape. These natives occupied the Delaware Water Gap and various places along the Hudson River Valley including New York City. The island of Manhattan was said to have been purchased from this tribe.

The secret brotherhood of the Order of the Arrow is based on a legend told by the chief of the tribe, an elder or two and a medicine man who give instructions to the young growing youth Indians and teach them the ways of service, brotherhood, and devotion to these ideals.

The organization has special meetings that take place and occur all around the country and are in addition to the traditional camping skill and scouting meetings that take place at neighborhood troop centers and parish meeting places.

These meetings combine the selected members from various troops to conglomerate and meet in their local area. The meetings are then divided into committees who have their own meetings who report and keep minutes and there are secretaries and treasurers of each group, committee, chapter, and lodge.

The organization has a special form of letters and insignias that it uses, which include supposed Leni Lenape language that is known only to members of the Order of the Arrow. The letters are W.W.W. which stands for Wimachtendienk Wingolauchsik Witahemuiwhich; stands for Honor, Service and Brotherhood or Wanton Cheerful Service in Brotherhood.

And these guys followed AOL and everything about the internet www the second it was on the shelves. And Martin then flipped and switched to worshipping Tarot.com. The Critical Mass talked about by the Celestine Prophecy was going nuts.

The guys from the scouts were all talking about psychics and being an energy now. And they were bigger flamers than ever. Bigger idiots too.

It doesn't stop there. The Order of the Arrow is signified by a sash that members are to wear to signify that they are members of the order when non-members or other members are around.

There are three ranks of stewardship which depend on hours of service. On the sash is a red arrow on the front and the back has a legend of a Leni Lenape warrior stitched to the back with ancient Native insignias that are said to be of the Leni Lenape original language.

The induction ceremony occurs after members are secretly chosen and elected by members of their own troops and home groups.

The chosen members agree to a weekend of two nights and one day of complete silence and service to a wilderness area, in conservation, without speaking and with eating only a little bit of food.

The Ordeal takes place at a camp where people will attend for the summer and the participants groom themselves with a service which they now commit to by becoming siblings in the order. It gets better.

After the days of service, the participants line up and get to the induction ceremony where members of the Order will dress like Native Americans and wear headdresses and makeup and old-style skins and clothing and give scripted speeches while taking on the roles of the Medicine Man known as Meteu, the chief named Allowat Sakima, and two other warriors take part in the ceremony. Damian, having native influence was considered the greatest Meteu to walk the planet, by many of the New York Lodge people but few remain in that organization.

Damian was coerced and forced in many ways to work for this secret brotherhood, and they took a lot of time, effort, and energy away from his private life to lure him into their sponsorships and purposes. They took for granted his gifts and offered him a position as leader in the organization. He joined under one pretense as they offered to teach him about Indian Dancing and the Ritual Ceremonies and the culture of the Lenni Lenape, but he was lured in quickly and due to a sudden culture change the membership dwindled and everyone dropped out except for a few people.

While Keith wanted to do other things, he enjoyed leaving his house and going out to meetings. He went to one meeting and was assigned more than five committees to which he could take charge and he was running events and going to training conferences and learning about business.

Too bad in a few years he would have a seizure and move to Arizona where the guys were calling him on the phone. And Martin would call him on the phone and bitch that he dropped out of the Order of the Arrow. And demand he comes home and sell crack and smoke crack and fuck hookers with him and a few of the kids in the troop.

And Keith refused. And Martin laughed at it. The style that Keith emulated. And it went on like that.

Martin decided that along with Nori and Marsha and Gale and Big Keith, he was going to help Patrick start a New Age cult based on voodoo-projected psychics creating schizophrenia and resulting in black magic hypnosis and reverse mind control. And he bragged about this on the phone. And this went on. People called about the cult, demanding that Damian become a part of it and that he delivers them crack cocaine.

Or help at the Pharmacy.

Or help at the Scout meeting.

Or help at the Auction.

And he would be allowed at Halloween. Where Gale and Mitchell escaped to smoke crack. And they set up a buyer for the big Christmas celebration and auction that was held at Aunt Arlene and Uncle Jack and John's place.

At Thanksgiving, Arlene would show up to pick up the buyer information physically and on Christmas or the Saturday before that, the buyer would put in their bid for the kids that arrived on the school bus with Gerri as the driver and without their parents to pick up presents from Santa.

And be picked out for future pick-up as the parents become indisposed. With a new job, with drugs.

Patrick did not see anything but an opportunity from exploiting people and making fun of mother fuckers he wanted to recruit for the cult. He was going off the deep end.

He wanted everyone to know that if they didn't sell crack cocaine to each other, they wouldn't be welcome to work for the cult.

They had to line up for a crack deal with a cousin, go all the way across the Verrazzano bridge to Gale's place, pick up some crack cocaine and deliver it to another relative, and even smoke some.

Then they would not be thrown out of the house. And they would know you were cool.

And this is what Big Keith did too. He would call Damian on the phone and ask him to go to Gale's place, pick up a small sack of crack on his dollar pay for it, and bring it to him to smoke.

If you didn't do it Damian it was cut off from Halloween and all that shit. He was cut off from Thanksgiving and Christmas and all the parties, weddings, and shit.

Until he smoked and sold some crack for Gale, he was just a drug addict according to Big Keith, and not worthy of respect as a person. Big Keith had been sobered in Alcoholics Anonymous for many years, but he always admitted that he was addicted to crack.

And Patrick did the same thing. He called LK on the phone, called him Damian without his permission and demanded he pick up some crack from Gale, fly home, and deliver it to Big Keith.

When Damian refused, he was ridiculed and made fun of. This was preposterous.

The world was turning on Damian for not smoking crack and even though he was living in Oregon and moonlighting in the music industry and working on movies now in Los Angeles, he still never had the opportunity to even see what Crack and crack cocaine looked like. He didn't care.

He had never seen or tasted anything like that before. He was always drunk and smoking pot as a kid, he figured his uncle, and his dad would leave him alone. But that was far from the truth.

When he kept on refusing to deal crack for Gale, Patrick and Keith both delivered threats to Forest and told him that if he didn't sell crack for Gale their sister Karen would try and have him killed if he ever showed up to visit and that he was not permitted to visit with the Flannery who were humorous cousins of his, but were also kiddie traders, or so they were bragging they were.

And this disturbed Damian some more.

It didn't take but a few weeks for Damian to finally get the remainder of his money returned from Patrick to the disability administration where they distributed the checks, but they only received fifteen hundred dollars from him. The rest he spent on bills but would not send the statements from the bank.

Then Patrick let LK know that he and Gale and Mitch and Marsha and Nori had fulfilled Frank's wishes and were starting a genocidal cult. Pat told Damian he was sleeping with Nori and that she was interested in smoking crack and hanging out with the cult. And that Patrick was now mastering witchcraft and astral projection to make Damian do what he wanted.

And Damian refused to let it bother him even though he could feel that the witchcraft was real. And it bothered him even more.

That his acting career was put on hold because of Patrick's unhealthy habits and his smoking crack, being addicted to wine and prowling at marijuana recovery meetings to meet potential cult members and recruits for his organization.

Patrick was overzealous about his opening his new office for Ed Jones in the richest part of New York and was selling crack for Gale and the paperclip factory of Strasser.

French immigrants produced the Strassberg who were paperclip crack dealers for all everyone knew. Actual German nazi scientists who were now selling crack under the guise of jew Frenchmen named Strassberg instead of just Strasser.

But it was all speculation. They were nazis though. And pretended to be musicians. And they were selling crack through their son now, and their family and friends.

And they were distributed everywhere from Boston all the way to South Carolina with several popular stops along the way. Shane was setting up residence in Washington D.C. and Philadelphia as well as secluding his friends in South Carolina. In fact, just a few weeks prior to a report in 2024, Damian called and texted Shane and had him meet him outside the White House to deliver some crack cocaine.

And one of them didn't show up and started a scene. But he promised buyers would be there in his absence and that their cousin Emmet, Karen's husband, was the supplier to an opportunity missed by Shane that didn't really exist.

Because Gale hates Karen.

And he knew that would piss them off. But there is a buyer there with a frisbee waiting to purchase. And Damian was off and running across the country.

But what gives? The Flannery gets to stay in the loop even though they won't sniff coke or smoke weed and that is because they endorse Gale selling that crack and there are people a thousand yards away from the president right now waiting to purchase some rock cocaine from Shane Strassberg right now.

With the blessing of Patrick Gilbride on it. And Russ Collimore. And Richie Hernandez. And Big Keith. And Frank Gilbride and Arlene and Jack Flannery. The 33rd degree mason skates are socially accepted since he supports

Gale sell crack in Philadelphia and downtown D.C. and all over NYC.

Just to think Mitchell works in a factory on Wall St. in NYC and Patrick was a broker and an editor on Wall St. and now operates Ed Jones and sponsors not only embezzlement, and trade with his cousin from the merchant marines, and the connections set up on tours of duty operated by Shane and his bright and sunny friends who also work on Wall St and the parties he would love to throw, that makes him a prime candidate for some coke use and instead he blows his money on wine, cigars and cracks to support metaphysics.

Instead of popping a mushroom, blowing some coke, and fucking some hookers, he sexually harasses his secretaries, gets complaints, smokes crack, and asks kids for favors. What a dirtbag in a suit.

Anyway, guys were hiding with Damian in Humboldt County, California affiliated with some of the catering trucks on the movie sets, who were bragging about hiding from the cartels because they were taking pictures with planes in Nicaragua in 1982 with official government clearance and they were growing seed marijuana plants, meaning they were growing pot plants to harvest the seeds and sell them to some Jamaicans in Jamaica.

Also, at this spot at the very mouth of the infamous rotting canyon known as Avenue of the Giants, was a woman who claimed to be a big dealer from Ohio who tried to coax D into a relationship but also was there to deliver a message from Sony.

When he tried to leave town and after he did leave town he was threatened out of town, and he told her he didn't want to be with her but had feelings for her and she got him threatened and then he told her he wanted to sleep with her and she called the cops, but it kept her from stalking him, which she blatantly was.

The Scam

What is wrong with the place known as this fucking planet? And they ask Damian to assume event planning and sit in the street drunk and get stoned and think of some ideas that would be great in some other lifetime. Because he doesn't' smoke crack despite his seizure and sells crack despite the hillbillies stalking he will never get rich or the place he needs to be in his career. That is the kind of advice Big Keith was giving.

The crackhead. The dude went to recover because his mother did, and she asked him to join her. So, thirty-three years later Big Keith is smoking crack and has not had one drop of alcohol the entire time. Nor did he smoke much pot. He was such a drunk, he would crave a beer if he did.

And Russ will only date white women now. Some of the white guys he knew made some comment or leered at a Black or African girl and man, now Russ only dates white bitches and sells crack. And some good fucking powder and some other shit too. But he doesn't' care. He got that spell.

And he didn't care.

That spell moves on.

And if Damian doesn't buy what he really got, he gets cut off from the Rasta. He gets cut off from his ganja and his life. And he can experience pain because he must help. He must help deal with that coke. He was sitting there wondering how the elite controls the planet and thought of Big Keith and Russ, the projection, the projectionists. The status quo. The reality of the turmoil.

The trip in the far direction. If you want to take a trip to the east Russ says you go to Russ, but he also says you got to follow Gale.

You got to listen to getting your life together only to deal drugs and sell serpentine solution. Sell a drug base and hope to get someone hooked so they will sell you their soul and give you money. And you will sell them dope, truth, independence, logic, and interconnection and of course love, freedom, and excellence. You can the excellence part. That was achieved by denying this world. And all on which it was based. But they didn't see it that way.

They not only talked about Russ, but they also wanted to know him. They wanted his product and him and too for him to deal their product and work with them and for them and that is only a part of it. Because they were addicted to the idea of serving as the nucleus for the rest of the world and taking over the planet with drugs and dangerous ideology and with the help of Bubba Rocco Damian.

And LK wanted nothing to do with it. And they tried to appeal to his form of mentality, which they have mistaken as simply a rule breaker or merely attracted to the esoteric and occult based logic, and they were wrong. They started getting scared with their plans to take over the planet. And it involved lots of mind control and there was the drugs and the drug trade, but that was for the addicts. They said so.

There was something else going on beside UFO's which were a big part of their original philosophy, but there is no way that anyone, including them can manage the effect of those UAP and UFOs would have if they started that religion. And they are risking it and doing that right now. Working to start this cult. And it is based on all the different estranged and complicated esoteric teachings that were left out of any manual and were passed around halfheartedly by some New Age enthusiasts and tourists who thought it sounded like a clever idea for a while.

Let's be clear, these people know a lot about astral projection and voodoo, and they can read people's minds and thoughts, but their religion has extraordinarily little knowledge. It claims to be metaphysical and carefully attuned, yet it can only read the physical world of someone they are targeting. It does not provide them with any knowledge or anything that can help them grow in life, which is not an aim of spirituality. They seek to integrate to make a point that their loved ones should not indulge in metaphysics. And they are sarcastic about it.

They are starting a cult to hurt people who want to embrace metaphysics or spirituality and don't have any formal training or awareness and they are targeting these people who are innocent and spiritually in need or misguided and even depressed and this group is endorsing their suicide.

They are trying to recruit people who want to die. And they are creating a negative religion. Thewy ill integrate various teachings that they don't understand themselves just to confuse people so that they may feel a sense of relief from the teachings and then experience a confusion where you can guess that they may do something they will in turn, regret?

They will use any philosophy to integrate into their system of spirituality and recovery. Any kind of uncertainty in thought or intention and unclear resonance in energy can result in magic by their incessant projections into someone's life through use of hypnosis and teaching of metaphysics.

They teach that they are more powerful than angels, more worthy than gods and are incarnate of the Living God and superior to the Creator because they are responsible for intimidating and tricking people into giving them power and cash to smoke them through cult teachings.

They believe in a false religion and a philosophy that is not backed up with any plausible or tangible science or proof of existence or has been judged to hold any religious worth, or have any spiritual value according to a practitioner or master of some form, their teaching will embrace these mistaken philosophies and teach them to others and have no idea but what it says on a forum or on the internet.

They confess that they practice astral projection and commit seances and voodoo to link to energy that will broadcast people's minds to themselves and to others without their permission so that they will commit suicide.

They speak of how they will project themselves into people's lives and minds to control their personal energy and thought processes and control the minds of everyone they meet and in turn everyone on the planet through their spells and astral projections.

They aim specifically to control people's access to their higher selves, by constituting their energy field through subconscious hypnosis that they are more powerful than the individual over their personal lives and more powerful than God over their spiritual selves.

They claim to perform human sacrifice on a Molokai altar and participate in various perverted and unsanctified ceremonies.

They claim to worship various Phoenician gods including the Goddess Semiramis, The gods Enlil and Enki, as well as Moloch. They also claim allegiance to the Pleidians and worship their neutrality as a sentiment that humanity asks and gives them permission to perform mind control.

They believe they are more powerful than New Age masters and deserve to be channeled twenty-four hours a day, through schizophrenia and personal aspirations of astral projection and spiritual realization through their organization.

They believe in controlling the minds of everyone on the planet. They believe that aliens will eventually take the planet over to fight with the robots as was cited in one of Damian's novels that they didn't fully read or understand, and they want people to give them money and worship UFOs for fun. They all confessed this desire. It started with Patrick on the phone and then Big Keith, both calling Rocco Bubba Damian Forest on the phone and confessing it.

They alternated and did it repeatedly, calling him names and demanding he join the cult.

They offered him a job as prophet and messiah over the population and all he had to do was teach metaphysics, live on the cult farm, and tell everyone to worship the aliens and for everyone to take the suicidal Kool-Aid.

Big Keith and Patrick told him to make sure that he poured his glass of Kool-Aid on the day of the ceremony and to not drink the one that everyone else was drinking or he would you know, die just like them.

And Damian scoffed and was ridiculed by each of them on several occasions.

And he denied his job as the messiah. And they laughed at him. It was a part of the agenda. He was not allowed to deny this. So, he was cut off from their parties, and if he showed he would have to show up ready to rumble and prepared to die like a man.

Or a coward. Or a killer. They were down with Suffolk Sherrif. And they were dealing with kids and crack at the White House. And this is still a true fucking story. Shane is lurking around Boston waiting for a ride to Philadelphia. And Russ is roaming through the bars at night starting a fight because people don't believe in Gale's coke. And don't care about that stupid skinny twit, that dumb bitch trying to bully and boss people around. And even people she never met before.

Gale wakes up at the same time every day and drinks a smoothie that she makes herself. She goes for a walk in Clove Lake Park and has done this every day since 1985. She then goes home, showers, enjoys some coffee, and gets to work, hitting that crack pipe and enjoying a fake pot. Then she pretends to listen to music, meets clients and sells her rocks and her dope and talks to her people on the phone. And they don't even care about what others think, so she endorses being a vegetarian and then talks everything about how vegetarians can't eat enough minerals and are unhealthy.

So, she heads home for lunch and takes a nap. She goes back and starts shit with hunters, hippies, and tourists and hopes to sell a house. Her son lives off her. He can afford nothing because he is a mutant, a crack-dealing hooker of hers and she pays his bills and his rent with his mutant money, for his genetic disorder he has had a disability since he was born and is a mutant because of it.

He longs to fuck some basketball man up his ass on a court. But his mom won't let him play. He'll cry anyway and get thrown out of the league because he is a butt fucking little bitch. He puts his cock into his defense and cries if he gets a second string. He is a freshman dropout and a waste of basketball camp.

His obsession with toys and trucks drove him to be his momma's sole possession besides her crack business and her Rotary Club membership. The same rotary club that threw D. Unknown out of the place the night Tower Records went bankrupt.

The producer lived a two-minute drive from Gale's houses, and it was the night that Nuri decided her witchcraft would arrive with her and after her and before her was the spell that forced Tower Records out of business forever, declaring bankruptcy for the first time. And she was happy the music industry was done. She had prayed all her days listening to Bob Marley and Jimmi Hendrix and

Ani DiFranco and the Indigo Girls and KRS One hoping the FBI and the government would destroy the music industry.

And she got her prayers.

She signed up with Patrick and told Damian she too was working for the cult. And Marsha did too. And Marsha even told the judge in the child support case all about the cult because she believed in it. And went to church on Sunday.

And fucked a preacher. And a couple of altar boys. And became a black supremacist member of a Black Christian church and continued to prowl on youths and white boys to try and lure them into witchcraft sex and satanism.

And she too confessed to Damian that she worshipped Enlil and Semiramis and the gods of ancient Babylon. And confessed to denying the word of God and the testimony of Jesus and that she didn't believe in it because she didn't like the Holy Spirit telling her what to do. So, she pretended to not worship a pagan religion and sought also to fool God.

And this didn't stop Patrick and Keith and Arthur, a former altar boy from bragging about conceiving Jacob, who they left homeless as he grew up because Marsha believed God told her to live homeless so that is what she did, with Jacob along for the ride in her back pocket and he was traded out with another kid who escorted Marsha around.

And no one put her in check. She just ran out of patience with herself. She eventually was paid off from her support and asked to not talk to people through a psychic anymore. But she practiced that voodoo anyway. And people were helpless to listen to the practices of this stupid cult that was winging it with a CIA psychic provided by the same people that gave them authority to sell drugs.

It's not just that they escape, but they keep getting fired from low-level government jobs and working in D.C. and supporting access to drugs and vulnerable people to manipulate into buying their drugs and taking part when it is ready, in the religious cult they hope to get off the ground.

And Patrick kept picking up harassment notices. And they set up in Georgia and were bragging in Delaware about paying off the cops for the trafficking operation. And they deal without impunity. And brag of dealing at the White House. And they brag of having a real psychic and pulling off these auctions and brag about not being threatened by the cops.

They brag about practicing mind control and laughing their asses off hoping to integrate the psychic vampires that bring people into their business that force people through fear of losing their minds to interact with this band of ridicule. They hunt for magic and recruit with tactics. They are trying to get into your decision-making process to control not only your finances but your relationships, your energy, your thoughts, and intentions.

They want you to give everything over to them and they will collect because you are willing to give it over to them. They will attack your subtle energies and talk to your brain, talk to your organs and your fat bubbles, your ligaments your muscles using energy projection, astral projection, magical spells, and all sorts of misuse of eastern teachings to interact telepathically and take over some aspect of your life. And will try not to laugh at you in the process.

They wait for a fly to land on your shirt and then tell you that you have fly shit on you. They will laugh at you while they sit as an adult on a kiddie ride in the middle of a mall or restaurant and yell "Hay O Silver, away!" They will tell everyone you are the stupidest person they ever met. They will have seven or eight courses daily at every meal and live in a white trash house and environment.

It looks littered with Linoleum patterned on the floor, the women wear literal house dresses, they still wear their hair up, cook pasta with every meal, eat antipasti, boil octopus, and have soup, eat meatballs and sausage with each meal, have salad, drink espresso and sambuca after each dinner and have a rabbit with the meal and then have a main course. And then make their clothes out of curtains and sew the curtains into pants and shirts.

Then demand that you work for a rabbi even though your girlfriend works with the rectory at the church. And the family isn't a Jew. Why do the kids have to work with a fucking rabbi? Why is it recommended? Then they all sleep with each other's wives, and it is heinous. That is disgusting. Especially everyone sleeping with a 700-pound American- Italian gypsy.

And she looks with the evil eye upon others and holds the All-Seeing Eye. They worship gods and directions, and they don't have any idea what they are doing except that it creates their image in an astral realm that lets other people know who they are without meeting, and they consider this famous spiritual enigma powers. And it is ridiculous.

Randy should pull his hand off his cock and kill Big Keith, but he is such a wise ass he would rather just front up and pretend he is LK's source of schizophrenia along with The Rat and his vampire girlfriend Amy.

Amy had lured in Rocco when he was just a senior in high school by inviting him to her sweet 16.

Now Damian had only briefly met Amy before, she was dating Steve, The Rat.

And they dated seriously. Now Steve for some reason was setting up Keith for no reason. He had Amy call Keith on the phone and invite him to her party, but he also pretended he wasn't there and that he was long gone.

When he finally took off, Amy told Damian that he had just left. And she had been flirting the entire time. Keith said he wasn't' interested and tried to leave it at that and she told him she was interested in him, and they had a conversation in front of Steve right there. Keith denied her and she also said she was suicidal. So, that was an alarm to stay away from her. The next night she called back and wanted to know if he was coming to the party. Everyone was going to be there, and he did want to go. So, he went and said he would be there.

He showed up and Amy and Steve greeted him and told him that Amy's cousin who was smoking hot wanted to hang out with him.

And he agreed.

They set them up in Amy's dressing room as the party was in a fancy wedding hall in a wealthy part of the city. It was in Bergen Beach or some shit near Marine Park. It was classy as fuck. And the girl was in a skirt and was smoking hot. So, they went to it and a few minutes later she went back to her boyfriend.

Then it occurred that they couldn't hang out for any more of the party. So, Damian hooked up with two other girls that night, one of them a twin set who would hook up regularly with the Catholic School kids, whose girls were friends with Amy. Some of them. And it went like that for a good night, and it was a great night for LK. He went home satisfied and well-attuned to his own life. He knew what he wanted and was happy to sleep at home, wake up another day, and have a decent memory of that party.

Then Amy called back, and Steve was there, and the same thing happened. And then when Steve left, she told him that he left. And then Keith got a little pissed off, but he told Amy they could talk and be friends that should be enough to get back at Steve for setting him up and not explaining his motives. And then it went down.

Amy called back and told him that she was slicing herself and cutting her skin and blood was everywhere. And then he got frightened. And then she kept calling every night and asking to talk with him multiple times, until she cut the cord several weeks later and he became codependent on her relationship with him intellectually and over the phone. And at school, they just talked the whole time, and he met her and walked her to class, and everyone thought they were together.

They weren't. though she was complicated and very suicidal, and she made the whole thing up. And girls tried to get with him and dumped their boyfriends and were smoking hot and he had to deny them because he was thinking about Amy slicing the shit out of herself and scaring the piss out of them if she got to know them.

And he liked her a bit she was compulsive and that spelled imperfection and she was ugly that spelled status quo check and she was absorbent and would fall asleep with him on the phone at night.

They spoke on the phone every night for hours for about six months. And then Steve found out and got angry and it never really picked up from there. D asked her among two or three other people to the prom, but they said no. He was incredibly happy with his prom date who turned out to be a girl he was dating for a few several weeks before the prom and after it too. And they got along well, and they were good friends for a while she was hot and slutty and was a good addition to his dating life.

He gained a bunch of weight, looked stupid, and invited her to his Eagle Scout ceremony. She dumped him that night because he was fat, clumpy, and dumpy, and he had gotten his lucky mole removed from his cheek. He was addicted to marijuana.

He started smoking at 13 and became that huge influence over everyone on the street through his promotion and protection from the big crews and for teaching the kids from the ghetto by the hundred and helping the thousands of Hassidic children learn wilderness survival and taught his staff how to eat and cook kosher and work with the rabbi when he had no idea how to do it himself and everything was done according to the book and their pots and pans never mixed and it occurred like that for several seasons.

Damian grew up Catholic, but he helped the Jews a lot. He had himself in a gang and several of them protected him and had influence over people. As time went by, his family was outcasted from the church though he was accepted.

His ex-wife tried to ring him in by splitting Christianity with New Age teachings, but he embraced her with the New Age at first and then secluded his teachings with Christ and her. When she attacked him, he left her and worked as a Taoist in a Healing Center where they offered him a job as a Taoist master.

But his masters were soon fired when they learned of their plans to promote Damian as a modern-day prophet and nicknamed him "The One" and 'Buddha." Not liking being made fun of or the object of psychic attention, he scorned the title of 'The One' and maneuvered to find himself situated in with the will of Christ who suffered and died for him, as those around him attempted to mass humiliate him in a new religion of satanism and projected magic and schizophrenia.

Where people were grabbing the electromagnetic grids of people and their organs through energy fields and trying to infect them purposefully with illness by saturating the particles in space with death and sickness and a plague of magic.

Their lives dependent on the one put into their energy, their brains or their eyes or their hidden eyes by the programmers who were now in large part delegating power through this cult.

And no one really gave a fuck. Everyone in society was interested in experiencing what it was like to be mind-controlled by someone other than the covert government agenda operating the same system behind their backs.

They wanted to see mind control in action and thought they could just escape from the repercussive acts of revenge and retaliation by whatever elements didn't agree with them.

It became a world where the Gilbrides could float in the space and talk to people through their mind to promote their organization through people and everyone wanted to know if they would get away with it. If they could prove that their mind control was real.

And they proved it.

And everyone was taking part in a centralized schizophrenia. And it went on for miles. Patrick claimed that celebrities engaged in generating the mind control and the psychic.

And the CIA didn't give a fuck. And he said Brad Pitt was an advocate of the psychic and the cult and mind control and so was Gene Hackman and George Clooney. But other than that, he didn't really know of any famous celebrities involved in the cult.

He believed that he heard a message from the celebrity gods, and they told him to demand from LK, that he pack up his bags and move already to LA where he went from Oregon on a bus, and Patrick told him that if he lived homeless, he would achieve greatness and celebrity stardom.

Damian already had a plan to become a working actor and it would not involve spending any money or living on the street. He could rent a place and live and work as an actor going to auditions and he was happy with that. Then Patrick stole the money from the SSI and left him in the street to prove a point.

Damian went to Arizona and slept in a monsoon and found out that if he ran from his schizophrenia, if he ran from the shadows of himself, he would run so fast he would fall and hurt himself on a rock and not pay attention to what he was really doing before, during that time he is frantic and he will not know what is ahead of him, will misstep and misjudge and fall and hurt himself. So, he learned to survive in the elements and rely on his relationship with his inner self, his confidence and with God and the center of the universe. The source of the entire creation is because the elements came alive after him. And he saw the world through its own mistaken identity.

He knows not to run on the rocks from conjures and voices and hopefully continues to be safe after hoping to walk safely amongst the elements he was facing. It's not easy for him. Bhim running and falling was an excuse for him to take a close look at what he was doing to himself. by taking the words of demons too personally in his physical demeanor.

That was an example he made of himself while devoted to something other than the source and center and running through fear; when he ran a few times and crashed to the ground chasing and running either towards or from away from his schizophrenic enemies. And he got there, knowing that he must pay attention while making and taking steps forward.

Careful attention must be paid not to ignorantly embrace or run from a voice in his head. He had his moments of Goddess worship but if God tells him to worship God as the Living Earth and as Goddess because God is looking temporarily for a form, then Damian would embrace the earth and the voice of her wholeheartedly. Under the guise of God as a woman, and if God chose that expressionist form for a while, then he would be subordinate.

But God does not consider this when hiring the spirits of the dead to enforce the codes of religion when God is worshipped as a Man and then reflects on the power of the Earth and its ability to scare the shit even out of dead people who think they can rise and make clever decisions.

The Goddess of the Earth is not the goddess Semiramis, as these gods were once kings and queens worshiped by their subjects and people and are often associated with child abuse and other forms of pagan idolatry not limited to psychic and physical abuse on children and those in their care.

They often pray to the devil and those who deny God's command if he serves his creation in the form of the planetary goddess under His command, then he casts those sinners into the lake of fire but holds them tight under his arm until he commands their remittance as he transforms into the messiah, which may not be the human being on the path towards time's evolution into the dawn of the second coming of Jesus.

If God wants to practice entering the world of his creation as a form of spiritual lightning before Jesus returns then why would he not take the form of a growing and evolving and angering planet that changes and regenerates and repopulates genera and species at will and consumes and kills and dines and promotes its purposes and goals over the dominion of its inhabitants, just as a god would in emulation of their creator.

And the gods call forth their psychics and their dead to humiliate the D. and make it profane to call them out. While Big K called himself God and told D. that Jesus was a bum and a punk and called the Lord a bitch and said that he was God, and that God was a bitch to him. He was stunted with his growth as God was blessing him with his health and his muscle evolution.

He was practicing denial and even weight training awareness activities when he cursed God and brought forth his son Liam through his wife. And years later he was still cursing and scorning his firstborn legal son Damian.

And God took the health of Big Keith and made him shrink in size. And for every inch he shrunk, LK grew physically half an inch. And his height grew, and his feet grew, even though he was over 40 years of age. And his feet grew beyond size 13 when he was just 11 ½. He almost needs new custom shoes now, Mr. Damian Keith Rocco. It was difficult to understand for his competitors how he customized his work as if he were designing and re-customizing an automobile into a fine piece of work. That was how he felt about his music, books, and even his photography.

He took his writing seriously. And people liked his ideas. And even his writing. But it continued. That he didn't care. He developed drinking and Vodka was not enough and beer didn't hit his head, so he resorted to Whiskey. Rum had too much of a headache, and he was sensitive to sugar.

So, he compared various forms of mid-shelf whisky and then went down to the bottom shelf before settling on Jack Daniels and either Boone County or Ole Smoky Moonshine. He preferred the former, but it was rare nowadays since the pandemic. And it was a form of 'plan-demic.' But let's not yet get off track.

Even though it was just tempting fate and evaluating the reaction of their interaction that was the experiment, despite how many lives were lost and how much prevention could have played a key role in the spread of the disease known as COVID. And to think I could still be labeled an overt conservative or even a liberal. I thought it was still okay to become an Independent Party member.

But will anyone vote independently since there is rarely some kind of place in the primary for more than one or two of our more serious candidates? That would make it easy, everyone just decides on one Independent political party candidate to vote for and agree with everything they say, vote unanimously for that one independent candidate, and then hope for the best.

They won't be corrupt and turn on our green energy ideas, will they? Of course, they won't. They will just lobby for the highest bidder and support your cause until the bill gets passed and then fish again for your vote. It's an effortless process. And no one is wiser. The world keeps spinning as long as the economy stays afloat.

Patrick swears that ethics are solely based on moral value, not that moral value is a secondary contributor and primary influence on decision making. Every good businessman should develop a moral code to attract more value into his commercial and legitimate dealings.

Noone is here to dictate someone's version of business or criminality, but when dealing with others it is necessary to attribute some value to the weight of possessing a moral code so not as to attract negative evaluation or resentment from those dealing in the legitimate realms without any consent to your business interfering with public or private interactions.

It's just principle not to burn bridges and harbor resentment or feelings of mistrust and leave imprints of negative interactions. These seem too much for a man with a business in the financial sector that has generated little capital and is in possession of zero clients.

Patrick must have an investment and payment option from the arena of experimental spy planes and technologically advanced drone prototypes. He seems to believe that his religion and cult should use their energy and magic and meditation and cosmic realization to serve the alien gods who operate in a world that is controlled and controls earth using UAP and UFO-style drone technology.

Not only did he call LK on the phone and demand he use his knowledge of Taoism and traditional indigenous civilizations and ancient religion to better the purposes of the drug smugglers, and child traffickers assembling forces for their new cult of destruction, which planned to desecrate the lives of hundreds if not hundreds of thousands of people whom Patrick and Gale and Big Keith would personally displace through genocide, murder and death. And no one even thinks twice about these mother fuckers because no one believes that they would say this shit in the physical. But they did. They all did.

Over the phone and the phones were plagued with static and beeps and crossed lines and people were talking shit over the other end without a dial tone and Patrick and Keith deliver the message from Gale and Karen. Not to step on their property without dealing crack cocaine and smoking some rock in front of a witness or there would be guaranteed issues of federally indicted violence, and it would not be pretty.

And the Times picked it up and sent the report on this group to some spy networks who influenced the Post to send it on through to some secret authorities and they found these plans mailed via email to the President of the United States and they sent the Washington State Investigators who were stationed in BC to investigate the psychic and the first thing they did, was arrest Shane at the military base in San Diego for screaming at himself about the president for months, and projecting through a living lucid dream infiltrator and hypnosis his desire to kill the president and he was responsible for helping ship soldiers to battle.

A few of whom died and he was at a funeral when he was arrested by military intelligence, Interpol and Scotland Yard and the Division of Child Support from Washington State, where Jacob was born.

Jacob's investigator was the same woman who arrested Shane and called Gale on the phone several times looking for Damian. Shane was partying along with Big Keith, Arthur Homan, and Patrick in the conception of

Jacob in Tempe, Phoenix, Arizona but Jacob was born in Seattle. And that was in Washington.

And Interpol followed Shane from B.C. and Seattle and went across the world with him watching to see if he set up coke deals from the U.S. to Thailand through Afghanistan. Shane was said by Patrick to be some sort of prophet for the cult. And the founders were halfway dying if they didn't follow orders for the stupid administering of the Kool aid on the cult members and followers.

And Patrick offered the job of Messiah to Damian. And he said no. Patrick demanded that he say yes. He refused. Patrick demanded he too, acknowledge that he put Damian under a specific spell that would hear only schizophrenia as punishment for refusing his job as a messiah to a suicide UFO cult of thousands of people who volunteered to commit themselves and then even kill themselves for the name of Patrick and Keith and Karen and they wonder why their bloodline was kicked the fuck out of Scotland.

And what was it, that the fuckers could condemn the poor son of a bitch for talking about religion once or twice and mentioned just merely once that he changed his name from Keith to Damian in the court of the clerk and the news spread like wildfire. All his relatives discussed and debated whether to call him Damian physically. Mind you, he said it once to Marsha, once to Big Keith, and once to Patrick.

He said it once to Joanna his grandma, and that was most of the people he said it to besides some comrades. Now, everyone heckled him, especially the high adventure people who wound up dumping him and screwing each other's brains in and breaking up each other's relationships, for the sum-part. And it looked like shit that no one could understand the person named Damian.

They begged to understand him and to know him and for him to teach them witchcraft and seances. But they didn't know that he worshipped the Word of God. And that he only followed the directions of the Lord of Israel and was like a prophet in a foreign land. In fact, many people considered him in exile. They did not know how he remained so resilient, not having a real upbringing.

When Big Keith finally agreed to allow LK to attend a cub scout meeting it wasn't just to enable him to go and socialize. Big K did not believe LK leaving his sight or leave the house. He was protective because he mistreated LK and left him alone for the most part, enabling him to use the microwave and gain lots of weight, which kept the acting and music agencies away from him because he had a mole on his face like his mother did and he had gained more than enough weight.

He was over 100 pounds by the second grade because the Gilbride cult fed him lots of Liverwurst, burned London Broil, Bologna, mayonnaise, and whole milk by the large cup, and poured lots of sugar on the cereal they ate with more than one or two bowls permitted.

He was quick with his blade after school, so Big K took a job working nights and realized he wasn't getting any ass or attention from LK. That was fine. LK was content and happy that each day when he got home from school there was no one there to bother him.

Although he got lonely, he preferred to stay alone rather than to spend time with Big K. He studied his books, read comics, played with baseball cards, watched movies and TV, and used the phone.

And his grandparents had talked to him about Jesus and his mother's family had talked and spoken to him about religion.

With the guidance of his grandmother from his mother's side, Joanna, he was able to discern the truth above the falsehoods promoted by the Catholic religion and look within the buildings they kept Him in prison within and found the spirit of God waiting there as if on purpose for him.

He obediently and ever so quietly embraced the spirit of God even though he knew the O'Hanlon's were vicious and evil people filled with mal intention and evil spirits that commanded them to do inhumane things and perform unsavory acts of criminality.

They praised other gods and followed the Babylonian gods of Nuri and Marsha. And Damian was left to suffer.

And throughout his early adult life, he was left to discover the meaning of humility. He was asked to endure for the sake of learning the humble act of selfishly sacrificing initial enjoyment for the sake of long-term investment into savorer and more sacred physical and spiritual and emotional experiences.

While he could have gotten a great job making very little money with his illness and skillset having dropped out of college for going to a five year school and getting tired while volunteering and working for ungrateful parties, even performing criminal activities, He was not dissuaded when he was asked to sacrifice so that he might obtain favor from the Lord and attempt to get into the movies and successfully land a resume working as a vocalist or a background television actor.

And that is what he did. So that he could ensure his future as a performer, he sacrificed the way God asked him to humble himself for the sake of being denied work at a regular job to get offered jobs in the music and film and television industry.

And he worked hard on his various projects and was asked to live in the streets by producers who knew of his sacrifice of paying a hundred dollars a month to Jacob, his legal son, and they asked him to sacrifice working for the most part in order to stay and experience homelessness so that they could offer him a job acting as a homeless person and mental patient for a pilot on TV.

This took a long time for him to get adjusted to. And the people guiding him began to stalk him and steal from his ideas and brag of threatening his family and they were connected to a big-time celebrity and an actress, just like some of the other scam artists and coke dealers and producers who offered him a deal.

And he endured and did as the producers asked. And he almost died from exposure a couple of times because he was being asked to be paid in an unfair and inhumane manner where he would receive a check weeks after he worked for a single day, and he would be paid through the mail by these big studios and movie companies. He couldn't even afford a hotel room because his pay got lost so many times.

He froze and had to sleep in churches and squat in houses and piss himself and live in a McDonalds and stay in a bus terminal and take a train out of state just to stay warm and stay alive while working as an actor in Los Angeles after years of struggling on the streets and trying to pick himself up and finally getting job after job in a small time movie and only to have no money and no place to live and no place to stay and no more friends and no more liquor and no more pot and no more cigarettes and no more girls and no more showers and no more beds and no more money and no more anything except bus fare and a wardrobe for the flicks to wear when you get there.

Somehow and someway, nobody gave a fuck about the cult, but every person he encountered, wanted to communicate telepathically to him about some aspect of the cult they were confounded with, either they supported it, or they didn't. But it wasn't that cut and dry. It caught itself in a thorn and didn't fly away. It just got stuck there like some shirt or a sock and it was impossible for it to be torn away, let alone learn to fly or unsnag itself on its own. And the thorns were sharp. And everyone was making it. Everyone had their beliefs.

Patrick was calm and cool as smoked those cigars and pledged allegiance to the religion of the Babylonians. And he was sure that everyone was going to fall for it. And they did. And it was complicated, but it just wasn't. Easily assumed by many that it was not complicated at all. And no one knew the wiser.

Pat went out and flew a kite and opened his gates and his door and worked on publicity and opened his shop and was there to supposedly make money and he was sitting there without clients and endorsing a religion either his by Babylonian rite, or copycatted from the conspiracy theorists and he was just throwing shadows at Damian.

Trying his nerves with counter production, uneasy negative metaphysics and destructive conversations attempted to blazon the giant guy into fury and he became enthralled with the audacity of the world and the ability to become lazy and not contribute to the betterment of society for quite some time. He was disillusioned. And he was angry at his family and friends for becoming cultists and for turning their backs on him. 'But they were always this way.' They would just say to him. He was just too young and naïve to notice and admit to himself.

Now it was too easy not to notice. He needed to get back with it. The way these guys treated him, and he tried to forgive but it was difficult to see one's way out of the fog and magic of pollution they created by saying toxic things to Damian and others. He didn't have to defend himself anymore and when he took off, they decided to start some shit with him to make him feel like they were necessary in his life. That he needed their approval and their presence otherwise his life didn't work out. And his spirit guides somehow fell for it. They didn't let him make friends with anyone except the actress and she hated him.

She played all his schizophrenia and all his memories like a puppet and kept him isolated from the rest of the industry. His ideas were big, and they were dangerous. And she did not let it go that she had received a billion dollars from his suggestions and ideas. But now, she ignored him. And pretended he didn't exist, and this made him furious. And after months and months of complaining he decided to take it out on a typewriter and Damian started typing away. And all the drug dealers wanted credit. And all the losers wanted his beliefs to be put away.

They could not deal with his accuracy without putting someone down for no reason just because they were right. The Lord knew this and kept piling on his insight as he grew increasingly humble and praised God with every right prophecy and psychic notion until the Lord was making fun of him that he was some kind of psychic mutant and freak himself. Then the world echoed God's awe at Damian, as the person refused to take it out on the actresses.

And he refused to demand his way into the industry and they forgot he had gone back to school to become a writer, and they forgot that they had set him up with a bunch of movies to act in and they forgot he was on the run and praying for safety when they were collecting their checks and he was out there with the lizards, the albino lizards and the scorpions and he knew they knew he was there.

And they watched him suffer in the sun as he ran for his life. They had threatened his safety and his grandmother years ago, and they told him he had to move to LA, and he was no longer living in NY. They approached her on the street said his name and told her to tell him to move to Los Angeles or she would suffer. And he had just done that a year earlier and was struggling when Patrick had taken his money, and he was living on the streets and camping in the wilderness. And wandering around between Arizona and Oregon.

And he has seen the alien, a group of black slugs after he arrived at rest for a second after getting off the Greyhound in Medford, Oregon and he went down the street and attempted to regroup outside of an old church for just a few minutes. He was going to wait for a bus to a local town and it would still be several hours before the bus would arrive. So, he thought it would be okay to wait there for just a moment to get his mind and direction settled. When he looked at the ground, the black slugs were moving briskly in a pack and as a unit toward him. He grabbed his stuff and started walking down the street. When he turned around the slugs were right behind him and he ran and took off walking more briskly, escaping the slugs but noticing how they looked remarkably like both the X- X-Files and Venom from the comic books.

But there was little more to that town other than it was where Ian was hoping to catch me out there and he was there the summer that Damian hung out with the homeless kids out there and they offered to jump him. And the girls there, two cuties who but seventeen offered Damian a threesome for a mere ninety-nine USD.

And he said no. Because that would be inappropriate. And although they were sweet, he often said no to girls trying to trap him. And he has been approached inappropriately enough by underage girls to make the prince jealous. And that is no joke, but he gained so much weight that girls won't ask him out anymore. And he has more peace but still, wouldn't mind a date or even a wife. Or some better friends.

The actress sent her assistant to bring a bunch of goons and threaten his grandmother, and that was a test of faith. For the right to commit vengeance, the Lord must fail Damian. He will trust in His might. He will trust in the force creator of Life. And the superseding of justice and the promotion of domestic tranquility amongst all performers and writers who choose to have their work shared with the world and are taken for granted by their production companies and studios.

She thought she was for hot shit when she approached Joanna again and told her some similar shit about Damian working in the movies. And the message was passed again. And Joanna refused to even see him anymore and she did not want to spend any more time with Keith as the actress and her goons and assistants were threatening her life and her safety in a way that was to be dealt with at some point and was avoided for obvious reasons. Damian didn't even feel that shit or believe that it was real. Until the actress sent her assistant and the goons separately to admit to doing such an act. And then, he was so busy, that Damian didn't put it together or take it seriously. Then he put it all together.

When the money was reported in the media, it was all a laundering scheme and they promised to set that fucker up and frame him if he didn't claim a whistle-blower. If the money looked a certain way and he didn't bitch they would turn on him like a rotten intelligence operation gone wrong with an innocent struggle for freedom exemplified over civic duty.

And then the nice guy routine when need be. Is that at your disposal? Do isolation and ice foliation have anything in common besides meditation and waking up in the morning to a cold plunge?

He always wanted to try it. He did that meditation thing and it worked out for his viewpoint and his health and awareness, but it never did anything for him socially. It was as if he was trying to convert Jews to Christ in the Middle Ages and they were still stoning Christians in Israel, very harshly.

It felt weird to be involved with any form of meditation and still be able to socialize with anyone but a beautiful woman who was so not into the fact that Damian wasn't driving around and he was getting plenty overweight, had an actress after him, was escaping a job as the messiah and a drug dealer, had feds looking at him, was writing for school, had an acting career people were looking at and had no real place to live. And yet, no one found interest in him anymore and he was completely and utterly on his own.

The Day Traders

By the fourth of July, the end of the auctions has taken place. More than likely an elaborate plan of action takes place between parties during the Passover each year. And its interaction varies a bit with the location. In the old days, the Flannery would host the auction on Easter for the final grooming and develop a relationship with the target's family for the final pick up.

This might mean a promotion at work or a parent breaking up with the family or getting addicted to drugs and entering a recovery program forcing the parent or family member away from their loved ones, leaving the children more vulnerable for a safe place to go. In some cases, the family might become addicted to substances dropped off at the target's home in hopes the parents will just abandon the kids in hopes of getting some more.

And then the cult practices begin to mold the target more acutely. And the parents become involved with the cult, brainwashed directly through drugs and direct physical hypnosis, and controlled subtly to stay away from their own family. Then, the children are left vulnerable and unattended.

A family member will notice, and the Flannery will have a scout there that will invite another spy or O'Hanlon to escort the family around and offer to bring the kids around to other parties socially. They will suggest the kids get dressed up in fine and unique clothing specially worn for the holidays.

Now the kids have nowhere to go except to the party with other kids and some people looking to become illegally adoptive caretakers. Of some small children. Who is going to the party with a school bus driver? No one is even close to being invited, even the parents except the family of the Flannery and their closest friends and neighbors and one or two other parties. These parties may or may not be silently bidding on the kids for a final bid and have plans to pick them up within weeks.

As they may have also met at the Christmas auction. The Easter auction has the kids dressed up to the nine's in their miniature shoes and pants and suspenders and dresses while the big Easter bunny sends them on an easter egg hunt and for three hours the hosts treat the kids to sodas and good homemade Italian and Irish food and all kinds of treats and cake and they are put on a giant auction block and thrown into the lives of a new family, maybe one they never knew before.

But not before they are escorted out by the school bus driver all at the same time and the party clears out, leaving the hosts to say their final toasts and clean up for the night, bidding everyone a terrific easter Sunday. And the kids have chocolate and candies to bring back to wherever they are meeting their parents. The kids range between the ages of three and twelve.

A dozen or so arrive on the Saturday before Christmas and wait to meet Santa in the same kind of style of dress with suspenders and button-down shirts and all the kids have their hair done and combed and they are there to play with the large number of toys that is given to them, and they play literally for seven hours there without their parents on a Saturday night. And the hosts and guests watch the kids, get drunk, and eat fine white trash NYC pasta and it tastes oh so good and is oh so nutritious.

This baked ziti competition with three people contributing and fifty people eating, this is a Flannery party. With the one buyer from Gale's Halloween celebration that had some guys from that Rotary club and the Senators and the scumbags and the waiters from the point dock.

The point they docked when their behavior intimidated him for once in his life and the last time if I remember; the point that ate out the culture of all music artists who are caught drinking free wine which is just courtesy of the record company tab, and to get caught on the night of the contract signing. The night when Tower shitheads when bankrupt and the waiters at the Rotary Club grabbed the wine from D. Unknown and they stole his contract away from him. And he went back to the streets after escaping from Nori and her Seaweed Monster.

And Randy was just a henchman. Trying to get down with the cult for fame. And so was Russ. He nor Randy wanted no part in that trading and dealing. But that was not really the case. They wanted in and they were almost considered Kiddie traders just for hanging out. Randy wanted to fuck everyone in the sex cult.

But it wasn't any kind of cult other than a bunch of dudes and ugly bitches saying they were worshipping Babylonians. And the gods that were used by pedophiles and deranged fucking black magicians according to the conspiracy theorists most socially accepted. And it was open information that the gods that the freaks were worshipping were the same gods featured in the conspiracy books.

The rumor spread that Nori had heard of the conspiracy theories from Damian and a few other people as they were the popular offbeat conspiracy theories of the Anunnaki and the Babylonian bloodlines owning the earth. And the same authors put those out over and over and are popular. She learned about its word of mouth and communicated it to the rest of Patrick and Big Keith, and they copied the Conspiracy Theorist religion without knowing anything about it.

Or they were practicing it and well versed in it the entire time. They forgot that the news announced the arrest of Enlil worshippers at KinderCare in the 80s at the very same time that Rocco had to threaten Pat and Frank to leave him alone.

And they planned to use his against him and knighting it into a religion in front of him that planned on killing thousands of people. And they were asking kids like LK and his cousins for hand jobs and to suck them off in the shower. And Arlene, the mother Flannery and her husband Jack, a Freemason, and their son John a Suffolk deputy, they all know what Patrick T. and Big K are capable of. They discussed it many times amongst themselves. But they could not rehabilitate these fuckers, could they?

And why did they want an alien religion based on black magic, astral projection, and mind control manipulation of alien races? This was so strange that these Babylonians were waiting to become a military experiment, a part of a private government project or be abducted by suicide and aliens. It took more class to pull this off, many can tell.

And the Devil may care. But it didn't seem like it. The religion had faded at this point, cults were no longer in style. Even though those purposes were of the overall objectives, they were not important enough to scare the children with or decide upon the parent's direct communication and influence.

The Flannery believed in the use of a psychic and a clairvoyant technology that can read and tear apart a person's thoughts, desires, forward moving intention, and their dreams, leaving them reflecting on their worth to stay focused in the game. Not focusing on the game to display your worth, they want you to own the room and demand those who are looking for a kid to show up at their parties and no one else other than the cover.

But they didn't care about Damian or Keith or that he was snitching, yet. Because Carolanne, John's wife commanded him to snitch when the time came. And after Patrick threatened him, he was open to a journalistic exposure for the family, even if it meant destroying their business.

But the Christmas party was always fun. There were never any parents there and the kids got some good presents. It wasn't like that when Bubba was growing up. He took off at eleven and started smoking cigarettes at the parties. He didn't care for them even if there was baked ziti and lots of soda pop and social interaction.

The Christmas party involved Angela from the parish, the vengeance of Big Keith for being social, inviting Angela and her sister the giant Gypsy Josephine, the demise of all of us, brought a big tray of cream puffs to the event. And they would spend days making these demons so that everyone could eat. And they would have trays of ziti and lasagna and ham and stuffed pastas and desserts and pumpkin pie and the grab bags. But there were walks and talks and Big K led the group around the neighborhood with Christmas caroling.

They would wear hats and go from house to house, while the kids were being auctioned and sing "Deck the Halls" and "Jingle Bells" and all that. People would sit there and pray and cry at "Silent Night" and Big Keith was the life of the old lady parties that were thrown. If it weren't an old lady party, Big K would be embarrassed to hang out with other guys.

Then the Super Bowl and then the birthdays and the Christenings and then the Easter Auction and then the Fourth of July and the Weddings and the family would gather a few times a month and break off into groups of those who smoked weed and smoked Gale's crack to religion and those that smoked weed and didn't smoke Gale's crack hopefully ever. And they were hated by Gale. And they were talked about and threatened by Gale. And she was in charge. And her house depreciates over and over by the day. Her net value dwindling as she makes fun of you, everyone, anyone, and those whom she admires. Those whom they hate.

The devil spoils them with the reputation of getting a free mind control and a gaslit pathway to sell crack outside government buildings in Washington. And they gave all their efforts to these holiday parties, forgetting they were lining up buyers.

It was easy to say that they were getting old and would stop soon. But the grandchildren are all growing up now and it's harder to see moving forward. So, they split all the family up and all the friendships and everyone moved as a nuclear family to their specific locations. Flannery split from New York and cut it in half with the girls and Jack moving down with Paul to Delaware. Then Michelle the daughter of Karen and Emmet lives to trade sweaters and kids down in Georgia. Big Keith took his family and moved to Florida. Arthur lives in Port on the East and Big Keith lives on the west.

Bus driver moved her entire family out to New Mexico except for the one kid and comedian, thinks I don't know their spying and eavesdropping on Little Keith's mind. And Shane covers Philli and Boston they all work D.C. Pat gets Bay Ridge next to the bridges and Gale gets Richmond Terrace, Jo stays in Brighton, and they own

Staten Island and much of NYC with their strongholds in Jersey and Court and the following they have in various locations with numbers of bodyguards and people protecting them on at most times.

They circulate also through places where people are vulnerable. They drink the same thing repeatedly mixing all the sweets with all the other stuff to make a funky mixed punch and drink. *They combine the Kahlua, with Bailey and Malibu, along with Goose and Johnny Red and that is the recipe for their lives. They guzzle that shit like its water and by the quart.* Smoking Reds and watching videos about the KKK, they reflect on the happening at the Mason meetings and the most insidious conversation about the situations at the meetings that involve witches and warlocks taking the meetings over.

And the pamphlet for the weekend 33rd retreat. It's sick how many people would just sit there and vibe out to his music, but the auctioneers want to control music through hypnosis.

And they wanted apart of Randy's astral projection, and they became a part of the guy's internal projector, he generated images into people's energy in order to make sure their energy was raped and any girls and women trying to communicate with one's energy were hit with black and green and slugs and turned off immediately. Randy projected the Flannery and the Gilbride and the Strasser into people's minds and gripped onto their energy fields with hooks, little studs and tacks and green energy slugs to which he would make someone's personal energy into a microphone and broadcast their thoughts in front of them and other people could easily read them and pick up on their thoughts. This was to make sure that madness and irresponsible outlooks were passed around and everyone was too busy getting drunk to pass judgement on such an idiotic practice.

And Randy just believed that no one would write anything like that about him. And they just happened to do so. Because he was an energy vampire who projected the image and images of the traders the Flannery and how they were connected to Shane threatening the President and screaming that he wanted to kill him because he was a brainwash. And Randy brainwashed the entire planet to listen to Shane's dreams and internal conversations and generated static into him, because Nori had told him that she was planning to sleep with Shane and that she was going to get gangbanged by the four of them.

And this was conversation and even gossip to not only Gale but to old lady Flannery. And she cooked with ease taking her chicken out for 45 minutes at only 350. And the chicken was raw. You must cook it for an hour and then at 400.

At least that is a short-term focus. Instead of paying the Flannery to register someone with the merchant marines and hoping they have nothing to do but pay 900.00$ to join and work six months out of the year on a boat away from home and have a vacation the other half of the year. Sounds like the perfect reason to raise a second family.

And is that not alright with what a person has already done and will it not please the Lord if a man offers all his offspring and raise his people the best he can?

And the world turned as the Flannery spread for themselves further. The grandsons were in the military, others were being their own and their organization was spreading itself nicely through the democratic world of synchronized government.

And old lady Flannery hated the government. Jack behaved like a comedian would, but as more manipulation occurred and corrupt credence the ideation of laughing at everything, he encountered took the predetermined path, that nothing did in fact make him laugh now. He felt unstoppable. But they did not count on the psychic that was generated about Shane yelling at himself and warning everyone that he tried to think about killing both Big Keith and the President.

And they didn't expect him to get arrested for that and even twenty years later they had just figured it out that the government didn't give them a free psychic and it was because Shane had misused his and everyone was now caught, and they used that one factor to investigate and surveil the rest of everybody else. And Damian just kept calling them and accusing them of crazy shit at the government building and threatening their lives.

And this irked the little planet that Arlene and Jack created for the little kids they were trading around. This has been going on long since the Flannery moved itself to the houses of Suffolk, NY and they were taking credit for getting their asses out of the Red Hook a long time ago. The Red Hook projects, where all kinds of shit happen. Including Big Keith ordering 6-foot sandwiches for New Years each year, while Barbara ducked down later that night from gunfire being let off from the rooftops across the street as she was living there in the early 1990s.

Even when LK went over there for one year, and he was playing with some of her boyfriend's cousins DJ equipment, and they were bumping over there occasionally. And boom at midnight everyone starts jumping hitting the decks, because motherfuckers was just letting off rattles and rattles of gunfire right up on the street side. And no one gave a fuck really. Noone died, and it was scary though, because there was so many people hitting the deck that no one knew if something went wrong. Thankfully, there were no more sirens.

When Little Keith Damian got home that night, his family had moved down to Clinton Street, just a mile over in Carroll Gardens, and he got a life back to his place where Big Keith married Angela and they lived in her parent's house, in an upstairs apartment in a brownstone on Carroll St.

Big Keith and Little Keith did the moves around from Sherman to another spot-on Sherman, down towards Church Ave, and then up on Liquor St. near Nelson across from the Gowanus Highway, and they moved it down to Caroll St. And this was before LK got thrown into another place and another and another all over town and all over the country.

Patrick does nothing all day but study finance. He sits in his office, attempts to find a date, has a wife, two kids but still needs to cheat on them. He's always right. A republican liberal, he has his eyes set on people opening their portfolios and sharing their money with him. He doesn't really enjoy a Monet but does live off the fat of the land. He spends about sixty bucks a week living off cigars, and smokes about twenty of them, all from the cigar stores down on Bay Ridge.

He likes to think about various spots of Bensonhurst and Park Slope and Manhattan and remember the 1970s. He and his friends and brother used to get drunk a bit, get stoned and he would listen to the Stones and some Van Halen.

And the wine. He likes to drink that decent wine. Usually, the Red and he gets to chill it too. He sits on his tiny porch with his picnic table and umbrella and enjoys the Bay Ridge sunsets. He looks at the bleak sky turn into orange and pink and watches the Cirrus clouds float on by like giant pillows of three-dimensional pillows, a cloud into the ride of the fourth dimension. And that is where Patrick was going. He wanted to take everyone on a ride.

And it was going nowhere. Really fast. Everyone was going to die. There would be thousands of people dead at his hands. And he giggles. Like Jack the Mason who sponsors that school bus on Easter and on Christmas and dresses up like Santa and the Easter Bunny.

Whoa. These guys have their own Easter bunny costumes. That is intense. And professional. Damian didn't like the Easter party for some reason. And Jennifer was always there. And Shane was into it. He lived for the Easter party. In fact, which is where his mom got the money to pay his rent every month. The big payoff. And the government surplus of disability from Shane's genetic disorder.

He likes to brag that his mom never once left him without 800.00 in his account. And she got that from stealing and selling drugs and using government money and selling houses to people. Wow. That's great. Get a job and get an education. People are watching you. As she uses her psychic, she does not know that Interpol is building a case against her for bribing the government. And they are investigating the government. By authority of the Scotland Yard, and the President of the United States.

They found out Shane had a government badge for a month or two and then screamed that he wanted to kill the president. And then projected himself into everyone's subconscious using a spell and appeared in thousands and thousands of people's dreams. They said it. And he said he wanted to kill the president for sending him to Afghanistan. And he cried at night. And drank his whiskey. And his mommy thought about him. And waited for him to get home so he could sell drugs through the government, and in the court building and in the prison and in D.C. You see, Shane worked as a prison guard, and was selling cigarettes to inmates in the prison, landing that job as soon as he got out of the military.

But Shane was only three feet until he was 16, and he wore the same overalls as he did when he was 8 years old. When he was 15. Then he figured out how to masturbate while attending Patrick's wedding. As soon as he got home from the party, he jerked off for the first time. And in months, he was over five feet tall. And then he was over six feet tall. And then he was on the College Basketball team. And in one semester he got kicked off. For trying to stick his dick in a player on the court and exhibiting bad sportsmanship.

He was crying over being benched. Tears rolling down his cheeks. And his face was all rosy. He was singing Johnny Mathis at Christmas and hanging out with his mom. And they set up shop in South Carolina and he got fired from the NYS Police after appearing on YouTube in court and doing some pushups. And crying at work. And they found out he tried to smoke the president.

After he got fired, he moved to Philadelphia. After Fentanyl took over, he moved to Washington D.C. and was waiting for buyers outside the White House in late 2023. He was smoking the rocks and waiting for someone to buy them. He didn't get arrested for that.

Patrick was sure he got arrested because Damian said something about the psychic in 2006. And Patrick didn't care Jacob, Marsha's son from the gangbang, was living homeless most of his days. Neither did Shane. Or Gale, who made fun of Damian for having his wife taken from him in honor of Shane and Arthur and Patrick and Big Keith gangbanging Marsha some Sunday, the week after Damian's birthday. Poor Leo the lion. He was so egotistical that even his own traded foster family left him and made fun of him when he wouldn't sell cocaine. The fucking drug addict that he was.

They didn't get it. That Damian never asked to marry Marsha, in fact, she threatened him to attend the wedding, had bodyguards posted at the door, threatened him to sign the papers, forced him into child support, hired the witness whom never met them before outside of business for the wedding and did not pay for or legitimize the marriage document, never had it notarized and the state still filed it, leaving Damian to flip the bill for the support. And he would have gone to jail and then did time for a long time because of non-payment, except it leaked through to the judge on the case that Damian was not the father. Jacob was born to other men because Marsha was screaming about it on the phone.

She admitted that Damian Keith was being played and made to pay for someone else's support and that he was going to get in trouble. And that he was not the father. And that was all the judge needed to hear, while they were on hold, they had the phone on silent and mute but could hear everything that was being said. And Marsha said it over the recorded line. And she said that he was going to suffer and never see Jacob again. And he never did. He had never seen Jacob after the few months after he was born.

Jacob was born to C section at over 10 inches long and 9 pounds and was three weeks late. He could walk in his walker for only a few months but could not crawl and would cry every time he was put on his stomach. He wanted to walk so badly. And he could talk. He said daddy in just a few months and even said mommy soon after. One night after they had broken up, Damian called old Marsha on the phone and Jacob immediately knew it was him and Said 'Daddy' right into the phone. He was only less than six months old.

But Marsha didn't like Jacob. She talked about him negatively. Damian felt trapped in a life that was not his. He used to cry that he wanted to break up with the old black lady and she used to complain that he was a white person and a kid. And she complained she was attracted to people that were still minors.

And by now, LK Damian was over 21, and she did not have use for someone who was an actual adult. She scratched him up when he went to the baseball game with two girls. And she scratched him up good. So good, he moved in with a coworker and then a lesbian from work, and then two girls he went out with, and then back to one of someone else's places and then he moved in permanently for a year with another coworker. And things calmed down. But they didn't.

Marsha would not let him see Jacob or visit. And he did not visit any more since she was so ignorant and mean about it on the phone. And now Jacob was not his kid. And he was confused. But Keith was calling him on the phone and calling him names. And LK was fed up with this shit. He was going to turn on these people.

And Patrick attended a conference or some shit in Seattle and LK was staying there, hoping to work things out with Marsha. Pat didn't want to swing for a birthday gift, but LK made him do it anyway. He wanted a sleeping bag, and some pants and Pat had a problem with it. He flipped the bill for the free hotel buffet breakfast and baseball game that the company paid for.

And Patrick bragged about hanging out with Marsha. And LK didn't care because he doesn't date black chicks or some shit. She fucked up big and he had no time for a loser woman, who was just fucked up and just playing the game and just playing a race card. And she acted like he owed her something. And she stole all his information, social security, and personal info and personal contacts. And Patrick and her had a little fling. Just like with Nori.

LK did not trust Pat and he never forgot all the bullshit that Patrick put him through as a kid. And the horror of all that he tried to do to LK. All those guys. If LK had turned out to be just the slightest bit gay, he would have gotten raped and beaten by the Gilbrides, they would have killed him and abused him. And he would have their dicks in his face. But he never faltered. And Patrick was going to fuck up big. He had no idea how bad he was going to fuck up. He thought it was his rite and his right and his priority to mess around with Marsha, who also was a pedophile just like Pat. And they would do the wild thing, so they said.

But no one knows if they really did. And Arlene and Gale were all about that gossip. And all about how that went down. And all about the auction coming up on Easter. Two of them now. Because Arlene moved from Huntington Station down to Delaware. And to two spots down there. Nice places. And her daughter and her whole family went too. The kids and Paul, who works for the merchant marines. What kind of products do they ship with the merchant marines? Drugs? Kids? Products Made in China or Taiwan? Sushi?

What do they have to do with anything? But now, the friend, the bus driver, the school bus driver, she knows what it's like to move to a tiny town in New Mexico with her whole family and wow, they must have a killer Easter Sunday in the middle of rural New Mexico. And the connections down in the south, what do they do on Easter Sunday? Is it a regular day like any other, or a regular Sunday like any other? Or is it a grand extravaganza where the kids are the center of the world? Where kids are the entire universe and their joy and their experience on Easter without their parents, with people who brag about paying the FBI so they can traffic. So, then were the parents strung out somewhere? And why is it important to spend so much fucking time with children?

And why was there now one nuclear family in each separate state? They must be starting their own units and branches of corruption. That must be the answer. Or it is paranoia riddling the brain and taking over the spine. That must be it. Except Jack Flannery giggles as he brags about the cops being in his pocket and taking over the world. He laughs aloud and does not stop giggling about taking over the world. And he drinks his Walker and bones his Ranger smokes his Reds.

And Jack is a real mason. Not just a Freemason. He fixed oil burners most of his life and it paid hardly anything more than minimum wage. So, he built houses and backyard porches and extensions on houses and ladders and decks for pools. He made money that way. And Arlene portrayed a hardworking Nurse hoping to become an RN. But she was just a secretary at the doctor's office. Not a real nurse. And her son was a deputy at Suffolk County Sherrif's Office in Suffolk, NY. But that was not Suffolk, MA.

And people in Vermont feared them, heard of them, and resented them. And New England stood on edge everyone wondering which of their Klan would travel through the region. And it was mostly Shane and Arthur and some of the Catholic School boys had found a home away from home out there driving around.

Dennis had a house out in Maine. And he had a family too. His other wife was named Johanna, while Damian's grandma was named Johanna. When LK was a graffiti artist, at an early age of 13 years, one of Dennis' step kids Matt, had some friends in the neighborhood. Even though Matt and LK were okay, some of Matt's friends jumped Damian, and beat him badly. A few years later, the guys who jumped him, all of them about 6 feet tall were approached by LK's crew and threatened over and over and told they would be busted the fuck up if they even thought about talking shit to him or touching him again. And things went on like that for a while in LK's youth. People stepping up to his enemies.

But Patrick would not heed the warning. He would drop off threats and offer him jobs as a tech Messiah, or a cult Messiah and try to hurt people in the name of Damian, Keith, and Rocco. And it was pissing people off. It was hurting the work and the reputation of these people. This person who was so massive, growing year by year in size and weight, some people grew to be terrified of LK. And he was growing increasingly frustrated and more and more filled with rage. He was going to flip out. Patrick kept on pushing his buttons and casting spells on him, and no matter what LK could not escape his schizophrenia from the cult. The witches would not leave him alone. And Patrick giggled. He thought he was safe.

Damian was receiving text messages from Patrick's secretary saying that Patrick was sexually harassing her. Even though he didn't ever remember knowing or meeting this secretary, she reached out to him anyway. He wondered how she had received or gotten his number. But she complained that Pat was cheating on his wife, had no clients and was not making any money. He asked her to the movies and freaked her out.

She said she was not interested in him. But she was on the phone with D., and he didn't know why and just figured he put her up to it. And dropped it. But he let her know that he had received an email from Obama's office, in 2016, letting him know that Patrick was under federal investigation, for embezzling and bragging and for starting a cult. And Pat was also reported to the SEC. Obama's letter to Damian stated that Patrick had been reported to the proper authorities and federal agencies were given a mandate on the reporting status of Patrick internally. That is, they were watching him and putting him under investigation.

Pat is weird. All about finance and Wall Street, but he snapped and turned into an offbeat Republican, and he was obsessed with Black Magic for a while. He was playing with Astral Projection against LK hoping the guy would just snap and join the team. Dealing crack for Gale, selling kids for Jack and Arlene and he was going to poison thousands of people for Josephine and Angela. This cult was going to make well over 90,000,000.00 USD just from its basic membership of recruiting 30 thousand people that were paying three grand a piece to commit suicide. And this was supposed to happen?

Pat and Gale and Big Keith thought they could pull it off. Mitch, Marsha, Nori, and friends were all happy to be a part of the spectacle, including Randy, Richie, and Russ. And Antoine. Who?

Antoine. The guy who attended high school until he was 21. He was 18 giving Damian Keith some LSD Acid tabs when the kid was only 16. And smoking weed with him and drinking and getting him some head from some Russian girls. And hey, Antoine was not trusted by anyone. He had a follower. A mist that followed him around and spoke directly to anyone he hung out with and told them not to trust that son of a bitch, very directly. And no one thought twice about that shit. They said that mother fucker off.

"I keep hearing that I'm not allowed to trust you!' and people would run off away from that son of a bitch. Cool and laid back enough. A fat enough black dude, with glasses and a beard, had freckles and he ran down at the Radio Station. Hot 97. He ran records for the afternoon DJ who he lived near as his neighbor. Antoine lived near the high school, which is in Midwood, a Hassidic Jewish neighborhood. And while most people commuted to the school, Antoine and Russ would walk home. And smoke up together.

Russ was a great student when high school started but he started smoking weed and he dropped out of school. He kept on reading and raising animals and he kept them in his home and worked at the Pet Store. He was great until he started dealing coke. And the attitude on the fucker.

He didn't take shit and Damian emulated him a lot because he reminded him a lot of himself. And Damian knew that Russ was not all gone for freaking out at people. A lot of them didn't make sense. But Russ would freak out as he got older. As the 21 st Century entered, Russ would fight a lot. Getting frustrated mostly by ignorance, he would take it up on himself to just fight. Daman identified a lot with his attitude. But there was shit that wasn't right.

The crew in high school had decided that dealing drugs was not for them, but some of them were ideally made for it, so they forgave Russ for selling weed and the crew was permitted by itself to sell pot. And some prescriptions in their name, it was no big deal. But Mike had started dealing coke and so had you known who, Russ. And no one thought about Russ doing it, but if you didn't buy coke, you couldn't buy pot. Even to his friends. So, he and Damian had a falling out.

Damian had been smoking most of his life and had medical conditions like glaucoma and pinched nerves which gave him pain, and lots of headaches, nausea, and schizophrenia. And a pando-cartitus spell, which made pot the perfect risk for all his ailments. He just needed to make sure he didn't have his heart swell up if he ran out of pot for a long time. The pot was helpful to his health. And Russ didn't give a fuck.

Russ liked to watch bootleg movies on his TV, but you couldn't see the screen. The screen was jet black, so he assumed because he didn't make the movie that it was the black thing to do, look at a black screen with radiation coming off his old-style box television.

The kind you must hit on the side to get to see the screen. LK felt like walking in and kicking the side of the TV to see if he could get a picture. And Russ asked him if he wanted to triple caked stacks of ecstasy. And he said no but wanted to say yes. He just didn't have the money and wanted to think about it. And the screen didn't change.

So, not only was he stealing money from the movies, he was wasting electricity, keeping the TV blaring in your face with waves and sound, having no screen to look at but a black screen and you can hear the dialogue. That was pissing Damian off. His roommates back in Jamaica used to sell those fucking things too. Stealing money from the entertainment industry while all the actors and musicians put in their hard work. Boo-hoo.

And besides the DVD's and cigarettes like Shane, he got all that immigrant pay of a few thousand a month and a free no tax off the books paying full time job, doing maintenance even though he got a permanent limp that is how he got that SSI and that SSDI. And to think, you can collect SSI and still get Food Stamps? I think they changed that law.

Well, at least the roommates didn't have dogs you had to take care of. A lot of crazy slutty girls with pit bulls have cases with the FBI for some reason. That included Nori and some others. Nori used to call that place in Jamaica and then call Patrick and have him cheat on his wife, in hopes as a Jew and self-respecting black that hated blacks, to destroy the white people. But they had made an agreement already and she couldn't destroy Lisa. The Legacy.

The fucking dog used to get cold and hide his face in the lap. And Damian used to freak about Betty, Russ' pit-bull keeping her face warm in his balls. And it was a bit frightening to chill with those two fuckers. Russ always used astral projection, and Antoine just followed what Russ did.

So, if Russ hated the whites and used his powers to manifest visions and energy of the KKK to pour into the minds of his enemies, any white people in the room, then Antoine had to pour some KKK visions into everyone too. And this is how people use their creative energy.

Pouring visions of the KKK into the minds of others, so that the other people there don't steal all the power, because nobody likes the KKK, and everyone can see them marching in through the astral realm. He was in like Flynn with Big Keith and Frank. They passed Russ a rite to passage. Gale wanted him to deal with her and put the word out on him.

So, as it stood, Russ the big-time dealer now, joined the Strassberg on some level, dealing and working for their cause of taking over the world.

Damian could not stand him anymore and told him off. After about 15 years of telling him he wanted nothing to do with him, Russ finally got the picture. And Damian stood against the ignorant son of a bitch. He had signed a deal with the devil. He pretended like he was a friend because he wanted to slang on the wrong side of the tracks and Damian Keith just wanted some weed for his fucking pain. And Russ needed to bring HA into it.

Russ went down to 2 Ave a lot to drink. And he did run into those guys. But there was a lot of history there, with Damian, and D was unlucky enough to have his stripes ripped down from that crew when their chapter was shut down in the 1980s. A long story that is for another chapter.

Anyway, Shane too hangs out down on 2Ave, but Shane was barred from spending time with HA, while LK was not. Shane was a big brat and pretended to know some guy named Lucien, who was a part of a song, by a group from back in the days in the 90s hip hop rap scene. There was a song entitled "Luck of Lucien" that was written and performed back then by A Tribe Called Quest.

Big Keith's sister Karen had bought the group's second album for LK at a summer graduation party or birthday party that was held at Gale's place. So, Shane was present.

Now Shane and LK weren't friends, but rivals. And Shane tried to befriend him and say he was family only to be there to destroy him and lead him on. LK always knew this, and Shane was always an experiment to him and treated him as such. I mean, there were always government doctors there and Shane didn't know about it. He was too young to remember. But again, for another chapter.

There was a guy at Shane's parties, he was Mitchell's brother so he was Shane's uncle, and he would show up on Thanksgiving every year at Shane and Mitchell's place. That is owned by Mitchell not by Gale. Even though she brags she owns it, she just runs the big mouth and pretends she has crack in her purse.

Anyway, Mitchell's brother and a family friend, he was Mitchell's mom's boyfriend, was a bald Frenchman named Lucien. This Lucien was not the Lucien from the song 'Luck of Lucien,' he was a different guy altogether. Except this guy was on the white end, had a big French accent and was bald for forty years, shiny bald, all day every day. Like the Kojak. Anyway, Shane got it to him to tell everyone that Lucien owned this bar on 2 Ave in Manhattan, it was a huge bar. It was a giant-sized place. He did but he didn't.

And not only that, Shane, told everyone that he was in fact the Lucien from the song, and that he was great friends with the group and was best friends with Q-Tip himself for well over forty years.

Then Shane told everyone that he worked for Belmont Racetrack as a horse photographer, and he published a photo of his of a horse that looked like it was a butt shot, it had no focus even for a 'drunk photo' like a blurry post card or picture that is a photo sarcastically when someone is drunk.

It had no focus you could tell nothing about what it was except that it said it was a close of a horse and jockey in a caption beneath it. And the colors of the photo were a big splash of brown and some green or blue and yellow some horse jockey shit that didn't focus on the presentation.

It was just a horrible photo, the worst photo ever published, by far. And I mean, by far. You can't find a worse photo I don't think in history.

Anyway, a screw is loose with these people. Shane is waiting to sell crack and cigarettes to someone. Hoping to drop some off outside a Congressional building or the FBI office buildings they have or near the Department of Interior. He would show up in the middle of the dark night and have a handful of coca and crack for me if I wanted it. But why would he even think that was a smart thing to do?

Pat sits in his office all day hoping to smoke cigars and sell some crack, but he doesn't see that he isn't doing business and that is not what business is all about. He has no customers, he has a trunk full of complaints, he has a plan to kill thousands of people with some drugs and Kool Aid.

The thing that really puzzles everyone is why they get to play with a real CIA psychic and why do they have to instruct people in their minds about mind control?

The sad thing about this is that this organization has not been shut down yet. They are in limbo. The authors of the text you are reading have shut them down plenty of times, but they are still trying to take over the world. They have a clear access to a particular technology that is dangerous. It is a multivariate astral projection, and it has a million different applications. It is something out of the Project Montauk. Or the CIA Montauk Project.

It promotes a clairvoyant psychic, equipped with accurate telepathy, facial recognition, streaming to thousands and millions of people at once through a mental highway, it is a mind control operative or psychic's dream, either one. A wet dream. This thing has a million diverse ways to use it and can be fortified with visualization, any type of ancient teaching can be altered to transform into a psychic and clairvoyant energy.

There are energy bubbles, wires, tubes, waves, forces all included in this particle worship, where the people can access the minds of those they focus on. And they consider it a form of people power. As in Power to the People.

And they choose to listen to Damian. Because Patrick tricked everyone and told them he was the Messiah. But he didn't. But there is this CIA technology.

A cloud or bubble that can reflect your mind to yourself or through others' minds, energies, physically, subliminally, and covertly, and this is what Gale and Arlene, and their family were passing out as a form of technology and rite of passage because they think the government wants them to distribute and traffic and smuggle. Making snuggling with the cute and sexy illegal.

They spawn their ears and their faces to destroy Keith and missed the Cosmic Energy, the information from the Pleiadeans and the information given to them by the God and Lord of the universe. They listen to the oil of the Dark One, the Satanic psychic that they use to listen to the mind of LK and Damian.

And Steve didn't tell anyone his mom was a cop, he said she was just a crossing guard. But her and her husband are commanders and wear a commander uniform. And Steve tried to say that Damian was a schizophrenic because Amy tried to seduce him, and he walked her to class for months, and they held hands twice and hugged five times and kissed twice and went on three dates that sucked the life out of him. And she bit his neck one night and drank a spot of blood. And Steve always resented it.

And Damian was labeled a schizophrenic by Big Keith and Shane and Patrick and Steve.

And Russ practiced astral projection until you bought some shit from him. And beat the shit out of some patrons with him. And stole some motherfucker's money with him. And stole some fuckers shit from him. And ran from the cops. And snitched to the cops. And look at Russ with his big googling eyes, all seeing eyes, watching all day all night in a spy in psychic powers he would see that man, Russ from Flatbush. With the fine powder.

Mike was selling coke the day he died. And he died with Antoine there just a few hours before. And no one trusted Antoine. Ever. And Antoine might have taken the LIRR home back to Atlantic and caught the D train to Ave K and walked back to his crib.

But he called Russ on the phone, after spending the night at Mike's house and influenced Russ to drop off a big bag of weed to him while picking him up and dropping him off in a radius near Russ' place. And Russ showed up and was hard and mad at Mike for starting shit with some kid he was playing basketball with, and Mike clocked a black kid playing basketball. And then Russ clocked Mike for some coke shit, as friends do to each other under the influence and circumstances.

Now, Damian can't pinpoint, he wasn't there. Mike died shortly after 9/11 with Antoine leaving his house, Mike was upstairs in his room and somehow got shot. Did Antoine climb in his bedroom and shoot him? Damian doubted it, but it wasn't farfetched. After Mike died, D got into touch for some reason with some guys he used to know, and they told him Mike had died a few weeks earlier. And that Antoine was there. And they all went to the funeral. And everyone thought that Antoine did it. And Russ.

And Gabe said it too. And Little Rob said it. And Adam Killa touch had said that everyone thought they did it. And Antoine always bragged about trying to hurt some motherfucker, but they loved Mike. But Mike was a half Jew Puerto Rican, they knighted the Latino to beef in fact instead of escorting them to sickle cell anemia and lives as light brown newly inducted black people. Meaning, Russ was just racist and killed Mike for being Spanish.

LK Damian seen Russ throw some Spanish guy around wearing a uniform. Trying to break it up, Russ flips the guy over and they flip the tables in the bar. And Antoine hates Haitians.

Damian thinks about setting him up with his aunt. Phil married a Haitian lady. Barbara's brother. Damian's uncle. The guy who was not there when Barbara left yet lived in their apartment, was not there when Danny beat and whipped LK, but lived there too and was there on weekends to take him away from Big K and them on days off.

And he let LK stay with him and got him into going to the movies on Saturday, going to the Arcade after, going to get Nathan's in Times Square, going home to look at Baseball cards, comics and make dinner, watch the game, watch a late-night movie, and go home in the morning. On Sunday. And he dropped LK off around noon. And a few years into that, after seeing every movie, Phil got married to Liz, a Haitian. And her mom was from Haiti, and she was born there, and they had a family. And they took on big families for no reason and there were a million people around.

But as time went by, Phil felt bad about leaving LK with those losers. But Antoine didn't know Phil at all, he knew of Pat and worked for Gale without even knowing why or for what reason, but they figured out that there was a cop, a psychic, and a psychologist, working for British Intelligence with full power to arrest using the Police in the United States and could pull warrants and had connections in media and with judges and senators; these guys were investigating the authorized American psychic that assumed it was in full jurisdiction to operate an operation that was worthy of capital punishment in the U.S. and was not being investigated by the American government. It was being investigated by the International Monetary Fund.

Shane and all of them were waiting to meet and do business together.

But it was not that simple. Shane was a big fake and had a problem. His mom thought that if you destroy the ghetto street education by possessing people's minds through witchcraft, visualization, spells, negative energy, viewpoints that hold front and energy claws, and projected negative intentions you can produce a hypnosis that produces direct mind control.

This bitch didn't ever care about offending the street and the ghetto and the Goddess and everything like the fact that everyone in the ghetto emulated righteousness. Were upright people unlike many scholars and brokers I knew. Fuckers. There were a lot of good-natured humorists and people there in those industries but all they could do is try to identify what real people went through daily.

\How they earned their stripes in front of the Creator and the Volcano and the UAP drone flying above, and their mother and their sisters and their brothers and wives and kids. Like real people did. These robots just wanted to sell you drugs, get you stoned, and probably just get caught fucking you up the ass while you dared to pass out in front of the cabinet. Oh, shit I'm the president, what do I do? I'm baked on Shane's crack laced with shit. Who knows what? Could be LSD or any of that shit. Fentanyl even. Deadly. Deadly stuff taking over the streets and the drug market.

Speaking of which.

Mitchell, Russ, Shane, Erin, and Julieanne, Jack's daughter, wanted to fill the ghettos with poison so they could steal your kids and take them away from you. And they still get to operate. Why?

What is it about these people that Uncle Sam and the Milk Maid from Canada approve of these people selling drugs in our neighborhoods and in Washington D.C.? They do this while walking and taking selfies, outside government offices and in our environments.

They are proud to disrupt other people, and their lives, and sell drugs and make jokes that they are stealing your children. They are doing this in the open and it is happening in front of everyone, and no one is saying anything. And they are giving lesser amounts of drugs to people and in a few months breaking up their families and spending time with small children involved, appearing as if they are more responsible and more white bread and offering to baby sit them and take them to holiday parties.

They are often laughing at society openly and have permission to sell drugs and trade children. They are bragging and hooting that they are pulling this off, paying the police, having no problems with the FBI, and dealing drugs in the park outside the White House.

Making deliveries from Boston to South Carolina with stops in Pennsylvania and New Jersey. Strassberg has a branch with Erin and Les the Karate teacher, in Central New Jersey.

They are hooting and hollering, especially because all this time when the world is falling apart to anarchy, mutiny within the government, we are finding these people at a crucial turning point in life. And they are in charge. And, yet they are pretending to sell drugs, trade children, and parade this information around the world.

As they wander the earth with nothing to do and walk around the government building in D.C. hoping to sell drugs and trade children while holding low level government jobs and everyone is just waiting to see what happens.

Meaning no one gives a fuck, they are allowed to deal whatever they want. Why does this family with their connections in Canarsie, get to mind control the entire world and follow Damian around through a hypnosis? Patrick called Damian on the phone on a landline no doubt and told him that he was reflecting his mind to him physically and projecting faces and voices into his ears and eyes to affect his decision making and to destroy him. He told him this directly. And Damian snapped.

And he called Pat at his house and left a message that Pat had left his wallet at the strip club. And Lisa, Pat's wife forgot who LK was. When he rang the bell, she said she didn't know who he was. And he was an usher at their wedding. And Pat said I will give you ten dollars every time I see you, if you leave me alone about the money, I owe you. And hey, that was another agreement that Pat had reneged on.

In 2020 Damian wanted to know if the investigation was still ongoing against Pat and his family. Except at this point, he didn't want to know. It was the pandemic, and he was happy he did not have Covid, and he did not hear Pat in his head anymore. And even though there were people there in Phoenix outside the Air BnB in a rough part of town, firing automatic weapons, and Swedish guys were starting fights with him and people talking shit to him were getting jumped outside, and all kinds of chaos was brewing. Damian found an ad online about joining the Wolf of Wall Street, Jordan Belfort in a new venture.

Damian immediately put together his demo tape and after 23 takes, he sent in one of them. In a few hours, he received a response from them, and he was in communication with that office for about two weeks. Let's just say that on the last day they communicated, it was a done deal that he was going to start training with Jordan himself and become an expert in Sales and working for a Security Firm.

During the conversation where there was some form of finalization before work started, a black helicopter hovers loudly over the house while Damian is on the phone. He did not turn around to look at the helicopter, just a few dozen feet over his head right behind him. He hung up with the woman on the other side gulping, and then the next day, the phone was disconnected, and he never received another email from Straight Line Hiring Service again.

And it was gross. Going there trying to forget these people. For him, it was turmoil. Every time he thought something, they would appear. And reappear. And he would remember, when Patrick called him and told him that if he did not join them, then he would be punished with astral projections of schizophrenia, fear, and voodoo, as well as all kinds of mockery and sarcastic self-reflection. D tried to ward it off as scam artists. He considered all these people scam artists. It was obvious that it was what they were, deep down. A bunch of scam artists.

Pat was a scammer financial broker. Gale was a scammer real estate agent. Jack was a scammer comedian and 33rd degree Freemason. Arlene was pretending to be prestigious by having a legitimate job in an office and was just scamming people's kids. Julie was scamming pretending she was going to school. Paul was scamming two families while in the Merchant Marines. Mitch was scamming pretending he worked both in manufacturing and on Wall St.

John was scamming pretending he wasn't keeping his ears open to the cops by being a cop. Shane was scamming pretending to be a salesman and government agent. Erin was scamming selling drugs through the Karate school. Big Keith was scamming pretending he was setting up a multi marketing Sales circle while attending AA meetings and recruiting there. Russ was scamming to get famous. Antoine was scamming to sell pot and smoke weed and get famous. Little Rob was scamming for his job. Gabe was scamming to become a vet, sell narcotics, and take over the world.

Gabe was more the kind of guy I took for having a big plan, but the scary part is that Frank's little idea, even though he wasn't officially an Ohanlon after he divorced Patricia and that, but he still was a part of it, she tried to throw him out of that family, but they overlooked his faults and he still was connected. But he died at an early age for a guy nowadays.

He lived his life as if he were an old man the entire time and died at a mere 67 years old. That is young. But to think that if Gabe had included his ideas into the foundation of the cult, how powerful they would be. The world would have ended.

And if there were witches there that knew what they were doing, instead of just some experimental CIA psychics, then you could even say that this group was going to destroy the world, and the real CIA was going to swoop in and shoot them in the fucking heart and terrorize and maim them for fun. Because these people are scumbags.

Despite it all there was no one there but scammers. Big Keith was a very unlucky kind of friend. He was there to make sure you didn't drink if that is what you wanted but that was not really what he was good at. He drove people to drink. He sold Amway, ran a Mitch Miller Folk Singing Circle, went to AA for years, got addicted to crack, thought crack and LSD and gangs were something you talk about nightly to young kids. Like a psychopath, Big K aka Modak, used to drive around in the afternoon on his way to pick up his wife at the hospital where she worked at the pharmacy, and he would scream obscenities from nis car, often racially motivated and aggressive towards anyone including Jews, blacks, Asians, Italians, and he was partial to Arabs and some Spanish people, but he threw them int too if he had to. If someone white cut him off he would call them either a "Mook' all day long, or some kind of 'bastard.' With a label on the front of it. Like 'you black bastard' or 'You Jew bastard.'

LK would wait for him to stop the car and often until they arrived back from the drive, to punch him in his arm or leg in the Charlie horse, leaving Big K to writhe on the ground, and he would give him noogies and something called 'gills; which occurred a lot in the 1980s when someone does something openly embarrassing or stupid, you can slap them in the neck or the back of the head, but you have to say 'save mine'. Every time or you get accused of an assault and even a battery.

So, kids would often, like punch buggy, jump at the opportunity to catch someone saying something that everyone thought was idiotic at the same time. 'Save mine, let me catch a gill.' And they would be first to slap or slide their hand on the back of the kid's neck. Then everyone could line up and give out a 'gill' one at a time. At the very rare moments, people caught collective gills but for the most part, everyone just lined up one by one and the person would have to bow their heads to get some gills. After Damian was in like the 7th grade, people just said it out loud, it became taboo to slap people in the head and scratch their necks from humorous 'gills.'

There were many types of gills. People would have to try and invent new ones, and there were all kinds of gills where cartoon characters were created. For the Chip n Dale 'gill' people would lay their hands on the back of the kids neck and say 'Chi-Chi-cha-cha-chip n dales' and sing the song to their cartoon theme and as they said the 'Ch' part they could warm up and slide their hand on the neck back and forth, and do a final follow through with the end of the sentence. The Mickey Mouse gill, kids would spell the name Mickey Mouse in a song, but would pull the ears lightly of the kid getting the gill with each letter being sung, and at the end of the song when you're supposed say 'E' at 'M-O-U-S-E' you can slap the back of their neck hard.

You could slide in on a skateboard and slap their gill and say 'Cowabunga' for a style of a Ninja Turtle Gill.

Big K was an open bigot and made fun of his own kids. He told them to save everything, to never leave home, and to only work for the city or for a pharmacy. Big Keith asked his kids for sex. LK hit him off every day with gills and Charlie horses and all kinds of threats. But Big K was an adult and tried to make out with him all the time and empty his schoolbag in front of his wife to try and make sure he was in charge and had the pants on. But as soon as she left, LK would drop that motherfucker right on the ground and beat him a bit, even kick him in the rib's arms, slap him in the shoulders, stomach hit him in the sternum lightly. Always drop that guy.

He used to work out and then try and start fights with LK. He had a lot of problems with calling people names and his wife had a relationship with Marty Maher from the scouts and the parks, who was just bad news. And Big K slept with Angela's sister and called up D. at some point on the phone and started bragging about it. Saying he slept with Josephine and Angela knew about it, he wasn't allowed to say anything. The problems grow with Big old K. He's sick and tired now and has a strange disorder.

He complains he has attraction to young boys. He traded coke for his son, demands that people sell crack for his affection and says it is the family business.

Now, that person is a piece of shit. I mean, does Abigail eat him on a cracker?

Does she dip her asparagus nacho chips in him? Is he a steaming pile on the side of a snowy road, that someone left to not shit in the car? What kind of piece of shit is this asshole? Why is he alive?

The President is Dead

The funny part is that G.W. agreed to let LK become a subliminal mind control through the desire to destroy the influence of Shane. And Obama sent more horses and king's men to investigate the O'Hanlon's who might just be big mouths talking shit trying to sell the shit out of their purses to make their mortgages. So, they don't have to go back and live in the projects. They got rocks, they got kids, they got cigs, they got stocks, they got land, they got apartments, they got houses, they got garbage, and they got pharmaceuticals, and Amway and bottles and all kinds of freezer goods. These motherfuckers don't want to live in the projects anymore. Don't you get it?

Because they get a pardon. They are allowed to deliver to the property line of the White House with some dope and they are allowed to hijack a fucking school bus and drive kids around in the middle of the night singing Christmas carols. Who the fuck are these guys? And we have not even gotten to the point where things are out of control. We have not even really crossed the threshold as to how unbelievable this story is. So silly. They crack a joke, drink beer and a wine and talk around the TV and have a giant meal together.

How ridiculous, because they believe that if you can sell this shit then someone will buy it.

They confess to Damian on the phone that if you look outside the window, you can see their image in a hologram that they are projecting that is not of an official technology. And then they will tell you that of course, you can hear it and it is talking to you, it is a form of psychic, and they have a power. And that Gene Hackman and Brad Pitt are helping them with their superpower to talk to people in a psychic way. And that is just like Fight Club.

I have not gotten to the point in the story, where I have told a lie, yet.

Well, it just so happens that some dumb motherfucker from the civilian corps of the CIA wanted to go into business with them and use a form of psychic telepathy that was being passed around through an experiment, and he created a monster with these people. And they believed that they would always have immunity. And that if they projected their faces into people's dreams and into their subconsciousness that it was possible to get them to do whatever they wanted them to do. And they projected voices and faces into walls and into public spaces and told all their followers that if they didn't do it and scare the shit out of people with telepathy that they would destroy and kill their families. And they practiced hypnosis a few times a week on themselves and lit candles regularly for years and planned out elaborate black magic ceremonies and disclosed this information to LK whom they were asking to join them and he refused and suffered an intense schizophrenia and gained over 200 pounds anticipating having to fight members of the cult and sought to outweigh and outsmart them simultaneously while fighting and defending himself.

He felt upset that Gale and Mitch and Pat and Karen had threatened him. And Big K and others there also wanted him down for not helping. Josephine had an affair with Big K behind her sister's back. And everyone had a tough time with the chief gypsy because she was around when people didn't invite her and didn't want her around and she took over everyone' s mind all day long. It's all she did besides make pants out of curtains and read Tarot cards. She was listening to psychic friends of hers she said, and Patrick swore she gave him the power to see the future and read people's minds. And he sought to establish the kingdom of Frank.

And Shane went nuts. He became a schizophrenic. His mom bragged to everyone that Shane was a powerful psychic. And Pat said it too. He called people on the phone and bragged that Shane was in the Marines and was a powerful member of the cult and would someday know his purpose. Not only was he a powerful part of the cult, but he was also a powerful leader, a psychic, a powerful psychic aside from being a cult prophet and a crack dealer and a spoiled selfish brat who was infiltrating the government, participating in antigovernment rhetoric, and working for the Marines in order to traffic children and coke to cook up some crack rocks. Everyone told this motherfucker to kick rocks since the day he was born.

Now he was just the same brat, but an identical giant. And not only did the rumors of Shane spread through the Oval Office in 2005 that he was screaming at himself and appearing to people in dreams and set the president on alarm that the New World Order was occurring in the etheric realm inside people's brains and minds and energy fields and was not a physical threat anymore. And Shane went nuts.

Screaming that Bush was a brainwash, and he was sent to Afghanistan to defend Big Keith who went AWOL and people like Pat who were seeking favors off kids and starting cults. And Shane didn't realize that Pat was a creep. And he was saying the wrong thing.

So, Bush instituted some mental mind control across the population. He started sending illegal messages across the world speaking through communist tubes and sending messages into frequencies like someone craving rhetoric and forgetting they can get arrested for thinking communist. And they didn't know any better when they asked themselves if the president felt better by trying to legalize schizophrenia and that alluded to the government generating voice to skull technology.

And that was how the Gilbride Strassberg Flannery, you know the Brooklyn O'Hanlon clan got along with life. Sending mind control through tubes and collecting people's minds from the atmosphere and space and devouring their lives and their souls. And Teaneck crew joined in, pretending to battle them. They called and lied to the FBI and went and met with the president over and over. Meeting with Bush and generating Shane in a magic, for the cult and to get away with it.

The funny part was that the CBS News crew in NYC was setting it off by putting out announcements and PSAs for bounties on anyone who used a psychic that broke the Patriot Act, or threatened the president, or saluted the terrorists and the 9/11 attacks, or that had a weird psychic over others, and worked for law enforcement. This PSA said it, every night, that if any psychic was hoarding information about this stuff, or planning anything crazy, and had to do with any kind of secret service-based fraud, or threats against the president, then both the psychic and the person not reporting them were supposed to get the death penalty. And this was crazy as this was an actual PSA that went on for a couple of years every single night on the news at 6 PM. And it was in a major city and on CBS. And NBC had no clue as to what the hell Damian was talking about when he mentioned all this shit.

But the secret service had shown up and arrested Shane for some story about him having a psychic when he was yelling about GW being a brainwashed. He was taken by the secret service agents while working as a marine and questioned about his viewpoints and his schizophrenia and his relationship with Damian. And he knew LK had said a crazy story, but Shane wasn't being arrested for trafficking or smuggling or killing or assaulting anyone or doing anything wrong. He didn't have the gun in his hand. He was just a schizophrenic from Patrick and Arlene and Gale and everyone in his family talking to him telepathically so that he could work for the cult. And he did not get it. And screamed at himself and went nuts for a while.

And the secret service took him to a facility near Camp Pendleton and injected him with some medicine that would cure his schizophrenia. And he stopped yelling at himself. And he became more lucid. Except he projected his own face and pretended to be 5 years old to himself in an imaginary friend scenario and then had this little baby kid crawl around him in an astral vision and it would talk and run around and laugh and hoot and jam and ham out, like it was an invisible person crossing through people's minds. And this was Shane's life. To pretend to get a job and be a retard dealing drugs outside of the White House. Like some idiot realm, he took overeating the minds of others with his own image and witchcraft and practiced hypnosis. And he wanted to get rich or die trying and he told everyone more lies about who he knew. And about the time he met his wife. When he was still a virgin. They met while he was deployed.

Shane was a good soldier, but he cried sometimes and whined and was like a big giant brat baby man. Like a kid who is a big old brat but is giant in size and behaves exactly like an extremely bratty three-year-old not just some bratty three-year-old. I'm talking stamping their feet and yelling and folding their arms and crying and screaming in public and private and doing it the same but as an adult. With the same face.

And the same mind. This fucker has a disorder and it's not a good fucking song. Using hypnosis and visualization to project his face into the minds of everyone who could train their inner ear to hear him, and anyone who could not train their ear to ignore him.

And he was just a big baby who had cried at Thanksgiving in front of Arlene and Jack. He cried with tears running down his face. He was crying and screaming while stamping his feet on the steps beneath him, 'I want to be a celebrity! Why can't I be a celebrity?"

And Jack was laughing at him. And Shane quietly brooded and tried to get vengeance by utilizing his gift of astral projection into people's minds and astral hearts. And he was still running off and telling God he was smoking crack. Everyone could hear him complaining. And he reflects to himself as to how he found his mom's weed and drugs when he was a baby and made fun of his mom. And he smiles. He almost got her caught. And yet, it paid his bills his entire life. How do you think he got baby food? And that house he lived in. And he forgot about his government doctors, and the team that worked on his mind and genetics with experimental drugs when he was a kid.

And he thought he remained present and smoked blunts. Yet, he fashioned himself as to being stylish in the 90's but it was the 2000's. And he feared men. And he liked to play ball, but that would interfere with his mom's operation. People would start to notice that he was somehow smoking crack occasionally. It was obvious. And people pretended like the guy was just a reject and he was just someone who nobody liked. But it went deeper than that. It went much further.

The secret service and the division of child support caught up with him. And he didn't care, and he barely even understood what he had done. That his mom set him up to die. She made him a schizophrenic by praying to anchor a psychic inside of him. And inside of his head.

In his spirit and in his energy, she wanted him to be a psychic. So, he was arrested for being a national threat, with thousands of people seeing him in their minds and in their dreams and hundreds reporting him, to escape death. They called CBS to respond to the PSA. They called the FBI to avoid the death penalty. They prayed that the schizophrenia would not destroy them. And no one could understand why they heard these voices.

Including Joe Biden. And Trump knew why. It was how the cult controlled the world. So, he told his followers in their dreams and spoke to them as if the Lord were speaking and consoling one of his prophets. And he told them to follow the psychic, that projected voices everywhere on behalf of the Strassberg. And Trump told his followers not to allow the government to own them, yet they broke the international ordinance, the same people who banned Communism, were hunting the psychic and those who projected schizophrenia and intentionally created Voice to Skull Technology. And they were battling in their souls and minds to take this ring down, but in the physical, it was a slow and delayed reaction.

They had nothing on them. Nothing. And nothing that could really stand in a court of law. So, the cult was just on paper, the assassination attempt was in their dream and psychic and the Patriot Act was in their affairs with little girls who had no experience in life or love and had a bunch of STDs. That was the target of a bunch of virgins who got STD's while losing their virginity. And the ugly bitches thought they had right with FBI because they had chlamydia and syphilis and weren't criminals by trade. They thought they stayed out of prison; they had something to live for. They bragged about staying out of prison but were only psychics. And tormenting people without being caught. And everyone wanted a problem, but no one took one. Except secret service and Scotland Yard and Damian. And the pigs marveled at the guy. He was so much of a unique enigma and the Flannery giggled that they weren't getting caught.

And Shane was followed around and was injected inside of a facility to end his schizophrenia.

How much crack did he smoke? As it was stated, Shane married the first or the second girl he nailed. But everyone knows it was the first one and that would no one gave that fucker the time of day except for a bunch of people who regretted it. They regretted giving him the time of day. There was never a person alive at any of the big giant events that were held to which Shane was invited, that ever walked away proclaiming that they liked him, as he was a little kid, cute as a button and three years old until he was about 16. He wore the same overalls for 15 years and was only a bit over four feet high. Until he was 16. When he more than likely jacked off for the first time that he noticed something, on the flower girl at Pat's wedding. Suddenly, he wanted some pussy and grew into someone else's shoes. Past a size 5 shoe.

Shane had visited the government doctor's office often. Barbara had noticed Gale there and had been there once a week to visit LK for an eye exam and he had had a pre glaucomic condition for most of his life. His eyes were stressed out. And he had eye treatments and they sat him in a chair and laid him on a doctor's examining table and a bunch of doctors would put him under and examine his eyes. And the visit took over an hour sometimes. Because he was under the influence of some kind of nova cane in case things went weird. And he remembered that. Damian remembered going to the government doctors to fix his eyes. And he still has that cataract condition that he always had. A side effect of the drops and treatments may have caused his eyes to turn green and reflective, so when he wore blue the eyes looked blue. If he wore grey, his eyes matched his grey tone and green and electric.

So, his visits were extensive, and Barbara took him for years and they got a few bucks for the treatment and that was when, right at the very end of the visits, after years of undergoing these treatments, the last four or five weeks, Gale had shown up. With Shane in a bassinet. And never did LK even honored that kid's life, because she never took him out and it was as if there were a doll in her bassinet. And LK didn't notice them, nor like them. And Joanna recognized Gale, but Barbara didn't. Even though she stayed hanging out with Theresa, Terry's wife. And Terry was Gale's sister. But Barbara didn't realize that.

And Joanna said hello to Gale and Gale started to talk to Barbara on the next week's visit. And Joanna ignored it. And then the week before the last treatment, Gale offers Barbara some coke.

On consignment. Just a bag. And she said OKAY. She'd try it. And then weeks went by, and Keith showed up looking for the money. It was true, it wasn't, and she paid for it. And Big Keith and LK met. And then Gale wanted Keith to drop off a big bag and bring LK over to meet Shane. So, they could be friends.

And it was outwardly the idea that Shane was the child of the Devil. And Keith refused to investigate his crib. And refused to meet him. And it went on like that for a while. For two years. The punks had gone to the island of Jamaica and didn't worry about fitting in Queens and Brooklyn.

They arrived back from the island after living on a plantation or some shit and bought a Volkswagen Beetle

Bus, and a house in Staten Island that in 2024 was worth 128,000$ out the door.

But they meant well, even by distributing coke which soon turned to crack in the 1980s. And the world spun forward, everyone trying to get LK to sell pharmaceuticals, build a UFO, and take everyone up to the mothership to become enlightened and live in the skies on LSD.

Now they had profited in on the fact that most of Staten Island in the early 1980's was undeveloped outside of the coastal areas.

There were a lot of apartment complexes and housing developments that were scheduled to be built. But they had not been completed or even started yet. By the early 1990's the borough of NYC had been filled up.

And most people assumed that it was filled with toxic waste and that someone would turn yellow neon green if they moved over there and they would get some kind of MRSA or Leukemia or Cancer.

It was joked that people who moved to Staten Island, could now glow in the dark.

It was an island that existed from compacted garbage and was put together by burning melted waste and mixing it with concrete during the Industrial Revolution and was made from incinerated leftover garbage. At that point, it was amassed and floating in the harbor past the Statue of Liberty. Developers assumed the responsibility of anchoring the island to the center of the earth and that does mean the bottom of the sea with some chains and anchors. And lots of concrete and Sand.

And after they set it in place, they filled it all in with moss, dirt, and cement and built streets on it. And slowly they perfected the landmass, that was designed to store the city's entire landfill for garbage. And there was one all the way on the North End of the borough of Brooklyn. All the way near the beaches in Long Island on

Nassau. And it was impervious that people wondered why or who in the world was going to move to Staten Island? As soon as you landed there you were either on a military base, or in an Italian American ghetto beach area, or smack right in the middle of the projects.

Or you would be in a nice little neighborhood but that was closer to the Jersey side of town. There was Tottenville, which was the far West End of the island and that is where everyone visited the pool. Even the local church camps and groups in Red Hook and Carroll Gardens.

There was a pool in the Red Hook projects, but it was pretty much guaranteed that someone was going to get into a fight there or there would be a confrontation nearby or outside that caused a disturbance, because even though the public pool in the Red Hook projects was nice, it had the potential to go really bad, if the crackheads or junkies could find a way in, or if a gang had chosen to visit. The church groups were big anyway, so they took a big van and bus all the way out to Tottenville to avoid the elements in Red Hook.

Hey, Red Hook had produced not only Barbara's tribe of Puerto Ricans, and Jennifer's tribe of Mexicans, as she had made the transition from Puerto Rican boyfriends to Mexicans in the middle of the early 21st Century. Patricia, Barbara's sister had already dated a Mexican. And Phil, he married a Haitian. Gale and Mitch went to Jamaica and married Cocaine. Patrick married a schizophrenic billionaire from Canarsie.

He married for money. And it was toasty on the other side of the river, the houses had heat and there was lots of construction going on, that Gale and Mitchell were taking advantage of. Gale had gone into Real Estate and Mitchell had a shady job over by Bowling Green.

One that when he lost it, he picked up another one nearby. He is in manufacturing, but no one knows what that fucker does. And that was the entire rent.

Worked there on some manufacturing line and took the ferry every morning. Hey, I would live and work for ten hours a day four days a week and take the ferry. But I would have to earn a little bit more money somehow. And I am sure we could figure it out.

But the houses were in development out on the Island, and it was the place where the government decreed that the entire five counties of NYC would dump all their trash there until the landfill was filled.

Big Keith and Frank had friends and family there, and some cousins were related to Frank who lived out there. So, when Big K met Damian, he started making him visit places in Staten Island.

Damian would visit and never look Shane in the eye, and people would attempt to introduce them, but LK would only ignore the bratty kid, who was obviously trying to set him up in some way. And that was true. As soon as, two years after they had initially started spending time in the same places, LK and Shane were formally introduced to one another. And LK knew that Shane was in to manipulate him to no end. Every time Shane had a friend to visit with them, as they started spending more time with one another, and LK was there to supervise Shane and teach him social skills.

However, when it seemed hopeless, Jennifer and Stacy O'Hanlon showed up and identified themselves as Shane's first cousins. And they helped LK defeat Shane. And Shane was hard to defeat. He would frame and lie and set people up to get into trouble with his mom. And his mom forever threatened to beat Shane with a wooden spoon.

She would say it to him every time they went anywhere, every time they went everywhere and if they were there to visit for three hours or so, she would say it at least a dozen times to him. "I am going to get the wooden spoon." And he would say "Oh. Ok. I'm sorry. I'll stop." And it would repeat over and over.

There was no place ever, that a person, young or old, adult, or minor, teenager or smaller kids and professional people, that if they spent more than a few minutes with Shane, they would immediately walk over to the closest group of people and complain about him. And they would say things like "I have never met a little kid that I didn't like. And that kid is the reason why nobody cares about or likes kids." He was extremely popular.

Jennifer and Stacy told everyone at LK's school, as they went to the same elementary school, about Shane. And the third-grade teacher who made everyone call her by her first name, Joyce, had her husband hired as the gym teacher at the school. Joe was the new gym teacher's name, and he introduced dodge ball and dodge ball tournaments to the lunches at the elementary school. And it was interesting that Joe and Joyce didn't have kids and lived in Staten Island. And Joe turned out to be Shane's baseball coach. And Joe and Big K got into it, when Joe started making fun of LK because of his now overweight status.

Whereas he grew up until he was about 7 with a skinny attitude, lots of big blonde hair, and was bright and sunny. He loved to smile and laugh. He was clumsy and fell down a bunch and he had tons of little girlfriends his own age, who asked him out and they would hold hands and hug and have relationships, that they were profoundly serious about when he was only three and four and five years old.

But as soon as Big K entered the life, there was no room for girlfriends, and he thought LK should have zero contact with girls and having girlfriends and he tried to turn

LK into a homosexual and possessed his heartstrings and his throat and his gas and brake pedals.

Whereas LK had learned to drive while they were in the countryside, Big K couldn't drive and was trying to get LK to be his boyfriend. So, they would go out and become men and visit with Frank's cousins who thankfully were nice people and didn't try to molest Damian Keith.

And he would watch Big K and this guy Bobby Tracy get drunk while LK hung out with a cousin that was about the age of Patricia whom he had become close with while living at Joanna's place. And she was a lot like an older sister for a couple of years.

When Barbara was on and off and when she finally took off permanently, Trish and Joanna were there. When Dennis the Native was dating Johanna, Joanna was left to raise Barbara's son. Everyone noted that they had similar names. And when LK moved in with Big K that February, everything changed. LK was not allowed to have girlfriends anymore and the girls were no longer as interested.

LK had a mole on his face by the time he was 8 that popped off through a zit that appeared as if by a magic spell and Big K was expecting it and placed it and looked at it and approved of the mole physically and mentally. And was satisfied.

And Barbara had moles on her face. And Big K entered sobriety. His mom Patricia, different from Barbara's Trish, started rebelling against alcohol. Patsy, as she was called, learned about AA, and went to the rooms to get sober.

After a few months of going, because of her issues with her new divorce; Frank had decided he wanted to get married to a woman from the American Legion who was known to hang out there looking for a husband. And they eventually started dating and they got married eventually.

Her son later jumped to his death on 9/11 and she and Frank moved out to Staten Island after Frank moved out and went down further on Sherman St. and then out with her in Bay Ridge before they purchased a Townhouse and moved out to the island. And it was the obsession that people were moving out there. In droves.

And the island stank and the kid's made fun of Arthur and his family for moving there. While Patrick made fun of the guy who jumped out the window once or twice, it was unintentional. And she was a drunk. And it led to complications between them.

Frank had developed into a conspiracy theorist, looking at what the government was doing to citizens through injustice and corruption and holding a resentment. And he would complain to Damian that he was not running from the right stuff and that he was supposed to buckle down and go back to school. And he ridiculed him for his life decisions.

And made it them of life to pick on Damian Keith for his immature status in the professional world on earth. As he didn't have a job. And he was in love with Thomas, his new wife Eleanor's son. His new son-in-law. Thomas had become a big banker and financial broker and investment consultant at the World Trade Center. He had money and was considered a top priority manager, with a couple of houses on the Jersey shore. Frank had a lot of affection towards him.

Patrick had gone to school for Finance and had served in the Marines. He joined the Marines at 18 and at 22 entered schooling at Pace University. He took 7 years to get his Bachelor and worked as a newspaper editor for the University Press.

He also worked at a financial firm known as Bear Sterns. Pat later bragged of his escapades in embezzlement and chose a job at a firm as a Tupperware reporter, who reported to industry executives on the new and innovative technologies run through bins, storage, and Tupperware. He had an expense account, free hotels and rental cars, free cell phone service each month, a MetroCard, and an allowance that gave him spending money while earning a 6-figure salary. He also had a rich wife.

While he had money for no labor, Frank could hardly tell people what Patrick did for a living. He was an industry reporter for Tupperware.

Across town, Patrick would show up in the 1990s at the Halloween party thrown by Gale with black makeup on. He had dressed up to look like Montel Williams. And no one said anything because he paid a few hundred dollars to do so, and they put makeup on his arms and hands, so it made it technically 'not black face.' And the parties were intense over there as time progressed.

Gale was selling cocaine, moving crack, and starting to advertise. It became mandatory to try and help her sell the stuff.

And there was no room to doubt that the Strasser lived just a few small streets away from the projects.

And there were two smokestacks out near Red Hook, that Arthur Homan the second, assumed Big Keith was admiring by living near them. Arthur Homan the second was ready to pass the torch of being a Sanitation worker to Arthur Homan the third. Arty the third was a student at Holy Name and was a catcher on the baseball team where Little Rocco LK was a pitcher.

Old Bubba had a purpose for Arthur when he used to spin sliders at him and strike out Billy Stout. Billy Stout's mom was the last person that LK and Barbara visited together before she took off. And Barbara went hiding in Bay Ridge and Arthur was groomed to think about her every day for most of his life, even emulating his wife about her.

But the thing about Arthur for now was that Arthur the Second had bought a house in Staten Island right across the street from the back gate of the Landfill. And when you looked out the window there you could see the giant mountain of landfill right outside the place. And when the sun rose, it rose over the landfill and the sky turned orange and pink like no other place before.

And when the heat turned on in the summer outside, the landfill could be smelled from across the river. As it was pinned behind the shopping mall that was going to fill up every day regardless of its location, Arthur Homan II moved his entire family there and they kept a room for Arthur III in Brooklyn so that he could spend time with his 'friends.' Everyone felt bad for Arthur, and he lived inside of their guilt.

Until the day he joined the cult, that gave him the power to project his face, including his eyes that could see his ears that could hear, and his chin that could lift itself higher than the mind they were invading. It was the sole purpose of the cult, to attach and control other people's minds at all costs.

It was necessary to control other people's minds because the founders of the cult who were working towards their goals, were controlling the minds of those who were controlling others minds, and it was set to work like a psychic and energy pyramid that the people at the top get to drink off of the energy of the people being mined controlled, who were at the bottom of the pyramid. And it was set up that they would also sell Amway products and sing Mitch Miller songs together, and move to a farm near Monticello, close to the camp. The boy scout camp.

And there was a boy scout camp in Staten Island. And Shane wanted to go, so he decided to attempt to join the twin brothers and Marty Maher from Prospect Park in Brooklyn Troop 237 to show him around. As Marty Maher was from Holy Name, he expressed great interest in getting to know Shane. And later, Martin would claim to be a founder of the cult.

And Nori would brag about laughing at Thomas from his jump at 9/11 and attempt to seduce Patrick give him an STD and that would infect his wife who would leave germs around from Nori's cists and the children would be infected too.

And that would be the Jews and the blacks owning the good of White financial families of America. And Bay Ridge would sink into the bay. On the ferries outside there would be whole tug loads of flowers flown in from the Islands and the West Indies. And everyone would be smoking crack. And the world would praise Nori for killing the white people. And the world would praise Nori for lying about 9/11.

And she would make it to G.W. Bush's speech while she was projecting Shane Strassberg into the minds of America and the world. And GW would look at her while giving a speech. 'Where's Keith?"

He would ask beneath his lips and into the molecular particle speakers, the vibrations of the earth and atmosphere reflected his voice and his face, and his astral projection and you could hear old GW ask, "Where's Keith?" And she noted and smiled and smirked as the world was hearing her witchcraft through the President's echoes of the world.

She was never going to do anything but be energy as a vicious cist or a disease. She passed her desire to destroy everything to her friends. She was collaborating with some people of hers from Teaneck she started following around Oregon and they would hide out there to fly out to Washington D.C. and raid events and all kinds of big parties and speeches.

And they started attending the Republican National Convention each year. And growing and hiding and listening to Keith from far away from Oregon. And George assumed that he was important enough to listen to the minds of others.

The other George was doing Kung Fu selling weed, getting robbed by his childhood friends and following Randy around, because he was raping women in Teaneck. Slurping the energy of everyone he meets, especially women, and gyrating his hips in public as soon as he gets drunk, hoping to cum and split his cock like a rooster in a hen house. Always crossing his breed by crossing his streams.

But doing it in front of anyone, including his girl, or bystanders, or acquaintances or dudes. He had to let you know that his cock was his biggest priority, and it had to be you to sacrifice the life inside your loins and the love inside your will so that he could feel a new woman from that and attract a woman to him by draining someone else's physical energy.

And laughs about it. He was a psychic vampire with some karma ahead of both he and Big Keith. Everyone wanted to know if the two of them would fight. And Big Keith knew that Randy even though he never met, was going to try and kill Big Keith. Just to get to LK. Because Nori licked him off in his sleep and Randy was just a little jealous.

But these other guys would fly between Oregon and Washington and Jersey, and they would get her what she wanted. Which was access to influential figures to report on to the FBI and to practice energetic mind control. Hey, this was the girl who studied and read about every meditation around that was commercially available and never practiced one herself. She would study every esoteric teaching but never be able to tell you how it worked or what it did.

Because that stuff causes changes in the body and mind, through a structured fluctuation of visualization and breathing through the lungs in a steady and deliberate mannerism. The world was not steadily breathing because it was not breathing steadily.

People were thought to have symptoms of subconscious fear and anxiety removed through the relaxation techniques of visualization and meditation. But as others sought to improve their mental and physical health and gain some simple quiet insight into a wide cosmic or spiritual based system of knowledge accessed through innate forms of breathing and coexistence.

But the Nori annoying presence sought to destroy others, with the knowledge that she gained from reading about meditations and drawing energy fields as shapes on pieces of paper and used that information, that data to compile magical spells and initiated rites of passage for those witches who sought to destroy others with the use of their minds, spirits, and intentions.

Their hearts are barren from the use of compassionate theories and devoid of any presence of unconditional love towards anything but their selfish desires to rule over others. And the bitch smells and hung out with GW and poured her hippie Ayurveda all over him. Her smelly armpit and crotch rot juices all over the President's new shoes.

And she scammed her way across the country asking hitchhikers for gas money even though she got her lesions from having sex with too many truckers while hitchhiking. And she didn't get it. That enabled Shane through spells to project his voice and intentions along with his face and his name would get him arrested by intelligence for not following the rules of social responsibility. When he was in Iraq and Afghanistan, he was buying cocaine and wishing he were home with his mom smoking crack in her bedroom.

And what was the resentment? A bunch of people were being warned not to use their psychic for an identity fraud on a PSA on TV. And Shane signed up to join the military and was sent to war. And his family had committed a psychic identity fraud against LK, using his wife's race as a reason to break them up.

They were lousy racists, always following through on the gang ordinance they attributed to; until the day all racism ended in the 21 se Century, they were racist until the last day in 2004. And they signed an agreement back in the 1970's with all these gangs and everyone was allowed to be a big white bigot until 2004. And they hated the 90s.

That didn't prevent Gale and them from being a racist kind of psychic.

They immediately hit Marsha up for her esoteric teachings. She teaches Big K and Patrick all about her form of Christianity that even though it is traditional non-denominational she leans towards a Baptist kind of teaching. And she attends the New Age church when it suits her.

Including the New Age bookstore where she regularly spends money to get advice from Tarot readers and attend classes on how to access the Akashic Records. And on Sunday she is going to where she wants to bed the preacher. She is attracted to God and thinks that Jesus would be better to have sex with her.

She takes it upon herself to behave blasphemous and turned the gods into her haven of pleasure with the righteousness of the Lord and his lowly human self.

, the one he needed to protect from sand, wind, and briar. And others like herself. She scorned the word of God, she said it. And she bitched and moaned she was a celebrity and that God deserved to give her the desires of her heart. And that the Holy Spirit asked her to do trivial things that annoy people and her all day long.

And that it was telling her the will of God all and every day. And that she was allowed to be a psychic. And that she was allowed to integrate an Asian version of micro and macrocosm into a psychic.

And send bubbles into people's spines to reflect their minds back to them and to others through a connection to the astral world through breathing into the atmosphere and throwing your voice beneath your breath. Illegal in many countries. In the U.S. it was determined to be worthy of death. Projecting magic and energy and realization into people's minds.

Spirituality and religion are aspects of the Entertainment Legal Department. In that religion follows Entertainment Law. It does not necessarily follow a religious sector of law, there are laws and regulative ordinances around religion and the institutions therein.

People are protected from their churches through the message that they receive because they don't have to contribute to their religion unless they feel they receive something in return, which would be a spiritual blessing. However, that is considered personal and not a part of the legal ramifications of society. Therefore, spirituality and spiritual experiences are considered legal entertainment, not specifically religious.

Religions must resort to taking donations by law, because they are offering a form of entertainment, and therefore they are nonprofits who are required to take donations for the solicitations of their services of that entertainment. That form of entertainment consists of religious experiences and religious practices, they provide song and lecture and consist of communication with others and a collective belief in their organization, therefore, it is required that they take tithes and donations, or they will be shut down by law.

In this way, tarot card readers spiritualists palm ladies, and psychics, all are required to have a transfer of either payment or in some states, barter is accepted. However, each state has its laws regarding the use and practice of a psychic.

Several federal laws protect people from being preyed upon by scammers and those seeking to get to know them to solicit help and spiritual remedy but are trying to get money from them eventually.

It is law that whoever is using the psychic for their own purposes owes the other party compensation. In states where it is illegal to pay for psychic services, it is also illegal to barter for psychic services federally. It is federally illegal to solicit psychic services without financial compensation in the form of cash.

Federally, psychics and Tarot Card readers are mandated to accept money and cash only for their services. In states where the transfer of funds is illegal for psychic services then the state may legalize the use of a barter system for the use of psychic services to protect its residents from federal laws that can persecute them for hobbyist usage of a psychic or psychic-based service such as reading palms, tarot cards or channeling divine beings and energy from crystals or other physical or mystical sources.

Breathing and deep breathing is always legal if the visualization does not interfere with, connect, or use of other people. And this was hard for the cult to grasp. Even the founders. That the use of a psychic or the claimed use of a psychic for the purpose of stealing money or one's identity for financial or other gain and purposes was considered stealing.

And, it was announced on CBS NY News, that the use of psychics for psychic identity fraud spelled the possibility of receiving the death penalty, even it was announced, for members of the military and law enforcement.

They are not allowed to use a psychic for identity theft or financial purposes without being considered by the international intelligence community for the death penalty.

Sounds crazy, but there are crazier laws in the world and people have been killed and have died for less.

And this is the kind of shit that Marsha was caught up with. She believed in all these kinds of esoteric and strange philosophies, and it just so happened that the cult was being lined up for its usage of magic and a worldwide telepathy and a psychic that could project into people's minds, tell them what to do, and steal their information and use that to follow them around and destroy their lives.

And she doesn't care what God thinks. She thinks God is a traditional viewpoint endorsed by religions and nuns and racist people who hate others and preach hate and it's only for black Baptists and white yuppie traditionalists that attend church ceremonies and have nice lives.

Everyone else is a realist and they can't understand her plight. She projects chaos and psychics wherever she goes. She thinks she can wear a seven-dollar weave and call it some dreadlocks. That she can hate the fact that she had a kid at 47 but could leave the poor fucker in a homeless shelter or on some farm and lug him around the map and not depend on dropping him off somewhere else. Instead of with his legal family.

Who loved him and wanted to raise and help him and teach him how to grow and become a nice guy and live to become a self-worthy individual and a renaissance man who was hard working and had a lot of noble characteristics and could learn to generate wealth.

But that is not what happened. Marsha took Jacob, left him on a farm, and hired some other kids to pretend they were Jacob, and she went back to Washington, where when Covid hit in January of 2020, her apartment complex was the first property on the US soil to be turned into a Covid 19 facility. How is that for karma, because she was on the news complaining that night and it hit the national circuit the next morning. She was living right next door to the U.S. first Covid facility and she was there to suffer the wrath of God by watching those people pile up. And then she disappeared.

And Obama had written to Damian and told him that Patrick was under investigation. It wasn't ten years earlier that the investigators from the Washington State Division of Child Support, identified themselves as both British Intelligence and United States Secret Service and they had arrested Shane, the prophet and soldier for being a psychic that wanted to kill the president.

She was pissed that they didn't support Jacob and left him to die in the streets and had called him a n___ behind his back.

This angered Damian because he knew he could teach Jacob the right thing, with his background in teaching kids for the ghetto and helping as an orphan and working his way to feed himself each day as a youth and work hard in his organization and was still a gang leader simultaneously whom people feared and respected. And he never hurt anybody.

But Marsha would not allow him to take part in Jacob's life and bragged that Shane and Big Keith and Arty and Pat were Jacob's real parents. And this tormented LK and made him depressed and cry and pout and scream in rage and break things and fill with fire and fury.

He wanted to kill all of them. Very badly he wanted to destroy them. And he wanted to kill them for saying that Jacob was not his and that Damian had married some black people and they all called him on the phone and physically called him a n___ lover and that he was going to regret marrying a black person. And having a black family.

And he complained that he never liked Marsha or legally married her, he felt bad for Jacob. And Marsha did not see to reason. She believes God asked her to live homeless and to stay outside and she took Jacob and lived outside and went to the shelter in downtown Seattle. But they didn't care. And they didn't try to help Jacob or

Marsha. And she attacked Damian and warned him to stay away. He did, not seeking after a kid that wasn't his.

While he went searching for them a few times over his life, he eventually heard from Marsha, and she was the same as the day he left. And she was proud of Shane and Arty and Pat and during that conversation, she got caught by the judge for cheating again and the child support reduced to 75.00 a month from about three or four hundred plus a back payment. It went to the square at 75.00.

And they praised winning over whitey Damian in that era of the race wars.

Gale and Shane had this battle that they could and could not become subliminal racists, but Shane was not knowledgeable enough in street style sociability to reprimand her correctly. He was this freak of nature who did not even attend school but told everyone that he did, but it was almost impossible for him to get by without a lot of home schooling, I could imagine. He was only three feet high, and he had no clue as to what was going on socially and culturally around him.

When Damian and Jennifer used to visit him along with Stacy at gatherings and parties, Shane was busy playing with toys like big trucks and army men and stuffed animals until he was well over 13 or 14. And this went on for a long time, so people thought they were visiting with an 8-year-old, when he was in fact almost 15. And he was playing Mario Bros. on the original Nintendo for a good 13 years daily. It was his whole life.

He wore the same coveralls and striped shirts for like 12 years. He was walking around in high school at barely four feet high and wearing Osh Kosh B'gosh the same as he did in kindergarten and was still wearing the same size he had been since the third grade.

The sad part about it was that he was trying to become a professional basketball player, and everyone tried to believe in him the best that they could, but he was only a few feet high in high school and couldn't really make the team for a while but he wound up doing so his junior year and since he had spent every day also playing basketball in a broken hoop in his backyard, people seen it as an improvement to his former status of being a brat to everyone he met, including the elderly and guys with families and what not.

Most people not only just weren't fans and not getting along, but they also had a tiff and were not interested in spending any more time with anyone from the entire family ever again. And this was back in the 1980s when they were just getting along and getting going. Their parties were off the chain in that everyone had a great time. There was always music and a room with kids and a TV and someone in a game room and a big dining room. And the food, everyone brought their favorite foods to enjoy, there was always Italian Bread and French Loaves and bagels and rolls and cream cheese and lox and butter and all kinds of baked goods and savory dishes and casseroles and everyone was fond of one another. It was a big family, and everyone had a great time, most of the time.

However, as the kids grew into teenagers and started to prepare for lives of their own, the older kids stopped going to the parties and there was always Shane wherever Gale was invited. She wanted her family with her, and Shane was no way able to watch himself at all anytime he was growing up. There always had to be someone close by, and the kid was out of control. He had the habit of just doing things to piss people off. And he wasn't that big into pranks, but he couldn't take care of himself. He could not use the microwave for more than a minute, he couldn't make a cup of coffee even at 16 years old he never learned how to use the coffee maker or the waffle iron or the pans and could not even pour his milk and cereal. His mom had to do that for him. And as he got older, his family brainwashed him.

They gave him an option the same way they gave Damian an option. If he sold drugs for them and helped a little with the cult or the auctioning, then he could stay and live there and have his parents and he could move out and roam through the city after a while. And after college was over, he joined the military and after that, even getting into trouble for being a psychic, he didn't get discharged or anything like that.

It was a shake-down. And the agents that were investigating him were investigating Gale before that for a long time.

They had called her numerous times to look for LK, but LK hadn't lived there yet, and he only stayed for a few weeks. And he did not use them as an emergency contact or anything like that, so no one knows why they were calling Gale on the phone if it didn't have to do with her bragging about gangbanging Marsha. But Gale had enough guilt now about sending the fucker over to war a couple of times. His job was to man the helicopter before and after they sent and deployed a unit or battalion into battle.

So, Shane's job was to clean the Helicopter and make sure all the soldiers had their gear stored and they were to sit and stand and not fall off the helicopter Shane and his crew would drop them off into battle and fly away. Shane would clean up the Airfield after the units had been dropped off or picked up for the day. And he was okay at his job.

For some reason, when a couple of guys got killed after Shane and the helicopters returned from their run, and were charged by enemy snipers and attacks, several men were injured, and some even died. The unit was brought back to San Diego at Pendleton. The funeral proceeded when Shane was interrupted by the lady from the Washington State Division of Child Support who was investigating Jacob and Damian's case together. And the same lady that was calling Gale on the phone from B.C.

and Seattle for years looking for Damian; she was there, at the funeral putting Shane in handcuffs and chains in front of his comrades. And he was embarrassed.

The rumor is that he was inoculated after being questioned and they found him to be unstable and gave him another inoculation to cure his instability and he was released back into the battalion after sending a subliminal message back to Mitchell and Gale.

This enabled Shane to go back to school and he got a master's degree in digital marketing which was useful for about 10 years, then everyone realized that someone had stolen the rule book from Adobe Photoshop and everything about that industry became obsolete and everyone hired on Fiverr. The end. When Damian hired this guy, it got returned for revisions a few times. And then it worked out. It had to be redone soon after, as it was imperfect. And so much for digital marketing.

Shane became a recluse, returning to work as an NYS Court Police Officer. After getting caught selling cigarettes, starting fights with prisoners, offering to deal coke inside the system, and being on the YouTube channel doing pushups with another officer in uniform. The officer looked identical to an officer who harassed Damian in Oregon and again on the streets in Illinois in a small town where he was walking on a divider over a freeway on a busy road that turned into a bridge. The guy just rolled up and told him it was illegal and sped away on his bike asking him to use the sidewalk.

Looked just like that guy. He used to show up that cop at night when Nurelle was insulted and Damian didn't want to sleep with her and she would scream and howl and rant and cry and yell and wake up the entire neighborhood because she wanted to sit on some dick and suck on some cock and he wouldn't give it to her without falling asleep first and then he would wake up to her riding his shit and he would let it go and fall back asleep while she was riding him.

But their relationship was not worthwhile in the fact that he was just appeasing her and seen her as a psycho who was committable and ferociously unaware of what she really wanted in life. She was always on that vegetable base added to your dinner made of grain but there is nothing worthwhile there. She only eats vegetables and pretends she is gluten free, so you know it's not going extremely far. You can't have any kind of bread or meat or regular cow milk or your own kind of frozen treats and no yogurt without her dipping her ugly spoon in it.

And it's gross.

You can never have regular cheese there or she will freak out and yell and cry. She will say that her skin is going to sell up and her body is going to implode from swollen glands because she can't hang with any kind of gluten. But she can eat her favorite shit that has gluten in it. And by the fucking bucket and it's a waste of fucking time. If you cross her, she calls the FBI and pretends you did stuff to her that you didn't.

One day her and Damian had an issue and D wanted to walk to someone else's house for a while and he was not interested in sleeping with Nori. And she said something, and he started bellowing at her just on the slight side of the right and she was up in his face as he was standing at the top of the stairs. And she knelt on the top stairs and slid down the stairs face down and feet first with her leg's half folded on the stairs. And then she said. "That's it. I'm going to call the cops and tell them you pushed me down the stairs."

"Nice try. If I threw you down the stairs you would not have slid down on your legs, because you would not have touched the stairs and your back would have slammed into the floor and you would have cracked your head and you would be laid the fuck out unconscious or unable to move because you are not strong enough not to pass out. You wouldn't be able to move. You would have slammed your back against the floor," Damian said to her.

"No, you wouldn't have." She resented him. She was nothing but a little jealous twit. She didn't know anything. And she smells. And cast spells at him in the movie theater instead of blowing his cock like his girlfriend did. She looks at him like she can make sense of what he says.

'You underestimate me."

"I don't. You're just an asshole. And a fucking loser."

"Fuck you."

"Fuck you."

She confessed that she worshipped the Darth maul and the Chitahuri most of her life and that she emulated the Illuminati and wanted to be one. She said she heard about the conspiracy theorist David Icke, that she had known about it that the conspiracy was real, and that she was one of them. He thought she was talking shit. She was a nitwit who worshipped Harriman State Park. Home of the mauling Black Bear and the Gardner snake. The armpit of the Appalachian Mountain range. A true piece of shit fucking town. Everyone was meant to be her minion and she confessed to practicing mind control and talking sexually to Big Keith and that she wanted to meet Arthur so she could have sex with him. And it was Satanic.

"I don't give a shit." He spoke. "I hate you and I hate that motherfucker. Fuck you."

"Fuck you, too."

She finally let him leave Oregon and he had to move across town to make sure she wasn't coming back. At that time, she was talking to Pat on the phone, and they were doing sexual stuff over cell phones. He said so.

And Damian hid out in Ashland for that winter of 2005, and Patrick hit him off with the agenda of the cult.

And Shane was away in the military. And he had yet to be arrested when Patrick told Damian that Shane was a prophet of the cult and that they needed Shane for his leadership and that he was so unbelievably valuable to the organization or group, whatever it was. And that they were worshipping self-worship through particle infusion in the human mind along with their voodoo Phoenician astral projection of their intentions along with the guidance of the Pleiadeans and the Ascended Masters, they would crash and burn only having controlled the minds of everyone on the planet.

And Damian told Pat to go fuck himself. And Pat giggled. 'You see my image there outside your window in your mind?"

"Yes. I see it. It's you in my mind in an image outside the window."

"Okay. That's us. It's not schizophrenia. It's mind control. You can see us, and we have celebrity guides, and you can see them and hear them, too. Gene Hackman and Bradd Pitt."

Did he have these holograms patented or something? He had access to holograms with Bradd Pitt like Fight Club? Did the celebrities know about it? Who else did he have as holograms? Everyone was so curious as to how their mind control worked. Even the president.

In early 2006, while waiting to go down to LA, Damian contacted tons of media agents and news agencies and magazines trying to promote his album. And he later, after getting ripped off by Patrick that summer, wandered around between Oregon, Arizona, and Southern California. And he eventually found a way to explore the experiences he had in Northern California previously with Nori at the hippie farm.

He had a premonition that the guys at the farm were doing something crazy like building a nuclear weapon. So, he went out there on the whim from Arizona where he was camping in the woods and getting into Gawker blogs about his travels, he was considered a lunatic by many of the reporters there at the Gawker agency. And he scored a couple of articles in Defamer.com that described some of his exotic travelling and camping experiences, and he was considered an artist and a talent at the time, still living off his reputation as a vocalist for Tower Music Group in Greenwich Village, NYC.

And he was okay with that. But he went up to Siskiyou and checked out the hippie farm and he got thrown off within minutes.

He told them he was a NY Times reporter and that he was doing a piece on the guys at the farm building nuclear weapons and that he was reporting to the Army. And they immediately asked him to leave. And they followed him up the road with the hillbilly he was hanging out with who was cool about things and was familiar with the territory.

And the world kept turning.

Damian went down the road and camped at a free campground and went up to Ashland and hung out with some homeless people and girls and kids in the park and stayed at the hostel there. He had a good time and went back and forth to Siskiyou.

While hanging out at the library, he documented his entire journey for the past four years and included some stories about Shane and the cult and started an email campaign.

That summer he sent out a few letters, a dozen little articles about his schizophrenia and its relations to the cult and how everything was progressing. He then went up to Ashland and stayed out there for a few weeks in the summer and then down to Cali where he stayed in Garberville and ran into Billy Crystal's personal assistant who was driving down to LA.

Damian rode with him to one or two exits and ducked out to drink by the river. And have fun. And then he in a few days, caught an Amtrak out of Garberville in California and went down to LA. But he had to take this route that took an extra day.

When they got down to the station in Bakersfield, LA was only a two-hour drive south. But the bus took the detour route and went all the way West to Santa Barbara on the country road and then proceeded to drive to Los Angeles and arrive 15 hours after it left Bakersfield. Damian sat next to two blondes from Sweden, and they wound up all staying at the same hostel in Inglewood after they all arrived. And after a couple of weeks of them hanging out together casually in the same facility and getting to know some more people.

The others there were mad that the guy was playing with changing his hair color with some dye. And he got a little depressed in LA. He thought he was going under quick. And he was there, just selling sodas each day on the beach in Venice in Los Angeles.

When he realized, he was going to go broke. He took all his stuff and moved it down from Inglewood to the beach. And in a few hours, he was sitting on the beach, and he got an interview with a daytime show on CBS. And he had an interview just before that on a Travel Channel show about his novel when he was walking and camping in Sedona, Arizona. He walked away from the interview, and he got a spot in the crowd at a Borat scene that was used in one of the follow-up episodes of Borat.

He was eager and found a way of getting onto movie sets for free. The music industry was about to undergo its final blowout and close all its stores and he instinctively reached out for a film career.

He scored a couple more interviews and was told off by a few reporters when he tried to cash in on the article and combined all the stories into one mega story that he sent to everything with a news desk in the country. And he filled up a few blogs with people making fun of his other letters and such and he was posted on a few anti-law enforcement blogs after the cops started harassing him and celebrities were following him around. It seemed like it, but he found a spot in Santa Barbara County where they were flocked together and he wanted to become a part of the scene so he made a deal with the devil, that if he slept out the world would acknowledge him in the movies.

He had already been in one part before he left Ashland, he was in the movie Conversations with God. He met the author and was scheduled by Dahn Hak the Korean Yoga company to be scheduled to tour with Walshe the founder of the yoga organization from Korea.

But that didn't work out and after the movie was released, the spiritual books by Walshe moved on to other countries and the novelty of his work was vintaged in the U.S.

So, Damian was on his own. He was now navigating through Southern California, and he was invited to a movie entitled 'The Comebacks." It was filming in Fullerton; CA and he took the train there from Santa Barbara and showed up at the stadium. He checked in and went into the film and then immediately left to find the crew and producers and asked them for a part in the movie.

He did not show up the next night but stayed close by because they told him it was the last two nights of filming, and it was the last scene of the film. And there was no more to do. He took that and hung out there and got stoned on Cali weed and drank a little bit and then went back to Santa Barbara in the morning after two nights of hanging out at the set.

It was not long before he wanted more out of life. He sent that sarcastic report out it why as a satire of Gale's psychic and the combination of the visions and the voices that everyone could hear, being repeated, the feds put out a warrant on Shane and collected him.

The story pointed out how Damian went to Siskiyou to the hippie farm and in the two years since he left he was hearing voices and seeing crazy visions, having dreams and a lot of them were all about the loser drug dealer named Shane and his protection from his mom, Gale and how she created a psychic energy field that she could destroy others with through her use of drugs and heavy narcotics and she spent all her time outside of work building this thing, she said it. And it took years. She created a clever clairvoyant method of Astral projection that she could freakishly hear other people's worlds and generate the phenomenon anywhere she wanted.

She knew how to create voices in people's minds and hear their mind and their activities from far Away. And LK hated her very severely. And people were being coerced to pass this technology method on. And she decided that the phenomenon was too tangible and scientifically provable because she could call the shots, that she wanted to use it and teach others how to be psychic and use LK's mind against him, in a shared public micro and macrocosm of his thoughts and activities focused on all day as the master of their spirituality and she wanted to start a cult.

And they went off the deep end.

And wanted to listen to everything LK did near and far. And they were smoking crack and setting up for the future and wanted to start a cult that would take the world over and instead of letting him be an artist, they tried to make it into a profitable business by anchoring his spirit and his prophecy on his life and to even eat and try to put an end and a formal communion in front of the world and exploit and commercialize Damian Keith D. Unknown's listening in his ear and to capitalize on his mystical connection to God and the universe, by asking him to become an innate brainwash, and to pledge allegiance to a plan that held him accountable as the Messiah. They wanted to vacate the world's religion and institute Damian as the messiah. And they were hounding him to come up with plans and lessons to recruit followers and make money off the agenda. Which was set to rake in over 90,000,000.00 USD.

They had a plan in order, by 2005, to administer to the whole world a semblance of their final saga and plan to institutionalize spirituality through a camp that they built. And they wanted to vacate religion as we know it today, and have known it, and combine all the faiths into an interfaith metaphysics, that will take its followers quickly through the initiation of enlightenment, but they must follow the protocols of the cult and follow certain Christian traditions which attempted to have no purpose religiously to the cult organization.

The reason for following the Christians again, had no basis to their actual teachings supposedly, and they openly admitted to that, it had no significance, but was there to cloak their purposes from the public eye and the law of the land.

The cult would plan to start a farm in the country and in the meantime, meet at various religious institutions and churches where cult members worked and volunteered. They would gain responsibility and lie and say they were entering a seminary, becoming the ministering deacons, and taking religious and metaphysical classes.

They lied to the pawn and had them attend Lutheran and Non-denominational Christian services on Sunday. Then during the week, they would attempt to meet at the churches in the middle of the night and perform black magic ceremonies. How typical. And oh, so 21st Century model!

It was hard to deal with, the ideas that the world was being tricked in order to trick you into becoming a version of the antichrist, albeit as a blind slave and follower of showmanship and miracles or was it the type of shit that got them in trouble hosting some motherfucker who pretended to be the second coming of Jesus and Jesus himself to the Jews and this was ugly.

And Patrick didn't care, he was helping Gale and Mitchell by promoting this shit. And the start of everything was to deal some crack for Gale outside the White House and Damian would be let in as the Messiah and he could get a wedding that was over 60K and have his parents at his side and spend time with his brother and sisters and all his friends and cousins.

And then it hit them all. Damian wasn't going to help.

And he went from King Solomon to the 40-year-old Virgin going a couple decades without one meaningful relationship. And there was no reason why he couldn't splurge and get sane with someone occasionally. And people liked him, but they couldn't get with him. He was becoming monopolized.

And this story went on. How this musician guy that was homeless collecting cans for his studio time in Tower Greenwich Village in NY and he was caught out there worshipping some kind of Merkabah or crazy Taoist energy and he was committed, and they let him go. And this cult of traffickers was now running a drug trade of their own with full government authority and they wanted him to become the Messiah.

And they even admitted that it was fucking fake. That it was all for money. And power. And the kind of power I am talking to you about is way more than you would every expect. It's beyond spiritual or religious and financial or based on any kind of semblance of righteousness and is meant to show everyone who the fuck is boss, and it is an unseen fucking hand, and everyone is supposed to fucking bow. And they admitted to it, that it

was a plan to commit mass genocide. And they asked
Damian Keith Unknoen to commit genocide in the name of
the government and in the name of destroying the
government from within.

This spot as messiah was going to land him a
guaranteed spot as U.S. President.

And that was the offer. And he said no.

They were pissed.

There is no way that anyone worthy of their status
as a movie star or public influence would ever succumb to
that kind of temptation.

They didn't just have a couple of ideas or some far
out fantasy about how they were going to commit this act
and carry it through to the end. And they said they wanted
to kill upwards of 30,000 people. They didn't really have a
number but they said they were going to recruit a few
hundred people at a time, keep them on a farm, charge
them a few grand to learn metaphysics and then make them
drink Kool Aid, with some people or everyone knowing
fully what is happening, but Damian was specifically
warned those times just presenting the idea, that he would
have to pour his own cup and survive in order to escape the
fate of the participants.

And he didn't even think about calling the cops. He
wrote that shit in that fucking report he sent around, and it
wound up getting back to the Washington State Division of
Child Support investigators who learned that the article was
sitting being read by the president himself.

The presentation of the offer was from Edward
Jones office in Bay Ridge, Brooklyn.

Patrick was very clear that Damian was to send
himself on a plane at his own expense, go to see Gale, buy
a sack of crack, and deliver it to Big Keith. Big Keith then
confirmed this by calling LK on the phone a few days later
and making the request for this to occur several times over
several years. And Big Keith said he was addicted to crack

cocaine and that he was still sober and did not attend AA meetings anymore. His mom had dementia and lived in a hospital and couldn't keep track of what he did. So, now he was still sober because he would lose his whole family; because he drinks like a loser would drink. He can't hold his shit together without starting some smack and cutting someone the wrong way, getting the fuck into it, and passing out. And waking up and finding he raped his whole fucking family.

So now, all he does is smoke crack. He smoked four packs of cigarettes a day, drank a dozen cups of coffee at least, and worked from three in the morning until two in the afternoon supervising garbage collection in NYC. He couldn't smoke any more pot even though he lived on the shit while growing up and said it would make him want to drink.

Big K could go to a bar and could go out to eat but he could not have alcohol in his food. He never tried penne ala vodka and does not choose to eat penne because of the connotation it would make him drink through temptation or ingredient and he would crave a drink. So, he went to parties and people drank and his wife would drink twice a year. And this was his life sober, but he also complained a lot about having credible feelings for boys that were under the age of 18. And he would confess this a lot to Damian as a youth and as an adult. He would remark that he had some kind of problem. And this was enough to keep Damian LK away from him, for the most part.

When Big K would call him on the phone between the years of 97 and 2012, he would curse at him, call him names, make fun of him, and call him a piece of shit, loser, this, and that. At some point that switched around and Damian had had enough, but that was a long way away. And that is how it is in 2024, but it wasn't that way in '05. And Damian took the hits, knowing he would get even with them at some molten point in their relationship when the fuckers would straight up mess their way up. And life would strike them up and down.

And Big Keith would back up the agenda that Pat laid out. And demand Damian fly home and deliver him some crack rock. He stopped being polite and offered him some even though he flipped for the sample and the flight home. And they started fighting. And this went on for a while and Damian cut them off once he moved to Los Angeles.

He was no longer welcome. They had laid it all out. What he had to do. And no one gave a fuck. Conspiracy theorists feared him, and people started compulsively following him around as if he were both a key to the cult's destruction and the messenger meant to save them from evil because he denied his role as a cult master. And this was the second cult that offered him a spot. And there were others. But he would not keep track of that shit, and this was the worst, they had taken over his foster family.

He always knew they weren't really related but were his legal family. Everyone celebrated that fact. It was a consensus that no one was going to figure out what they were doing. And then it happened. It occurred to him that the uncle he had begun to think of was complete and selfish yet articulately selfish, and that made him seem both selfless and humane.

And he behaved as an intellectual this Patrick. He not only smoked his cigars but drank his wine, which was all cheap and shit, so it made the experience cheap. Unless he lived with humility and with a humble sort of demeanor as if he were either poor or compassionate, but even *as if.* He assumed the worst and scoffed at the thought of providing a product or providing products in a store or environment that sells products and makes deals and moves forward and looks to present the world with something it can walk away with, thereby generating capital and revenue.

He lives off others' wealth and attempts to steal what they have earned and to say that it is a form of Robin Hood-type behavior is Ludacris in thought and attempted action. To only offer portfolios of other people's earnings and not bring anything to the table for those people to walk away with something in their hands besides knowing that they gave their money to a crook does not constitute either a smart, nor sophisticated or good and reputable business.

They are haunts stealing money and offering services to kill your children, take away your thoughts through hypnosis, and attempt to sleep with your wives and loved ones, male or female, young or old. They are vampires, haunting people in the night. Destroying any form of mind that people can hold onto to that they cannot reach with their energy and intentions and tubes of generated lust and devilishness. They eat fine orders all day and all night and only think about themselves and how everyone else is inferior.

They practice spelling and generate their image consciously into the dreams of millions of people on purpose. Saying that they conjured it while on LSD thirty years prior, but it was the plan of their dead father. He collected a pension all through his whole miserable short life and he planned on overthrowing the government. He did it with his plan to sell drugs, sell and smuggle kids from school directly into his bed and into people's lives whom he or they never met, and he wrote the plans to take over the mind and start a camp and a cult that would participate in a suicide ceremony.

Patrick offered to orchestrate it when he died. And had zero forms of guilt or ethics when it came to collecting that money and giving a taste of that Kool-Aid, enough to kill your baby sister or cousin.

And his family started selling drugs in Philadelphia in 2005. And they planned to expand their market of trading kids to an outpost they started out in New Mexico and did it like it was nothing and like it was non-participatory.

Everything was subliminal if someone they didn't know was listening. And they practiced telepathy and stayed awake on all the new trends socially, technologically, and even religiously and didn't take part in it and told the youth to do so. And they upheld their end of the gang war and stopped being so racist for a while.

Everyone except Arlene who used her witchcraft to occupy Nurelle, the crater of energy in the macrocosm of the earth that was left behind by the Towe Records music industry bubble. And this made no sense to a lot of people.

But it made sense a year and five later when the stock market crashed, and Circuit City went out of business. And Virgin, and Nobody, and Sam Goody and Toys R Us, and anyone who sold music on their shelves. And mom and pop music stores were invited to reopen. But this does not concern anything, or so it seemed. Until the history and manipulation of Damian extended through the music and entertainment and political industries.

As people from places in the south were starting to get involved in the career of D. Unknown now D. Unknoen Emcee. And people didn't see it coming, but people from the town of Franklin, TN who were involved in the movies, attempted to start controlling the moves of Mr. Unknown.

It was felt that things would come to a head, and this was interesting because the politicians who lived in Franklin, TN had lobbied in the early 19802 to shut down the music industry through a congressional hearing in Washington D.C. where rock artists were put on trial for the content of their music and the government created the rating system for the musical content and established the PARENTAL ADVISORY EXPLICIT CONTENT LABELS AND STICKERS on every piece of music that had explicit content and it was considered a breach of constitutional expression and artistic motive, but the lobbyists were attempting to shut down the music industry completely. This included future White House people and their families who were pushing to shut down the music industry.

Damian was cornered to enter the film industry after his family was threatened and he attempted another crack at the music industry showing up on Santa Monica Blvd. selling CDs and giving them out at the record companies on the south end of town. Now there were other people involved and he continued to push the issue about Shane and his antics of becoming some kind of religious warrior and hero and prophet to a bunch of alien and UFO worshipers who were trying to commit suicide.

Now it was the whole and the entirety of the entire planet. Never mind that people later emerged telling me how to go about manufacturing my stealth plane and flying it around, only to have an influx of giant UAP and UFO drones flying around fifteen years later. And again, at a later point.

It was neither later nor earlier when the plans were ignored, and this dude moved to LA. Even before his family including Joanna was threatened, he was there for the music industry and to dabble on television, he had it in the plans, and he wasn't stressing about movies. He had the feeling TV would show up and there would be his music that he was slanging and trying to sell at a big price. And he forgot about the letters and the blog, but he didn't. And he ran out of money and fell and went up to Santa Barbara. And his movie career was introduced to him through some unconventional means. He didn't necessarily like the way it was going, but he was guaranteed a movie spot in some form due to what was occurring.

Someone kept calling the cops on him because he was bumming around homeless. And the police and sheriff of Santa Barbara took a special interest in him and wanted badly for him to just leave town. And he didn't see that as an option. At least not for a few months, and he knew he could and would just be thrown out of that town right away, not that he was ever in his life before approached and asked to leave a whole town. But he knew it would happen. He could just tell the wind was burning at his ass. And keeping his arms cold and it was pleasant to breath in the air continually, as it shifted. And he knew, right there, that he wasn't' welcome.

He liked the weather, but he was not prone to being absorbed by it. Just the notion, he knew it could just turn out to be a quick visit. Well, he was about to start it out right, and there were celebrities showing up. And what do you know, he decided after sitting in town for a while and mailing out the composite lettering that told of Shane's psychic projections which said that he was "Going to Frame Cousin Keith for the assassination attempt of George W. Bush in the name of Shane Strassberg First Battalion Thirteenth Marines."

Now this was a recurring loop as a waking dream like a recording in space, which was supposedly put there by their cult and their connection with the psychic from the CIA. And this voice and loop played, and people were hearing it, and reporting it. And it was some kind of phenomenon.

And in NYC at CBS, they were broadcasting this announcement across the screen in writing with the anchor repeating the different ways that psychics were to be reported to the FBI and get this, if they weren't reported in the correct manner, then anyone who heard it could possibly receive the death penalty. And they were not having it. No one believed in that shit. So, Shane obviously heard this announcement and used his family psychic to torment tons of people including Damian and the fucker put it in his story.

The agents from the Division of Child Support for Washington State used it to become incognito federal

Secret Service agents and with a cooperative effort from Scotland Yard and British Intelligence, they took down Shane for having his own PSA about framing Cousin Keith, where there were at least three or even four different Keith's that they knew of in his family, including celebrity Damian the brainwash. It went to the point that people were complaining about hearing voices in the walls and becoming schizophrenic and the news was putting up reports about people using psychics and witchcraft to destroy both the government and other people.

It was obvious that people were protecting themselves, the PSA said if the psychics weren't turned in and if people were misusing their psychics than there was the possibility of the death penalty. And the news was at odds, not honoring this imperialistic bullshit, but the people were being rounded up by Stop and Frisk policies being instituted, and the feds hear this also from other places.

Like a journal or from TV or other spots. People reporting to them from the obvious places. The president's desk, the vice president' s desk, the CIA, the FBI the Daily News, the Newsweek, Newsday, National Enquirer. Like the bugged conversations that Pat and Big Keith had and the ones that Arlene and Gale had with the same parties, and they included Arty Homan in the conversations. And brought him up quite often when speaking with LK.

And it went on from there. That many people were talking about this stupidity, as Patrick was offering people a slot in the cult with Shane as a psychic prophet. And that was included in the report that went around. And the feds hired a task force not to bring down Shane and them but to watch them because they didn't have anything on them. Shane was accused of using his psychic to intimidate the president and other people that he was going to commit to smoking the president and moving up the political ladder to become a celebrity and thereby gain access to negotiating himself for a career doing whatever he wanted.

Perhaps become an actor or a singer or basketball player on second string for the NCAA or NBA somewhere. But he could have just applied himself and not quit the team. Anyway, these people from Washington State were now secret service agents with a bunch of militants from Scotland Yard, and a big, huge budget. The budget included a private airplane, and free lunches and expenses and all kinds of shopping in Beverly Hills and Santa Barbara on the weekends by the female agents who were trying to meet celebrities and wanted to get to know Damian.

He had been reported speaking just recently to both George Lucas and he said hello to Stephen Spielberg, he sat at the table uninvited with Jennifer Aniston at a Mexican place near Goleta, and he had seen Gene Hackman over there who coincidentally, stopped his car at a light and Damian was waiting for a pickup and Gene and he locked eyes and said hello. And the list went on and on, as the celebrities started sitting next to him and saying hello to him in the past few months. And the cops didn't leave him alone. And they bothered him every couple of days for no reason, reading his ID out loud all the time, every time.

The cops there, they called him names and they cursed at him, laughed at him, choked him, threatened him, and gave him the low down on his career. What he was allowed to do in the entertainment industry. And every time they showed up, they pretty much brought with them a lesson or a message from one of his producers who now owned him from Nashville. And that was what they said. And he was under investigation until he left town. And he was just getting going.

They threw him on the ground. They called him curse words and names. They made sure they told him that they would kill him if they had to. But they also called him a potential and future movie star, they told him they would put him in the movies and TV and make shows about him.

And they told him that they would include him and his work and his books not just some movies and stuff he writes for the studio, but his work was scheduled to be included in the wheels of life. At schools and in the real world and his ideas were meant to work. And do things, resurrect the music industry, and involve practicality and fashion and common sense and spirituality and science and application. It was a huge deal.

He lost a big deal at Tower Records, and they asked him to step away from the music industry. They were the producers there and they announced the bankruptcy and that he was just a last-minute addition, that even though they expected to make billions off his music, it wasn't going to be produced and Tower was not working a deal for him anymore with an independent label. And he just flaked on his own. And he didn't know why. He was told to step off and he did. When he got to LA, the phony actress from Nashville made it clear that she would not enable his music without him working in movies.

Three years later, he got busy. But for now, he was stuck in Santa Barbara and was feeling the pain of sending out that article to so many news agents. And the actresses kept checking on him. And the lady from Nashville was up chilling with her friends having lunch with the ladies from the White House and a bunch of people there. And that continued for a while and the cops kept harassing D. and wondering what he was doing all the time.

Sometimes they brought cops from out of town just to meet Damian and shake his hand because they wanted to meet some real Hollywood motherfucker scheduled to be included for a movie star nomination, but that shit didn't happen more than once or twice. And Damian was holding it down in downtown Santa Barbara. A few weeks later, the lady from British Intelligence showed up and told Damian, at the police station in Santa Barbara, on a Saturday, the place was empty.

She told him that Shane was arrested, and they released him, and she wanted to know if he had written a letter that was on the President's desk. And that was all she asked, she didn't show him anything or the letter or ask him for any specifics. He said he wrote it anyway. And she said "Okay, that's what I thought. We arrested Shane. And we're investigating every matter inside of that article."

Well, even though the harassment from the cops continued for the months he remained there, the police were more pleasant to deal with and less dangerous for the most part than the Sherriff was. The Sherrif Department of old Santa Barbara is crazy lunatic motherfuckers at large, no doubt. I could not stand here and say I could openly disrespect them to their faces or behind their backs, but I will give it to Damian, he was not afraid to talk to them to their faces and tell them what he thought, even though they were disrespectful, he didn't necessarily disrespect them.

Well, the secret service agent from Washington State, from Seattle, had brought in a couple of them that dealt with Damian. One of them was pretty mean, they had pulled him over for walking and getting some exercise and he was walking around a cul-de-sac when a deputy pulled him aside from a patrol car. Another giant deputy truck pulled up with a deputy that was at least 400 pounds no exaggeration.

He was in a massive vehicle and had a tent wrapped around him. And another one of him pulled up like a clone and they were all around Damian on this street, the weekend of Thanksgiving. Now, they brought him into the station which was filled with graffiti on the outside and they badgered Damian. And he asked for Gene Hackman. And the deputy who pulled him over, Rogers, handcuffed himself to Damian and they went to the bathroom where Damian had to piss in a cup. And the deputy got to watch. And they filled that piss cup into a drug test, and it turned bright colors red and blue and green, and they said, "The only thing you have in your system is THC."

He said, 'That's not illegal."

And the deputy said, "It is in Santa Barbara County unless you have a medical from Santa Barbara County."

"My medical is from Los Angeles County, sir."

"We don't accept Los Angeles County medical prescriptions for marijuana. You must get one from Santa Barbara County."

"That's not a law.' He spoke.

"It's our law, here in Santa Barbara County."

"Can I go, now?"

They eventually let him go but Rogers had to drop him off at the storage unit. And that was his first encounter with Rogers. And the other deputy they brought in for questioning for hating the president. And for being a psychic. Deputy Jenkins. He was assistant to Rogers. And Jenkins thought it was funny to use the astral projection mechanism and to hate the president under his breath and joke around about shooting him. And Damian when released, he sent an email about Jenkins to the news, and the news in Washington D. C. sent it to the agents from Washington State that Jenkins was beating up on Mr. Light and drug testing him, and that he was talking to him using a projection and astral mechanism and used a psychic to pretend to communicate that he wanted to shoot the president.

And the lady agent brought in Jenkins to see if he wanted to kill the president.

Between the months of those two events, Damian being detained by those idiots and the agent bringing in Jenkins, they bothered Damian all day long. He was harassed sleeping in public, drinking coffee at the coffee shop, walking around at night, sleeping at the park, walking near the public throughfare in certain ways.

He found a wallet and turned it in but looked in it and Rogers showed up with Jenkins and tried to arrest him.

He received tickets for paraphernalia every few days. He never stopped buying a new pot pipe when pipes were illegal in California and made it the point, because he loved to smoke but the woman who threatened Joanna, had told her he had to smoke pot, or he would be thrown around. And he battled the cops and smoked pot. And he would be thrown out of court with his pot pipe tickets. And slept around the gutter and lost his mind.

Thinking he was insane, he grappled at the voices in his area, and he realized that the family was taking over with their astral projections, and they were getting easier to egg, but would they take over or would they take off he couldn't tell.

He wanted to yell at them. And he refrained from calling them to Santa Barbara. And the world spun but it started staring at him.

And another deputy put a gun to his head and threatened to shoot him. And told him to get out of town or he would beat him and taze him. He demanded he leave the county and repeated his threats over and over. And it went on for a while. The police were nicer than that sheriff. And after about three months in Goleta, he was thrown out by Perez, and he went and stayed downtown.

And the agents showed up and told him about arresting Shane. And the rest of his family had remained under federal watch and international ordinance required them to be under federal surveillance and it was mandated as electronic surveillance. And they were out of luck but remained afloat because no one bought from them, even though they were selling.

A few weeks later, in downtown Santa Barbara, this guy walks by surrounded by Mexicans and he is staring directly at Damian, and he has a circle of men around him and he looks into Damian's eyes. It looks like GW Bush in a giant handlebar mustache and orange make up. And they scurry away. He doesn't know nor ever officially believe that it was the president.

After he finally left Santa Barbara, he decided to hitchhike back to NYC. And he was plagued with cops from Ventura County all the way to Chicago. He met a cop every couple of days and was thrown off a couple of roadways and driven around to truck stops and out of town by cops. It took two weeks to get there from LA. That was with stopping in Reno. For a couple of days and moving on from there, broke. He survived the summer, getting jumped in his own neighborhood of Park Slope and starting a war fight with Pita Pan whose food he begged from a neighbor and then criticized, and the owner swung at him and tried to fight him.

Damian ducked and scurried off but started some shit with the guy and even went in there and talked with him, called him on the phone, talked with him, and went on and on through the web making fun of the restaurant and filed complaints with the health bureau. And told his friends about it but they really didn't take him up because Pita Pan is a tiny shop in a stupid part of a rich part of the neighborhood.

It was a rough autumn after Damian made it back to Arizona and went to Tempe hoping to get his job back ten years later wiping tables and working as a supervisor. Talk about taking the red pill and regretting it. Out of nowhere Ron Paul shows up and gives a talk on campus to a bunch of students and Damian stops to listen. After a while he moves on, having nothing to eat and being overweight making the situation irritable for anyone to notice. As he walks back to the podium, a crowd ah gathered, and Paul is still off to the side talking to some students.

On the stage walks the illustrious Obama.

He smiles and the small crowd of a few hundred claps and gives him the attention he asks for. He shares his ideas. People are intent and Damian is marveled that he is now standing before the might Barack Obama. And the O stops during speaking and locks eyes with Damian. And then he continues and a few moments later, he does it again. And he doesn't do this with others. And then he stares intently at Damian as the speech ends. Damian ran back and was wiping tables the next morning at the Student Union where he had worked as a supervisor for a couple of food stands there. And a cop on a scooter gives him a mean look and stares him down and scowls and gets vicious looking.

Damian falls for it and calls the campus police to complain that the cop was coaxing him. And he gets thrown off campus by that cop. A few moments later. They target him and throw him off campus several times before he finally leaves town in January, some weeks later.

Many weeks.

And in 2016, he was at the Trump rally, ready to fight for Trump when he realized that he couldn't get anything from Trump because he had nothing to give Trump. Except for his common sense and advice as a consultant, which he could have helped Trump out considerably. But he was not considered, and Trump just noticed him for a second and did not communicate to him.

Just a few months earlier, Damian had heard back from the administration in power at the Oval Office in an email which informed him that Patrick Gilbride was in fact under investigation by several government agencies. And that it was being attended to his iniquity and his cult practices and embezzlement ideology and his belief in ridiculing any type of moral code and that included business minded ethical guidelines to protect clients and consumers.

And Damian stopped investigating Pat for a while. Hoping they would stop doing what they were doing, Damian moved to Boone County his favorite county in

North Carolina doing some construction for the people moving in for the summer, and that is where he ran into Trump. And Trump was not popular with black voters in North Carolina in 2016.

But Clinton and his producer shut down Tower records and his deal, so he was not voting for her. He was supposed to make some hybrid music for the people, and they decided that silence was going to be the exercise of the righteous while the patents to move human consciousness and use robots everywhere were being distributed through industrial private networks that ran American business.

And the CIA sold its psychics to British Intelligence, which is why they were tracking the Gilbride Strassberg Flannery network but did nothing about them dealing narcotics outside of government buildings and setting up shop for new religions and mind controlling America from within. Using electromagnetic frequencies embalmed in Witchcraft, the cult claimed access to the UAP then known as the UFO.

And there was no thread. Except when Damian went to Park Slope and attended an AA meeting and a guy who was from LA, owned a brownstone over there and asked Damian to help him out in exchange for a place to stay. And the guy told him that he worked as a pilot and airplane designer utilizing stealth technology and was stationed for a few years at Area 51,

And then he taught Damian how to get a job building stealth planes. And he gave him an interest in it. And told him all about the 80s Hollywood music industry. The guy hung out at the Viper Room, knew River Phoenix or some shit and met Keith Richards hanging out over there. He used to see the Stones play at the Troubadour and he still went to see Pink Floyd and Roger Waters when they were hanging out in 2010. And the world was noticing a little bit too much.

And the people wanted to join the cult. And they shut it down by joining it for free. Everyone started attuning their mind to the schizophrenia and the world went back in time again.

And as of January 2024, these guys, making who knows how much by delivering this illegal product trades and wondering why the government would ask them to do it. To run drugs officially with the government blessing since 2005. That does not necessarily correlate with the rise in opioid deaths and the amount of people killed from drugs with chemicals like Fentanyl with tons of rackets going up in smoke as people dwindle towards the streets that are simultaneously occupied by Shane Strassberg and the product of Gale. She will threaten people if they don't buy her stuff. And if they don't want to sell her. She really thinks she has it together in all, she is just falling apart.

Patrolling the White House better than some secret service agents, is ex-Marine, ex-NYS Police Court Officer, ex Department of Veterans Affairs and ex Department of Homeland Division of Digital Marketing associate, with a bag full of pharmaceutical grade cocaine, is Shane Strassberg. The bane of president of the United States since Jimmy Fucking Carter. Why was he targeting a Bush?

Was it because they made crack illegal under their banner along with Reagan? To continue the agenda of drug enforcement with hopes of one day eliminating the problem of dangerous drugs and narcotics in the hands of young people and those vulnerable to mental illness and extreme psychosis. Which the drugs induce quite normally.

It is abnormal for the drugs not to induce abnormal behavior or things like a psychosis in an individual, because prescription drugs prescribed by your doctor will also do these things as side effects, if the doctor deems that your illness is more important to treat than the potential side effects that are induced by taking dangerous prescription drugs.

Perfect for idiots who think pot isn't cool because it's going to be legal someday. And the dope fiends who don't know any better, and those that think they should just duplicate the energy and realization of actual meditation, which is what those drugs try and imitate, a duplicate form of meditative realizations.

But didn't the doctors in the office give Shane some drugs?

Which time would we prefer to infer to, the time when Shane was in the government doctor's office in New York City, working on some sort of experimental remedy for his growth inhibiting mental genetic disorder? Or was it the time when he was arrested in San Diego for being in a cult and screaming about the president and his visions of the occult he was having simultaneously, during war?

Never mind, the style of recruiting is reminiscent of a straight edge brainwash, brought to you by the enemies of Alester Crowley and the President of the United States, independent civilians who entered the U.S. illegally and are now representative of the CIA and its elite Law Enforcement division of field agents. Enabled and able to do whatever it takes to defend our American freedoms, and the prototypes being sent via UAP signature across the globe.

Now, Shane had a lot to handle as a kid, because he was this influence that was obviously malevolent and never let up on anyone or anybody ever at any time. And he always lets you know that he is planning to destroy you. And his mother is no better. She is there to lead him on to become a worthless motherfucker the longer he waits to get old. To make an object out of rarified plants and to believe in their properties is one thing. But to go and take a perfectly good plant and then cut it and cook it and cut it again and recook it and then distribute it, when clearly that dug is out of style.

That might be their personal preferences but that doesn't necessarily make the cultural standards, and that doesn't make money People will smoke what is in style what is strongest and what is putting them over on their knees, falling asleep or staring at the skies looking and peering towards the heavens as if waiting to be absorbed. The guy was standing there in front of LK Damian for two years, hoping to get him to be friends and say hello even once, but it was obviously to try and manipulate and control him, and there was an obvious energy manipulation, which was there to grab Damian over in some demon, and Strassberg didn't let up. Trying to get Damian LK to move on over and let Shane run the ride. But he refused to let the kid even introduce himself for a couple of years. Even there conversing right in front of him with his parents, he would never acknowledge the person. And people were intrigued that they didn't know each other yet were trying to be introduced and Damian would not even think about turning over. As soon Shane arrived, there were voices of apprehension and hiding and fear and protection, and Barbara left. So, Shane was not his person's favorite source of companion and brotherhood.

As soon as Shane was introduced as a psychic by his mother and then again by Patrick to Damian, he was discredited as an individual. While D might have thought being psychic was a novelty during his childhood, being an adult taught him better, and Shane wanted as much attention as possible and Pat and Gale and all of them wanted fame for free for being drug dealers and hard guys and criminals, but they were not and are not willing to do the time.

And Arlene and they lost it when they started laughing and bragging and becoming psychics. And Interpol started sniffing around because that PSA was created by the same organization that created the HUAC, House of Un-American Activities Committee, which persecuted communists during the 1950s and 1960s in influential organizations and businesses including the Hollywood Studios.

Anyone who was caught or rather who attended a Communist event or parade, or meeting, was put on a list and blacklisted from industry internationally. That was run by Scotland Yard and British Intelligence even though it was a Congressional Mandate and an ordinance prosecutable by law. Anyone who didn't surrender another for attending a meeting of the Communist Party, even once was blacklisted and imprisoned.

The same people are persecuting the psychic that cult built and was spreading around the government and the people through hypnosis and a link from one person's will to the particles and subliminal vibrations in someone's brain and heart, and people through biting through the particles and humming a vibration and speaking can echo their voice through the space and annoy the living piss and hell out of anyone they are trying to target through witch craft.

And that is what they were doing. Besides linking a child trafficking ring to the park outside the White House.

Since there are so many empty coke bags being found in Biden's White House, do the people outside the White House have anything to do with that? Is this the idea that we are seeing the governments of the world deal kids right at the front door of the government? The front door to freedom for many is coated in cocaine and cash money that they can grab from the federal reserve by bagging up for its employees at lunch. What is the government up to now?

You can lie and say this is why insurrection happens, but you can't say that anyone devising a plan of mutiny and malice wasn't sitting in a Republican chair and doing the same thing. It isn't fair that parties can blame the or there for things they commit as well, but so is the blame game and that is in a large part, polices and politics, it's a rival that is just political not only a political rivalry.

What purpose does it serve to pump this conniving bullshot down people's throats, when the government is pretending that it doesn't raise a blind eye towards this Easter auction and this Christmas Carol blinder, attacking the fabric of democracy when everyone is at their most vulnerable, which is when Cola companies decided that these particular days were more important than a sentimental celebration and now they are ignorantly enforcing the demise of American freedom at its finest, by teaching everyone to relax and drink a regular on the holiday. There should be an advertisement for Thrill Seekers drinking Diet, and not just Zero. As an ad gimmick, it could make a lot of sense, and keep people apprised of situations like this that occur the one day of the year that everyone wants to relax.

There is a dozen of those days per year, and people should maybe relax in shifts.

Is there a temptation to indulge in remorse when there is no strategy at hand to counter these measures of people taking advantage of a child's good nature and hosting them for very little money and for the sake of decriminalizing outward socialist concepts instead of giving thanks for the traditionalist view of their gifted days, where and when they make money off of some family that got put through turmoil for the rest of their lives, having to struggle with drugs and a potentially kidnapped and beaten and fucking molested like a little doll that shouldn't speak back and these guys are grown adult pedophiles. No one seems to point out the importance of a low paying child trafficking ring that exists outside the government office and has a cult attached to it that resembles other cults, where things have not ended up the right way.

Now everyone wants to know if Gale is selling crack to the Biden family or to people at the White House or in Congress?

These master cult artists are just allowed to trade people and endorse genocide and ask to have sex with anyone they can feel like or imagine because they said so. Like some outdated 70s pimp, that attitude has gone far enough, especially on this planet as this is the end of placating this particular auction to take place without people letting others know about it.

If it is fake, they should just keep their mouth shut and not brag about it. They probably just smoked crack and traded a couple of orphans. Now they think they are the mob or some bullshit.

Because Gale is broke and can't sell a house, she needs to sell everything in her purse and that includes the keys to some kids house she was paid to babysit but ran out and scored some rock instead. Now she had some good shit and there is a cult alive in her name.

But what does the purpose of this elaborate Easter show with a bunch of kids that don't have parents? Why parents aren't invited is beyond anyone's explanation or contemplation. It's a shame to throw such a party every year and yet no one says thank you to that poor old woman who put it all together. While they were mad Damian dressed like the Easter bunny for thanksgiving on the Deay of the Lord's resurrection. But instead, they were mad that we brought our legend to the mall, taking pictures all throughout Lent at the mall with moms and people bringing their kids to take photos as the Easter Bunny.

And Gale meets the kids down at the Community Center who stares her down when she goes to sign her kid up at summer camp. They know the freak is going to cry. And boo-hoo he needs to be an astral supervillain, so everyone knows who he is he is Cousin Shane, meant to deny himself no further other than on that five or ten dollar bill you have ready in your coat pocket. If it crips, it better be folded. And don't worry about the cameras, we got this on lock down.

Gale will stab the shit out of you, or least that is what she'll say. "I'll stab the shit out of you." She says, to people who smoke pot, but not her pot and whom she didn't approve. "You must buy my pot. I want the name of your connection. Tell me who it is."

And when Damian gets arrested for smoking with some 16-year-olds down the street, she'll warm up to being cold, and say it again. "I'll stab you the fuck up. I said no smoking pot without my permission. I am Gale. My way or the skedaddle old Freeway." She let loose thinking she was his spirit guide or something She would keep LK in her house, make sure he got a job, keep his schedule, and follow his bus home and then play witchcraft with the bus driver from far away using her government privilege to coordinate her telepathy. And everyone thought she ran with the government.

What kind of profile is this, when a kid like Shane gets thrown out of a party with the motorcycle club? Man did that put his mom in a bad spot for a while, and for the rest of her life. Because when she got thrown out, all they had to do was remember her kid and she wasn't getting back in.

There was no way anyone would risk losing their sanity to meetup or spend time with that kid. It was less than an hour before he was asked to leave, and he was three years old. It was convinced that he was just a little kid, and no harm was being done. A few hours later, he got his last warning. Some time at the next party, the kid was asked to leave, and Mitchell had to pick him up to go home.

No one knows what he said to people, but they would stop to talk to him, and he would get ticked off because he was preoccupied with some stuffed animal or a toy that he played with for hours, that he would say a couple of words. Then the other person would talk, they were an adult, Shane was three years old and then, it would transfer.

Within a few seconds or a couple of minutes, sometimes it took a few interactions between them, but the person, usually bent over to talk to some cute little kid, would snap right up and start barking. They would walk over to a crowd of people and start complaining and getting really agitated and fuming mad. Shane was satisfied and hid it well but not that well. It happened to every person that met him, most of his childhood, until he was about 16.

Then he started growing and his years at basketball camp paid off, he made it to the team. And he had heart. People gave it to him, the benefit of the doubt.

Arlene smoking crack and letting Gale do her planning and serving on the guest list. Might sound like nothing but not Gale has an illegal network operating on government property and Arlene has her tied directly to trading, trafficking underage toddlers, and using a network that operates on government property. Sounds like a big mess. With John eyeing the president through his connections the law enforcement database as a deputy of Suffolk NY.

Arlene sat up in the afternoon from her show on television wondering if National Security depended on a decision made while under the influence of Gale's narcotics and cocaine. Wonderful, it is fruitful to multiply. To produce such fine specimen of human creation and machine. I feel like I am within an advanced world deep within the future. Where the president doesn't fall asleep from the narcotics streaming through his blood.

Rumors abounded on the internet how Joe Biden was a mask and that a couple of junkies were just passing it off and pretending to be him each day. They were wondering what direction the country goes, since it is considered a corporation not a country, just like people are, and this corporation is a factory to produce an alien vacuum, meant to drain humanity from above its domes like a sponge, flying around invisibly over each crowd or group of people like a jellyfish or a sponge. And the girl on the plane wore a silicon mask of the actress featured in the movie "Snakes on a Plane." And everyone noticed.

Just like Shane wandering around downtown Philli and roaming aimlessly working for the Department of Digital Affairs in Washington D.C.

And the rite that grants them privilege to deal their crack and sell their kids at the white house also gives them religious rite over passage. They now have an initiated complex, but they have never even been punched in the face. Never been in a fight, never pushed anyone around. They just hypnotize someone to get their way.

People accept their hypnosis to see if they will fall for the trick of letting them control them, and people walk away being a vacuum for their will and their voices. They treat everyone and everything like a piece of energy they are going to absorb. And this works for them. They get what they are after and accomplish their goals, but they don't achieve their dreams, and they don't make anywhere near enough money to impress people. They married rich and their wives don't care what they believe, they want to be the very top of the elite in this country.

They had plans for LK to take the presidency in a number of terms from now. And it wasn't easy to break free from those fuckers.

They came up with one idea and heard people were buying self-help books and looking at New Age concepts and alternative forms of thinking, within science and alternate realities and looking into mediations and ancient knowledge and they went off the deep end, thinking they could profit and make money, cash off of people's spiritual enlightenment path, and they mistook questions of energy and emotional attachment as weakness and vulnerability and assumed there was a way to profit off of this vulnerability and people's weaknesses like they do when they sell drugs to you. And they want you to buy some more.

If the information every got out, the first thing the Strasser would do, is blame the president for all the local UAP and Stealth Drone mind control surveillance and data accumulation networks there actually were if they knew about it. Which they claimed to know about it. And that it was in a movie that it was the president's responsibility so they couldn't say that it was true, but they tinkered with the idea that it is just his or her responsibility and therefore must be held liable for its existence.

And in small towns across the world, some Ukrainian company partnered to utilize U.S. designed superpower drones to perform data accuracy surveys and geological mapping surveys, utilizing high tech surveillance and infrared and ultrasound equipment. In towns like Williams, Arizona there are such experiments, and for some reason Gale and Pat supposedly know all about that stuff without being able to pinpoint the locations of them but will start preaching that they know all about UAP and how to use it as a religion.

Now, UAP is a form of drone either built on earth or in outer space by ancient astronauts and even aliens themselves, or even perhaps a group of elitist reptilian beings, or some earthen scientists and politicians flying around in space. But none of that is probably the truth. The rumor went around that people were building the drones and calling them UFO and UAP as a form a little green alien vehicle.

What is more a likely is that some people with immigration issues who are released back into the U.S. until their court date are notified of government jobs available in the private sector. Some of these jobs are in advanced aeronautical engineering firms that operate popularly in the U.S. and those firms hire people who are legally allowed to remain in the U.S. and give them jobs as aeronautical engineers, to build planes and design planes. Someone must do it. Of course, some experience is required in the field of engineering or aeronautics.

However, these drones are also designed by the hiree, who has a team and others who are pooling resources and they each design a plane and some drones as planes, and besides from choosing traditional models of airplane, the now CIA badged project helper and airplane designer, gets access to the facility. And if it withstands science, they can design any kind of experimental plane, with any look, color, technology, they can integrate into the warehouse and the budget and ordering system and have the resources available to construct the drone or plane that they want to design.

Basically, these jobs are given to people who want to experience something great by designing planes. Some of these people are technically illegal immigrants and they live off their salary with their fringe benefits for the project duration, while they design and modify and proceed with the building and construction and application of the prototype. Lots of people design a plane that no one has seen or used before, to get a cut from the sale of the prototype.

If someone wants to get a job building planes and after they design and build and testify their fighter, they may have time left over for a second project some experimental and technologically futuristic or if they want to build a stealth with a futuristic look, the only thing stopping them are the requirements of their project and the desire to build and fit it within the inventory contracts and resource lists.

When the chips fall, they can put together a sleek design that can withstand the tests of science and time. The ability to shop for resources and search through inventory lists for potential materials that one might find beneficial for their craft, is always going to enable a builder to stand out, if they can maneuver through the resources and stock lists and supplies, like a scavenger.

These designers can put together a plane that is technically a prototype that technically does not look like a plane. This drone can be just that as an unmanned craft playing by remote control and towering over a town to gain access to the x-ray capabilities, the infrared and fever medical camera capabilities and its ability to scan geological data and landscaping issues that may have the ability to identify a problem leaning towards society at an alarming rate.

For instance, there are weather drones that are considered balloons, but they are made of metal, so that they can withstand weather, including tornadoes, hail, heavy rain and lighting, wind, and weather balloons are not always going to be made of cloth. Someone designed them thinking it was cool to have a drone that they can design and use and they patented it when it was perfected and now other people can buy it and use it or manufacture it and license it so that they can sell it to those who want it, making it a profitable venture and it has a hidden demand. A lot of people who aren't interested in drones are asleep to the interest level that people who are mesmerized by technology in drones have about the subject.

There are many hobbyists who would jump at the idea of designing a weather balloon or a drone that looks like a pyramid that can fly around and even use antimatter and turn invisible and run on rocks or petroleum or nuclear energy or fans and crystals, water, or sunlight. People will jump at those ideas.

But there are idiots like Shane, who will blame the president for those kinds of projects. Where people just want to design and build their own drones and then companies buy them and use them for either malevolent or non-interesting purposes.

It's not all well and good for patients at the institutions for rehabilitation in southern Arizona. Unfortunately, their branch of the government has volunteered them for a data participation survey which enables the facility or whoever is conducting the tests, to utilize an X-ray technology that reads infrared and can scan various parts of the human anatomy through a processing of information.

This drone looks like it has multiple large cameras and lights and can hover as a drone would but does stand over ten feet tall and is well over ten feet long. It stops at certain times to hover over the institution in Benson, Arizona and explores the waves and infrared and x-ray camera capabilities over the patients who are approaching bed down or are asleep.

When the government sends a steel weather balloon to examine a jet stream that is 100% predicted that the tornado winds that erupt from the cloud stream that buckles through Arizona in order to try and map data that could perhaps somehow influence the coming storm, is that the president doing their job, or is it just a conspiracy that the steel made shell drones, as weather balloons will withstand the winds and tormenting pressure of the clouds, when they fly by?

But shouldn't people be educated that on the existence of experimental technology so that they don't fear for their safety if they come across it, or is it preposterous to think that if anyone thought it was something other than an alien in a UFO they would just go and build their own craft and fly it around? Which was more dangerous?

No one wanted to risk giving this knowledge to just anybody.

But now people are chased around with Men in Black with remote controls and the number of prototypes for geological survey drones and weirdo weather balloons outweighs the demand, and the number of experimental planes they expected to sell to Ukraine and Czech out weighted the demand.

Few people need a bunch of those. They are like Lamborghinis in a Police station requisition. They're cool but they don't do anything except a function which is used in rescue and dangerous situations. Yet, it's probably more than likely going to get stolen. You don't need a bunch of those to perform the functions of the job.

But if they are after you in a Lamborghini, you might need a lawyer. So, drive one for a few people to pretend you are rich and they will either fuck off or want to compete and then you've got a problem.

They all pretend to be cops, the drug dealers, the traffickers, the Interpol investigators, the security guards, and the people at the deli. They want to know what you are doing with that quarter pound of American cheese and bologna in your bag.

I'm going to trade it for crack.

With these people. Flying experimental aircraft in restricted airspace ladies and gentlemen. Children of all ages. The guy who told me all about getting a job at Northrop Gruman and Lockheed Martin to build planes made of stealth materials for Area 51, he's a junkie. He was shooting heroine up his veins when he told Damian this story. He had a needle in his arm, was buying bundles down in Brooklyn Heights and was sure he was going to get there playing guitar, going to AA meetings, and watching videos about planes and air fighters.

This mother fucker designed the planes at an office in El Segundo and then went to the middle of the desert to build it and then flew it around Area 51. While he was designing the planes, they would work and commute from Hollywood in the Hills. They would go to the bars on Sunset at night, meet celebrities, get drunk and go to work in the morning. And then they would do it all over again each day.

When the planes were funded and produced for designing and they were ready to be built they were put up at an Airforce base or a house and then they would go to Area 51 and stay in the barracks and fly their planes around and modify and test fly them. And drink in local towns around there with CIA and Air Force Clearance culturally, at least.

At least this is all taxable.

And you can go and get a job there and feed your kids doing the deed in aviation. And if you go to Walmart in Vegas you get to the gate of Area 18. And if you go to the racetrack in Vegas you get to see the flights of real fighter jets right on the street at that Area gate. So, it's just an experimental testing zone where they now keep bones of people who break in there in the middle of the night. And they won't even start comparing stories or the DNA of past culprits because they would be liable. And so would the president.

It is not the president laying up hoping 30,000 people would make us all rich so they can ask people to hurt them and then kill them with poison Kool Aid, which would be his or her job to persecute those people to the utmost.

So, dealing crack and hating the government is not enough to tear down this organization because they have members who are in the Masons and Rotary club who tear apart the righteousness that those organizations might portray to their society and followers.

The world caters to them for having big mouths and lurking around the White House hoping aliens' trick everyone and take over their minds. It is possible that these people are just at home in a mental institution.

Dealing kids at the government statue, Arlene hates the government. She hates the U.S., and she don't like people that want to buy her product, which is some orphan dressed in some nice clothing.

Not like Shane, who takes pictures of himself outside the White house wearing tuxedos and showing up at a bar wearing a pair of knickers and corresponding half pants tucked into the knee-high thick socks.

Dancing and prancing around with a beard and his resume posted online, with his phone number attached.

A California phone number that has been in service since 2002 and has barely been in the state of California since 2007. That's a number he uses for his digital marketing company that outsources and contracts to civilians and private corporations. Crack.

The Dream Factories

A couple of wild beasts try to and maul one another outside a McDonalds, in a wilderness area near the movie studios in Senoia, GA. LK is asleep in a pit in the back behind the parking lot as the two beasts collide in midair while roaring and growling at each other, slamming into one another. The thundering echo of their chests piling into each the other, is what wakens the 318-pound freelancer.

He was trying to get a job at the studio or on the set of the Walking Dead TV show, and after all the hype of the movie studios moving to other states, he didn't assume that it meant an up close and personal with the National Geographic station. They fought those wolves and mountain lions, he hoped it wasn't for his soul and his body, because that spot was where he contemplated sleeping that night even though he didn't have a tent or a real blanket.

He opted for the construction pit, there weren't' any vehicles there and there sure wasn't a bunch of people over there. He should have taken the ride from the hottest woman he had met by far in a year and a decade. And this was during a break he took from his self-written complaint and lawsuit that he filed without a lawyer against the Boy Scouts, because of the trauma endorsed by the twins and Martin Maher. Who were also a part of the cult. Martin believed in his newfound power as a psychic and of course had called Damian on the phone and pledged his allegiance to the cult and to the parties and he confessed they were smoking crack with some kids pretending they were on a camping trip.

The statute of limitations has not been overturned in NY State yet, but it would be later that year, which transformed the case entirely.

The complaint was filed in Kings County in NYC, and it was over 50 pages long with well over 1100 notches in the text. They were charged with over 1100 tort counts without any of them alluding to sexual misconduct or any type of molestation against him directly.

Let's get this straight, that no one very molested him but it was always a matter of discussion with the same parties over and over. Big K was a cubmaster and that wasn't the entire issue, but Martin made it the issue and showed up naked a few times, talked about misgivings, threw some parties, jacked off and stared while D was shagging, getting a bj from a prostitute that was ordered and there was a certain amount of play fighting which was pretty hard and there was some issue of Mark and Joe trying to masturbate with Damian and when he refused they kept harassing him for permission to masturbate with Arthur and his younger brother. And this was an issue because Mark and Joe were over 21 and over 16 when all this started, and they just were not very socially admired and accepted at some of the camps that they worked at. And it was difficult to get through working with that organization for Damian.

He did a lot of work and worked hard and there was a lot of labor that physically took a toll on him that he had to do because he volunteered, and he wanted a promotion. If people were assigned workloads by him that they thought honestly was too much for them, he would help them do their task and take a lot of the pressure off having it done on time.

Things like heavy lifting and digging and fixing fence posts, carrying rocks, raking, and cleaning and scrubbing, those kinds of jobs where help is appreciated, he often showed up to show his appreciation for others' hard work and would lend a big hand for a while.

He also coached team building as a teenager and ran a pretty good store. People trusted him and let him have a free reign and he was usually given the right to take as he pleased form most people because he worked hard, trained others to work and how to do the job and got it done effectively and there was a lot of overtime and other assignments that he would shou up to help especially when no one else would.

Marting didn't care. Martin had two events that he felt were very important. Each year he hosted the Irish Fair Concession Stand which was one concession amongst a hundred or so, and he served hotdogs and hamburgers with sodas and chips.

The other event was the Irish American Day Parade which was different from St. Patrick's Day, it was a Sunday near the same seasonal time, and it was mandatory that everyone had to show up for no reason but to walk down the street. Or they got made fun of, barred, and had their stuff thrown into the trash and laughed at to a bunch of hot toasted women.

They had a few drinks and were just looking for it, Martin would get wind and tell you to go fuck yourself. He is still a virgin besides his hooker whom he got busy and dicked once and now he just lays there like a blob, when he gets his head on, he can lay there like he did when he ripped his pants off at the Parish Center with a bunch of moms and little kids running around. Passed out like a blubber choked beached whale.

He called Damian on the phone and pledged allegiance to the gypsy, the 800-pound curtain pant suit lady who pretends she can cook some Neapolitan, she can't.

But he was a part of the cult now and when the statute of limitations had kicked in, Damian had just decided to drop the case after getting the okay from the judge to rewrite the complaint and include more present and forwarded information that had influence on the entirety of the case itself. It was almost thrown out until he mentioned that when he was in Senoia a few weeks earlier, that he was looking for food at a local pantry, and a guy showed up who was doing something else elsewhere on the property of the church with the Scouts. He approached and asked Damian what he needed. And he responded that he needed some food, he heard there was a food pantry there.

It was early summer, and it was extraordinarily damp and hot and there was a lot of sun and rain, and it was clammy. The guy said he had the key he was helping a couple of scouts. He didn't work at the pantry, but he could grant access. So, Damian agreed to wait by and in a while, they all went inside, into the cool basement of the church and the guy asked him which kinds of food he wanted out of the goods. And he had a nice little pile there, it was making his day, and he was satisfied that he had some food. He wanted to go check out the movie set some more and try to find a job.

Anthony, the guy who was helping him, was calling people around to see if he could get Damian a shower. He found a place in another town and wanted to drive him over there to take a shower. It was about a forty-minute drive. He said no thank you and the guy was insistent. He had his two kids with him who were both around 10 and 11 or 12 and that was taken into consideration.

Damin had mentioned that he had been an Eagle Scout and that he had a lawsuit against them, and it was almost awkward, but he thought it was okay to mention and he thought Anthony would let it go. So, Anthony offers him a ride to this other town and there is a shelter there. He says he can drop Damian off and get cleaned up, he must do some chores and he can stay the night and have a meal and take off or stay or whatever he wanted to do.

He keeps insisting on driving him. So, he reluctantly agrees to go and get some sleep and take a shower at it another day. Calculating his safety, DK aka LK aka Damian sits down in the car and Anthony had revoked the food that he offered him to eat. So, he said there would be food there. Okay, they all left.

Anthony mentions his daughter played the supporting lead in a Paul Rudd movie. They talked about the movies for a while. And shoot the shit.

To add fuel to the fire, as Damian was earning his credits being thrown out of Senoia, GA, he was dropped off at a farm in a nearby town. The house was basically a big place with a couple of bedrooms with dormitory style living situations. And the food was basically gruel, not really grits and eggs, but more like a gruel and there were lots of hotdogs being served with fruit punch.

When he showed up on that Friday night with Novak and his kids, the world changed when after breakfast, he assumed that doing some mopping and cleaning was the end of the labor and that the day was his to spend. They were all taken and loaded up in a van and driven to yet another town. In that town, they were put out into the sun without water and food and asked to trim the grass and do all of the landscaping. Then they were paid but the organization was paid, so nobody doing any of the work was getting any money. A few hours later, the guys who collected the money and drove everyone around arrived with a thermos filled with tea. But that was it. There was no food or lunch or any water. So, the Boyu Scouts sponsored this homeless work program where people worked for ten hours in the sun every day and weren't allowed to leave the property and they weren't allowed to get paid and they didn't have any good food to eat, and they had to painting of walls and fences and all kinds of illegal labor that was deemed okay by the BSA leaders who stuck to their guns and yelled back towards LK that he had to deal with it, after they convinced him it would be a shower a meal and some chores for a bed. He was again being ridiculed by the BSA.

This was 2017 and Damian had already been on TV a bunch and in some movies and nobody noticed him in any of those parts, but he did some small-time stuff that was appreciated artistically. He had some slots on big TV shows and some major movies. He was in the movie Conversations with God, and played a protective spectator who was stepping up to fight one of the author's hecklers in the movie. The author was the main character who lived homeless in Ashland and became a Millionaire writer who drafted books about talking with God as if He were a person talking to him in his head.

He was in Communications and Entertainment school and was about to graduate. Again. The people he knew in life brushed him off as a dropout. A loser. And that's not what he necessarily was, they were all dropouts and losers. He wasn't. He took a different route. He wouldn't bow and bend to Martin Maher, who had gone to his house and asked him to move out of his house with Big K and Angela and move into his place with a couple of guys from the older generation of the Troop and his brothers. There was room for one more.

Damian LK thought it was a good idea. He didn't bring it up to the parents at home because he was like, going to wait for martin to say something as he had requested. He said to be quiet about it and he would take care of it. When martin showed up, they asked LK to wait in the other room and they just brought him after they finished talking and said he could leave at the end of the summer.

They never once asked him if he wanted to leave. And he never said to them that he did. The day he left to work at camp again, Martin showed up and picked up all his stuff without permission and when he got home at the end of the summer, he didn't have any of his stuff there. He had to go and live with Martin. This was all in 1996.

And Big K and Angela resented him and threw it in his face that he left and that he was never allowed back. And that was when he told them to go fuck themselves. They have never had a good relationship because Big K brought all these people in from the parish and the scouting when Lk was just a kid and they never left.

Angela came over for a sleepover as a den mother in 1988 and she never fucking left. It was a piss off point. And especially since her sister Jo, forced voodoo down everyone's throats and they became those people that craved being psychic and complained about being schizophrenic.

Big K was just pissed off he had to share time with LK and LK was tired of spending the Friday night alone and half of the weekend by himself. He wanted to play baseball and get to know other kids and go camping. Big K had a problem with it. It took until a friend of theirs showed up at school and recruited for the cub scouts so that he could even get a message through to Big K.

Damian threw his arm out because they let him throw screw balls. And breaking curve balls, submarine pitches and some crazy loopy pitches. And he threw that shit out before baseball camp. Big K would only pay for one week.

He was saving his money for a woman, and would never spend a dime, he pretended he lived on a five dollar and hour salary budget. If it didn't have food he pulled a paint job, if the fake budget didn't pull gas, he tried to work for an old lady and maybe score or get some tips for his help.

He had a great ethic, but he lost his courage to communicate by getting sober and endorsing drugs. He endorsed gangs and gang membership on a nightly basis at home and that was what he liked to talk about. He wanted to talk about gangs the whole time and when he was younger in a gang. And it was his whole life.

Every night. Or Affirmative Action and the Liberals. They believed in Sanitation these guys. Now, Keith lived in Carroll Gardens which was mainly Italian still back in those days, it had a lot less hipster vibe to it than it did now.

And basically, when they moved into Carroll, they were the only people there who were not Italian. And everyone there was a first- or second-generation Italian American, their parents arrived in 1913 as a small kid or some shit and it was still the effect to live like their grandparents did. And they had to deal with that shit. All day long, they were the only guys who didn't grow up eating the Lard Bread for their days in like a two-mile fucking radius.

And every Guido int own had it in for the fucking kid, Damian LK the one Bubba the Buddha. A couple of the hottest girls he ever knew by far, liked him a lot and that might not have played in his favor because a lot of girls liked him, and he never got with those girls over there in that neighborhood and they basically told him to fuck off. One of them wanted to marry him.

One day he was coming home from school, and he was badly coming from a bender, and was stoned and they threw a snowball, and he threw up some gang sign, called them n____ and he got beat to the ground. Pretty bad. His face was all swollen. Big k went around town with a baseball bat he used for practice still and then they called the cops, found a couple of the guys, and put 'em in cuffs. They were mostly all Italian but had one guy that was Latin. A punk. He tried to steal his bag, but D. didn't let it go.

And the cops wanted to go to trial and file charges. A couple of friends at school went to handle it the next day. The following day, the first thing they said was 'drop the charges and it will all work out, ok.' And they repeated it, and in a week or so, he had the charges dropped and that was the last time he heard from the Italians, although they did scare it a few times, it kicked in quick.

By the next year, everyone was on the same team for some reason, and everyone was polite and cordial. Damian had been initiated for over two years into a sort of crew that was protecting him on a major level. And he moved forward with his life after a year with Martin, and denying Martin's parties with the guys a year younger doing the same thing with the strippers and whatnot and moved his ass out to Tempe, Arizona where he would decide that he was better off in Los Angeles if he wasn't going to get a good job out in Phoenix, Mesa and Tempe.

He was prying to the gnostic God of the Merkabah and fasting in Sedona Arizona when some guy noticed him in the bookstore and offered him a room free of charge. Now, the guy didn't hit on him at all and helped him out a lot. He offered him a permanent place to stay and find a job. He was going to take him up on it. It seemed like a good idea.

But he was called to go to Seattle. And he didn't really want to go. But he wanted to go to Seattle and check it out. Turned out to be a groovy kind of city in some spots. But he was on the payphone with Big K in Sedona, and the fucker didn't tell him he had a gangbang with Marsha. What he told him was that Marsha called on the phone and was pregnant and that he should go and meet her in Seattle.

And Damian was coerced after they told him to go. Both Big and Angela said it was a good idea and the right thing to do. He bucked up and went up there. He wasn't going to get hitched, but she beat him to it and threatened him into putting his name on the certificate for just a short while temporarily until he could get it annulled. And he thought it was okay until the kid was born, they would get a divorce and that was how he got stuck owing the IRS and Washington State and Jacob some child support.

And the lady from the Child Support agency pounded on his door in late 1999 to serve him his overpayment notice and to serve him his paid summons to not appear buy pay arrears. And his turmoil began.

He joined the Korean Yoga which was Korean Tai Chi, and it was a deviated and more broken-down form of Tai Chi and the headmaster there, he authored books but didn't speak English, he had the books translated into English.

He taught this one lesson when he showed up from Korea, and everyone paid like 365.00 to meet him and do a *bubble capsule exercise*. Basically, you have to breathe a bubble around you, and it protects you, and you have to say, Capsule Capsule Capsule to yourself over and over.

And then the guy would sever your ties to astral conditioning and clean your meridians with like a zap to your forehead just like a preacher would put his hand on someone's forehead. And people would collapse. And they would teach everyone that it was better to collapse when he touched your forehead. And they had really bad Korean accents. They spoke worse than Jackie Chan.

And in time your meridians would clean out. And this was one special program. Damian didn't have to pay for it. They offered hm a spot next to the headmaster and to tour with Neale Donald Walsh as a Buddha figure. He didn't pay to meet Master Li and he didn't pay for their New Human School either. He had to do basically nothing for months and months of book training and classes and physical training all to do with the philosophy of the program and was the premaster program and was all about the union of mind, body, spirit, heart, and brain and was unique and very informative.

Well, a bunch of students were paying for New Human School and rumors went around that he wasn't paying. And they were paying like 10,000.00 for the classes. And there were all kinds of weekend retreats and all sorts of special training that people were going all out to pay for. But most of the people had some money. And he was invited to Master training for free to become a full-on Korean Yoga Tai Chi master, and that didn't happen.

He brought a bunch of students to a hippie festival, did LSD and his master got fired and left just before the trip. When they got back and he was back a week later than everyone else, there was some new female master's there, and they immediately refused to let him in the door. And he was asked to leave the program. Chris, who paid full price for the school guarantee, sold him up the river and told on him. That was a different Chris and a different Amy.

That was when Nurelle and her boyfriend Chris L. brought Damian back to Seattle and Chris took off to screw his aunt or his cousin and Nuri was jealous; and every time Chris' aunt was around, she would start sucking Damian's cock. In a private corner of the house, she would lay a wet hot blow job on his dick when he least expected. And she would guzzle his shit. They still hung out with Chris after they started hanging with one another. Chris stayed around for the entirety of their relationship. But she and Damian couldn't last. He was not so into her. And she was too suspicious of him, and it took way too long for that to occur. He wanted her attention earlier on in their relationship and she wouldn't give it to him, she was still hung up on Chris.

And Damian didn't really want to be with her. He was always into smart, pretty girls who were socially adept in big circles of Guido's and jews and had lots of money, protection, and people who looked after them. And he was confident no one was fucking with them. And they were sophisticated.

He didn't wreck with pothead girls. They didn't get it. They just wanted to pretend to be open-hearted and spiritually open minded and make everything cool. He could be friends with some girls, but he didn't know if he was looking for a pothead girl. He knew he probably was not interested as much as a girl who wore light makeup, clean and mature clothing and smoked regular popular cigarettes.

Girls that smoked American Spirits were proud to tell you she was telling you to fuck yourself in front of her friends.

This bitch was even worse.

She'll ignore you all day long and will fuck a stranger under a dirty tree and shit on the ground and piss on the lawn and ignore the signs and order someone else to clean the shitter or latrine at the farm that she will herself ignore to use and disrespect and use it as well and not offer to help clean it. But will tell someone else to do it.

And in 2004 Damian took her to long island, or she drove him out there to meet his ex-fiancé at this point Jennifer and man when they met, the two of them, it was like devious. And when he was unloading the boxes, some actor came popping out from the car she was with, and it was a big-time new actor, who Damian recognized from Derailed. It was the same jacket from the movie. It was Clive Owen without a shower, and he had a scotch-tired look on his face. Of course, Jenny preferred to work full time in a store, and live in a tent.

Rumor has it that he stood in the rain waiting for Jenny for a few days staring at the store and trying to get to know her from there. The other rumor was that it was her ex-boyfriend, and he was stalking her outside her business, a thrift store in Suffolk County near Melville. And he was staring down Damian hard, very confrontational.

So, good luck with that. We were just moving boxes.

Needless she died her hair brown and got a reduction after they guy left. She was a redhead and to someone she liked she had a magnet attached to her.

And this guy had an attitude.

And Jenny started hearing voices, like a bunch of people did. And she was scared of gangs in the area always hurting the Mexicans or each other, so she was kind of nervous all the time.

She told of a story where she was working at the school bus garage where Gerri worked, the bus driver from the Flannery's. She complained she got raped on the bus there while she was there working. She was a driver. They know the guy worked there.

She was now a store manager of a local thrift shop at the time she left Damian. And it was hard to let the old pimple butt go. She had nice hooters and loved it, but she would screech every time she laughed, and everyone would look over. And she would give out some love in the restaurant under the table to Damian, but she would start a fight if they couldn't plow and there were women there in public. She was a public skewer. She demanded it in the bushes and all day every day, but she had no buttocks to admire. She was mean spirited and spent thousands of dollars a month on vegan food. Waste of time really, but she was fun and nice for a little bit of time. She had crazy beliefs and talked to Big K in her head.

She would freak out about schizophrenia and say she heard voices in the wall the entire time and that she was pissed wasn't enough to cover it. She wanted to get even. She was furious that people were crowding her body and space and talking shit. They were always looking at her and talking to her from another dimension. She finally complained that it was a guy talking into her head from far away and showing his image in a trench coat while haunting her dreams. She said it physically over and over. It was getting a little frustrating dealing with her and everyone else's open schizophrenia.

The Thrift Store was on the same street that the Flannery's lived. Damian even watched Jenny and John the deputy on the same line at 7/11 which was also on the same street that the Flannery's lived.

John was a good funny guy, very friendly and always told jokes, Problem with him is that he used to talk about mind control. And he was pretty bent on talking to Damian about Big K and his use of covert and overt control over other people's minds. When he joined the Sherrif Department, Damian was renting but not paying for a room at Arlene's place in Long Island. It was at the edge of Melville and Huntington Station and was not a bad area of town crime wise, but the elements were there when Carolanne, John's wife, was caught following Damian with her mind intently and talking to him and calling him two people while he was sitting there and speaking to him as if Keith Lk and Damian were two different people. They weren't two separate personalities, and they were ideally the same person with a different name. LK never told Carolanne or Arlene or any of them about changing his name. He never said it to Gale.

Yet they all demanded to him physically that he become a part of a mass hypnosis through a request through Big K, Patrick, and Gale. And their business continued for a while after Carolanne approached Damian and told him a couple of times that the family was trafficking kids. And it was a big joke, but it wasn't. It wasn't a joke she said, but it does look that way. Convincingly. 'You must tell us. You have to snitch on the family. Rat. And turn them in. You'll see. You'll do it, you must."

And he didn't want to believe her. He kept it to himself for a couple of years dismissing it as a joke. But deep down he knew he would have to do the right thing eventually.

And she approached him again and told him that again, and he didn't ever talk with her after that ever again. That was in 2002 and it was rediscovered with Big K and Patrick had admitted to this over the phone several times, and this pissed off Damian. He was going to eventually have to say something to somebody, because he knew the way he was brought in, that someone else would not be as lucky as he was to get past those people.

When Big K took over LK and his caretaking, he was aware that there were movie producers who were interested in working with LK. They had said it. He was a good-looking kid with big wiry hair, and he had a big giant heart and a huge smile, and he would start a fight with anyone who bullied him. It was obvious that he was going to be in demand being that his mom had such a big plug.

But Big K and Gale and Frank had conspired to take LK and Patricia O'Hanlon had finally decided to walk away from Frank when Big K decided to bring LK into the picture. Even though she hid the truth and was a slimy rude woman, she didn't agree with him being mistreated by Big K and Frank and Patrick.

But Gale had set Barbara up at the doctor's office and gave her what was needed to keep her coming back for more. And after one or two bags, Barbara was stranded with some guys thinking about joining a cult, so she left with one of Big K's cousins' friend in Queens and started a small life with those people. Big K found out about it and she and Mario didn't get along anymore.

Barbara went to get clean and was dropped off at a NA meeting where a cult leader took her in. And they were going to cult meetings and the members were taking a drug going into a trance and sharing a vision about their master, who was performing enlightenment exercise by a lake or in some woods; and they would share their visions of the master who was walking around upstate New York supposedly using Remote Viewing capabilities. And they could see what he was doing.

It sounded ridiculous. But when they tried to kill the K-9 dog Barbie called the cops and she was outcasted because she ratted on them trying to kill the dog and they were starting to prepare it to get dead and die.

And she went to the police station to get some answers on her safety and file a report. While there, the cult members were in custody talking to other members on the phone. When Barbie came back with a sandwich, it had some Ham and Turkey on it maybe some Roast Beef and the cult member was looking at Barbie and said, "It's eating meat, now." She fed some to the dog. She thought it was hilarious.

Well, before all this and before Barbie and Big K got back together before he met Angela, they were together for the sake of their recovery, going to NA and AA meetings together for a little while. Well, Big K learned about the auditions from Joanne, and she was interested in helping Lk get his acting career together. He was only 6 years old, so after that Big K decided he wanted to become a movie director.

This would buff out LK's desire to produce a film and become an actor because that was what he wanted to do for fun and thought it would be great. Big K got some people together and a few showed up, mainly some Gilbrides from Staten Island, Bobby, and Richie. The four of them went to Prospect Park with some other people and filmed a horror scene where LK was scared because Big K and Pat jumped out and tried to attack and eat them as a monster from the wilderness. And it was like the Wolfman.

After that, Big K lost interest in editing the film and he charged LK to do it. When LK was about 8, he threw the film in the garbage can because he thought it was exposed and didn't know how to develop the film himself. Big K offered to pay but he threw the film out.

He had started gaining massive weight and had acne at 8 years old and wasn't having a great feeling about the movie even though it was still in his immediate desire to see how the movie had been made. And he never saw Richie again. It was devastating to lose his friends when he was so young, and he couldn't talk to his real cousins and stuff, but he was forced to hang out with losers who were pretending to be his family. And he was open to starting a fight as a kid.

Later on in life, Big K was supposedly contacted by some guys in show business, and they were supposed to keep it quiet and Big K wanted him to succeed but, his wife was also interested in them becoming rich and also famous with the rite of being introduced once or twice. What happened to Richie, no one knows except his neighbors and some of his friends and family, and luckily, he had some people that still cared about him. LK was in big trouble. He was going against the grain, and Big K, after he stopped drinking, he gave LK the keys to the apartment and left for a while. And LK went to school and went home and ate dinner and Pat called him on the phone and became his buddy. He apologized a whole lot for what had happened with people and him asking to team up on Little K and they became closer as almost friends, but LK never really trusted the guy. He knows he said the wrong thing.

For instance, Patrick called Damian on the phone and said that celebrities were telling him to project his mind across the whole world and take over everyone's mind individually from an office in Bay Ridge, while he pretended to map out a decent financial portfolio for you, he would try to get you hooked on his cousin's drugs, sell your kids to his other cousin's friends and then attempt to steal all your money and if he couldn't do that he would try to recruit you for his mighty suicide cult. Then you would die. And this was orchestrated by the hidden minds of your favorite Hollywood showmen except, it might not have been.

Fight Club style, just astrally, in a vision mind you, and they will let you know what you are doing right, or maybe what you're doing wrong? Maybe, maybe man.

Everyone assumed that because D was in a record/ movie deal with Tower and worked on some movies and TV that the whole psychic experiment was sanctioned by show business.

And the hits just kept on coming. Damian got rocked writing graffiti on an ice cream truck when he was 12-year-old, leaving him to realize that fame was not the source of power and light in life, and it was only good if it was worth health, wealth as knowledge and money. It's not worth anything else.

Without knowledge, health and money or cash on hand, the entertainment industry is worthless. Everyone singing my songs and telling me to shut the fuck up, they don't want to pay for it. Music is free/ Music isn't fucking free, and neither are actions based on a dick, cum, or some cock they always have consequences that can't be taken back.

Never mind, they just hear you are a millionaire because of a rumor in their mind or an impression or because someone had to pay someone money, or the industry owed, or it was just some value added to action and behaviors that benefited society in some way or provided an ample amount of sincere product that people found of very entertaining value. Entertainment is a preoccupation to some but some business and art to others.

It does not have to be the way that conspiracy theorists say, but there is perspective and people's perceptions and the fact that society is government by people and people partaking culturally and against the grain in some ways that they follow and get frustrated and turn against the crowd and rebel and become an elitest, thinking that the world is a horrible place and people deserve to be punished so they brainwash them and attempt to get them to pay them.

But sports are just competition, and acting and performance is a thrill for expressionists and philanthropists who study external artistic communication as a physical expression and journey of experiences.

When people like it and it makes money, advertisers are hard to turn down the opportunity to sell their provided products and services. And it is really the food industry how it took a turn for the worse under the Great Depression with the institution of the frankfurter and Hot Dog and the exclusion of the United States and its prophetic campaign of death by providing Corn Syrup based sugars in beverages and foods.

That is what makes entertainment artificial, political, and selfishly motivated on greed and materialistic viewpoints and perceptions. Most celebrities quit their jobs because of this projected schizophrenia created by these kinds of people. Preying on innocent people, laughing, and receiving a joyful rejuvenation from being psychic vampires, creating visions and sending out voices while trying to gain an advantage politically, financially, and sexually while destroying the earth and all its inhabitants with their thoughts and intentions.

Strassberg and Carty, Gilbride and Flannery, Diroio, Hansen, O'Hanlon, Robins and Harrigan. These groups of people believed in their psychic and infected humanity with an ideology of psychic awareness as a prowess to gain thousands of followers for their financial gain.

And the practice of using people of color for their psychics and energy transmission didn't cease. They used a unique energy field that was created during their meditations and seances and they practice spells to create grids made of energy, and reflective energy through spells, and they did it over and over, looking at maps and globes and focusing all their energy and trying to take over the world using their metaphysical discovery.

And they could anchor and take over the space around someone's body and their environment; and talk and speak and listen through it sunnily to the power of their minds. They were known for seizing a whole environment through the capture of its energy fields with their hands in their minds and they would use this power to talk to people and raid an energy grid and transfer different energy fields from around objects and people and make them speak to another as if they believed that a god or God or the devil or a demon or another person or an invisible entity was actually speaking to them, and they would do it from far away. So, the most corrupt vile and evil psychics, spies and enemies and allies of British intelligence started investigating them.

While Patrick assumed the responsibility of relaying and reiterating the messages of the cults that Kieth had started conveying, things took a turn. People just had their share of being manipulated because they all travelled around and tried to put a mind control energy field up and above every place and around everything they visited and then went about trying to control the drug trade by dominating the human subconscious. The pharmacists working for the cult advocated the cults message and projected their own form of drama into everyone's mind wherever they went, so it seemed like they were absent mindedly starting arguments and controlling the situation unnecessarily with extreme arrogance and lots of times, excessive rudeness.

But the audacity was that Patrick was proclaiming that people including celebrities were manipulating him and telling him to tell Damian what to do, as far as his career and living situation, to make it as a celebrity, which pissed him off, too much in fact that he blew a gasket and hand a nervous breakdown. The guy had taken all his money and used it, however, and paid off Damian's credit report and but didn't pay for his rent or anything like that. And he said he had the right to convince the universe to surround Damian's energy field his mind with his mind and energy fields and project it back towards not only him and a few others but into the minds of thousands and millions of people like pouring water into their spirits and possessing them. That's what they were after. That was the goal.

Making demos across the county, LK got into it with some shady girls that were talking to the FBI and trying to frame him for any old ordinance including making Mix Tapes, having too many friends or girlfriends, producing music over someone else's music, meeting black people who went to a mosque, along with a lot of bullshit psychic trickery and basic deceit. And she is hiding shit in her hand made purse, like tape recorders and stolen weed, delivering large garbage bags filled with processed leaf that no longer has THC crystals and was a big waste of time, planning and hoping to put maggots into the food at Black Bear Farm hoping to sabotage people's food and the visitors there.

Her friends, Songbird, Laura, and a couple of others were all there getting jobs in Dade City by an Orange grove out by the Renaissance Fair in Tampa. And Damina had a job there as a runner, but he was tired of hanging out with those girls. He did not want to spend hours in the car with them. So, in revenge for him boycotting the Renaissance Fair and boycotting their dumpster diving, since they only brought back rotted vegetables and yogurt, he wasn't interested in scavenging with them. He stayed back and overheard them a couple of times plotting to change his name to Sarki Abdul, and he thought it was interesting.

They were all on this farm across from the groves and the owner of the farm had a fake cult and did this therapy exercise called Satsang where people like meditate a little and talk about their week and like have a pow wow and get to communicate with others and they do a small eastern vibration prayer mediation thing. All well and good until Damian's boss asks him at work if he knew Mohammed Atta and if his name was Sarki Abdul! What a coincidence.

And, as Damian was a writer, he had written a 600-page sequel to his novel entitled 'Light of A New Day: The Calling". This was a grand feat for him. It was all about spirituality and this and that, it can be found in photo form, on Facebook. The issue with this work was that he wrote 600 pages, in one month.

Beginning to end. One draft.

There were literally zero misspellings, and it was written on a typewriter. It would have been formatted and published save the letters N and R or T, one of them, are broken halfway through.

You can find it on Facebook, some of it is just blurry and you can't read it. It's a text that was 300 pages on full 8 ½ by 11-inch paper; but he prints his books in little, smaller …and that will cut the pages in half and more. It's a big size book it's not a pocket size but fat, it's still 5 ½ by 10 or 6 x 9, cut the words up a lot.

Anyway, he was bringing this manuscript wherever he went for like 18 years he carried it around with him and stored it in lockers and had it in a bag. He had coffee spilled on it.

He was showing someone who was a guy living in an old RV and playing guitar and the guy said he wanted to retype the manuscript because of the broken letters. So, Damian agreed to let Ken write the script over against his own, if it was word for word. And the guy was doing it anyway.

Nori walked over thought it was an arts and crafts session and started retyping the same chapters that Ken was typing. And they both retyped the same work over again and it had multiple copies that they could probably try and junk and take for themselves.

Nori did that with a roll of camera film that she didn't take any pictures except of Damian close and tried to steal his award-winning photos. She was plagued by the media, she said who never printed her just talked about her behind her back, and only to her, no one else knew about that except for Randy who was trying to beat off on some energy. And moaning to himself because some girls were walking by.

He likes to reverse the energy girls give back to him. And send it and start a conversation which is smart and typical dating, but he possesses people's minds and asked to join their cult, so he don't get no respect. Damian went to the club with that guy, and everything was okay, except the guy wanted to trance out to visions of the cult and was arrogant about it, making everyone suffer from him being the magnetic electrical magnetic nucleus that he was, just from using his black magic in a negative metaphysics and projecting it around the room.

They like to bite into the space and pretend to be vampires, then steal actual energy and portray that they are not actually vampires yet, and make people look into the past, it's how they create magic and illusion without pulling any actual cards.

They try and tell people what they are doing, without knowing or looking, and repeat madness into their minds, so that they can create the illusion of being powerful so they can be in control and manipulate events by throwing up smokescreens as they get to know you. And they will deceive you and pretend they are doing you a favor by laughing at you and trying to get over you. They are communicating without speaking, it is a form of signal of those who participate in utilizing nonverbal communication to get what they want, which is usually some selfish gain that doesn't serve many people or purposes other than a selfish gain on behalf however many it takes to provide their safety and clever manipulation. So, the more than the merrier.

This was the girl Nori, who wanted to hang out with Damian and his friend Mike, and they also knew that she had something up her sleeve. But they just went to Connecticut and smoked out, and Nori Damian knew was dropping some kind of negative vibe. Either she was talking to the feds or her friends or playing with magic and trying to manipulate people's minds and energy body and moving along disturbing people's psychology by aiming to manipulate and alter their subconscious. Maybe that's why Mike shot himself. He had her nasty voices in his mind. That was not the first time that people who played dirty tricks on their mind tried to team up against Mike and Damian LK Unknoen.

In 1996, Gabe received an invitation to a small party at a girl's place who was hosting another girl, and they lived in Brooklyn Heights with Janet Reno's sister, a block or two or five from the Court buildings downtown in Brooklyn. They wanted to meet LK and to smoke some grass, so Gabe brought LK and Mike because he had some good pot and he brought them over an ounce of Purple Haze. And they all smoked out and Mike said he was uncomfortable, and Gabe wanted to press to leave, and

Damian wanted to go because they wanted to go, and they were always weird about outsiders. And since Gabe wanted to invite and leave, it was better probably just to go, even though it would have worked out. But for consensus purposes, everyone left. And there were a couple of girls there that looked familiar.

A couple of weeks and months later Gabe brought it up to Damian that they wanted to meet him again, without Mike and Gabe can bring the pot. And that was okay, he agreed. And they got there, and Drew Barrymore was sitting there and started talking to her friends, and Gabe wanted to leave. And kept pushing it, and LK thought it was weird. He wanted to leave too for sure now. Gabe didn't like it and had invited everyone. So, they got up and left.

A couple of months later, Gabe brought it up, they wanted to meet again. He said no this time. A few years later, Gabe got in contact with him and told him that they wanted to meet again, and he said maybe, whatever you think. And Gabe turned it down. A few years later, he said it again, and now he turned it down for LK, who was curious enough to want to know what they wanted. So, he told them to meet him, but Gabe said no.

He was fucking Julia, who asked out Damian for two days and dumped him after a week and Gabe thought he was the man for pounding her for years. Pounding her brains out.

I mean, she's fucking screaming. His name and talking to him about LK. He had that kind of effect on women. Besides the fact that several major actresses had approached him when he was 17, and a couple flirted with him pretty heavily, on the street. He had a major actress whom he thought was the sexiest hottest women actress on the planet for a long time, walk up to an ice cream truck next to him where they both ordered at the same time and they both ate the ice cream cone together walking silently apart from his party, on the beach on the boardwalk and the entire time she looked at the ice cream cone. And all he did was look at her and eat the ice cream. She walked away and it happened again the second week in a row, and they did it again and went for a walk this time sat beneath the boardwalk standing for a minute eating the ice cream and then she wouldn't talk to him, so he walked away with his friends. And she appeared a third time and they separated.

She appeared several times in life before him, even the day she appeared in the News for riding in a limousine with a famous baseball player. And she appeared to him on Hollywood Blvd when he was on the way to an audition. And Gabe was there for the ice cream incident. And it was peculiar who Gabe was. He was probably getting caught dealing Animal Tranquilizer to CBS associates. He is a madman.

Everyone knew Damian was out to become a professional poet. He gained some awards for his poetry and got it featured in all the record books, so people would actually know him for his written words and his hard work instead of just his good looks. He was bummed out that he got thrown out of the music industry.

The night he was at the Rotary Club, and they closed Tower, he was drinking wine in the back, having asked the cook for a plate of pasta, he ate the pasta and went walking around. He thought it was a wedding hall and a big banquet. There was no one there. He was with the producer who played the Ukulele for the club for like an hour every week, nobody could tell you why.

The guy was a producer, Von Thadden, but Paulie was his first name, he was a music teacher and together, they were Paulie Von Thadden of the Apollo Theater and Tower Records and Music Group from W 4th. He was one of the owners of the record store. Tower ran a recording label and had music studios all over the place. They were every artist's initial record label and deal and then when they proved their faithful, another independent label would pick them up and make them into a big commercial success all around with TV and Stage appearances and nightly performances and commercials and cameos and magazines PR and all that. But Tower is where the artists go.

And Damian was no different even though he wound up getting dropped just minutes after getting chucked out of the Rotary Club and thrown out. Paulie was playing the motherfucking Triangle for some Guidos who were fucking practicing for some recital, like I knew that or was supposed to give a fuck when I was walking out with the wine bottles, er when Damian LK was.

The guy stopped him at the door. "What the fuck is going on?' He asked.

"What?" D responded.

"He's got a bottle. What's this?"

Guys came running over. 'What's going on?"

"This guy's got a bottle of wine. Who is he?"

"I'm here with Paulie, moving instruments and speakers."

"Paulie? Who the fuck is Paulie."

They find another bottle of wine in the sleeve. He runs out and moves some speakers in the back and ducks into the van. "Hey Paulie, you see some guy running by here?"

"There is he is." They noticed him in the van. Paulie was about to utter the word no.

"He was taking a bottle of wine, two of them, man. You're not going to be welcome back here for that."

Got dropped right there, because of his own cultural ignorance.

"If you want to make an album, you're going to have to do it on your own… Tower Records isn't going to survive the internet craze of Mp3. We got the call; we are going out of business. The company went bankrupt today. They filed for bankruptcy, there won't be a contract with you. You are the last artist to be signed with Tower Records. And you are the first artist to be cut from the New Music industry, there is no one to represent you, we are not bringing your contract. If you want to make it in the music industry, you are going to have to do it on your own."

They offered to give him a few free demo tapes and new recordings which they provided at no cost, except lunch, and to listen and work with his new music that he created. He couldn't get music from them.

He went to work right away and created a couple hundred loops and wrote a few dozen instrumentals and immediately was back in a studio that was not Tower Records. He made another meeting with Paulie and didn't show up.

That summer he went across country and was selling soaps and CD's out of his suitcase while hitchhiking in California. He travelled from LA to the Oregon, and the Nevada border on the east side of California and on the west, he went all the way up to Eureka and was up in the Marble mountains with the hippies and Nori. She said the most heinous things, but they rarely even spoke for months on end while standing next to one another.

While driving he would say literally nothing the entire time after she confessed to talking to the FBI. If he and she were in the car, he would say nothing. Because every time he was going to California to go to LA or going to NY for whatever or going to Seattle to try and see Jacob, she was there and wanted and offered to drive. Hundreds and even thousands of miles. Pay for gas and she would drive half using her vehicle. Okay. No problem.

And Warner called him while he was waiting for the actress in the coffee shop in Park Slope, called him back on the phone in late 2010 and committed to attempting to wire a million dollars into his account by mistake supposedly. They were giving him the account numbers for a million bucks, and he cut them off. He had gone back to them as he had gone back to Von Thadden who for the second or third time flaked due to his personal affairs.

He had gotten his break in the making with Warner at a Saturday audition for lots of musicians to try out and freestyle or rap up on stage. Damian the L got up on the stage and wrecked it for like two minutes and they was like, 'Yo, we got to do this.'

So, he went along with it, and they called him on the phone and asked him to sell some tickets for a show. And he knows how it goes, but he said he couldn't sell any, he had some problems. And they called him back and offered him a deal. He was into it. But they kind of lost touch for a minute, he went to their apartment down the block from Warner offices and these guys were bragging that their company was with Ms. Whitney Houston in the late seventies, and they were original group and all that. So, he was into it. He dropped off a demo at their apartment, waited around for them and this was in 2005.

In 2010 he caught up with them and he dropped it he said he was going back to Cali and Whitney Houston died at that time, right when he was going back to San Diego, so he lost contact with them. He could drop off his card or a postcard. No doubt. But he was like out of it now.

In 2005, he was being coaxed by Nori, while he worked as a mortgage handler for a chain mortgage group known as Southern Star, they were off Wall St. and he worked evenings selling and trying to get a mortgage set up for a couple or homeowner by setting appointments with them and mortgage officer. He called Arlene, got her social security number, and passed it to the mutual friend Rob, who was blamed for hanging out with Russ and for hanging out with Gabe and it being a scandal.

In 2005, he went out to Oregon after hearing the PSA on CBS News calling for the Death Penalty to anyone who had a psychic that was against the authority of the

Patriot Act. And this was over and over every fucking night, they said this shit. And then the actual announcer from CBS, her partner anchor, he partnered with her through thirty years of anchoring, and they would transfer to different stations together, switching from CBS to ABC and whatever at the same time. So, they left and took over the five o'clock news at the same time and did it every night in NYC for forty years.

This was like thirty years into it. She made the announcement every night for like a few years about this psychic identity fraud that was on the loose as a psychic assassin and it was an Al-Qaeda suspect, and it was all over the Patriots and the Acts and it was the death penalty for all these crazy psychic laws. And the cult was mentioned without mentioning them, every fucking one of those things. And whoever knew a psychic could get the death penalty by some government.

Noone else ran this story but CBS News NY and they fucked it up big. They ran that PSA during the News every fucking night and the anchor showed up at Damian's boss's club one night after the broadcast at 11 pm was over and was drinking with them taking pictures.

And the people were running for their lives that day and he took it seriously, but no one card when Sabrina had to run, she was this girl she had asked him out, but she was his buddy's girlfriend, and he refused. She made it out alive running for her life on 9/11, her office overlooked Building #7 at the site.

So, Damian took it personally that he absents mindedly turned against the country that kept him alive, gave him a place to live and allowed him to express himself as an artist and scholar. Not every country will do that, and he knows now that he took it for granted, and that it is worthy of defending, like so many people have sacrificed to do.

When he left the movie set of Conversations with God, he had a premonition about how to not behave on a movie, and he wanted to stick with that. Also to find a person there that he could relate with and do movies with, but for some reason it became hard to come by.

He was lonely and the casting agent operator from Explore Talent where he had seen an internet advertisement for acting and casting in movies for a low monthly premium, and he was interested in seeing what it possibly had to offer for his resume.

And he was talking about his background a little and after a minute or two, the operator got down with it.

The operator said, "If you give us some money (2,900 or some obscene four figure number). and we can get you to where you need to be in the industry. We can put you in movies. But you must decide if you are going to do whatever it takes to get on that movie set. If an old man wants you to sit up on his lap, you are going to have to do it."

"I don't think so. I'm not fucking doing it. I've been to movies before. I don't need to degrade and hurt my own reputation and destroy myself. Fuck you."

And they got hung up on.

He moved out down to LA a few weeks later and it was an interesting experience. What was interesting was that Gene Hackman was sitting there in LK's high school cafeteria like a bunch of times, and they locked eyes man, and Damian acted out in front of him. He noticed. /He looked at him the same way when he looked at him in Downtown Santa Barbara.

Besides from the resolution to face no one and systemically outcast himself, he put himself under the fire by going down to LA and distributing his CDs and then writing that article of sorts for the summer and then they honored him and then put him in some tabloids a couple of years later after the arrest of Shane and the garbage that went along with it, he was out of luck when it came to finding a job and getting a place to stay, he wandered around and got into trouble. There was a brief instance of living on Crenshaw, and he seen Brad Pitt over on Hawthorne or someone who looked just like him and he kept seeing him between Santa Barbara and Crenshaw in LA. Which is a big contrast and difference in environment. So, who knows what was happening at the time.

When he finally moved out of the mental place in Torrance he was in the fall of 2009. And he just had registered for a casting agency. He scored a bunch of movies and lived in his own mind control program filming a couple of his own style of documentaries and doing some extra work. He wound up on some pretty great sets with some CBS names and was on nighttime TV for a minute playing bad guys and SWAT team and playing protestors, and he got into all kinds of movies and television.

But early on, some people approached Joanne, his grandmother, on the street and started harassing her. Talking about LK and Damian and how they need to work in the movies. And they shouldn't worry about the music industry. It was all about the movie industry. And they said they were from a company out of LA but also out of Franklin, TN. And they said movies were the way to go if Joanne didn't want to continue to be harassed.

So, a couple of years went by, and he signed up and started doing principal parts and getting his name out there as an actor and performer. After Joanne was threatened a couple of times over the years, she told him about it and he brushed it off, he was acting all on his own now anyway, he just had a feeling.

And then the assistant of the big producer there at Type A Films approached him on the street and so did her boyfriend a couple of times and her brother and the boyfriend of another assistant. The assistant sent people on set to talk to him and his neighbors and to talk about Reese Witherspoon behind her back.

And he was on dozens of movie sets.

Her brother told Damian to drink beer and get drunk, sit in the street, and wait to do what the boss said to do. And work as an actor a little bit but to maybe work on some other kind of movie or write something. But he wasn't allowed to find an apartment or get a job. But they recommended he go to film school. And he did.

The boyfriend admitted to Damian on the street of being the skelly that followed his grandmother around. But at the time he didn't believe it and dismissed it as heresy. They told him that she was following everything he did and knew everything about him. And didn't stop. And that she married this new guy, but it was all business, and it would be over in a few years. And in a few years, it ended. And she started stalking Damian and then stopped. He was too into her. He fell for her again. A different kind of woman.

But they admitted to stealing his ideas that he gave to her via email when she reached out back in 2009 and she wanted an idea and complimented his investigation into their family and she liked his style of aggressively working against their movement, even though it seemed to be going nowhere. And they started to get along and it was a bit sexual via text. And it was impressive. She liked him you could tell, but she wanted what she wanted. And he gave her the comic book idea and it eventually generated a couple of billion dollars in three years and disappeared and no one really noticed that it was or was not around, it had already come and left.

And he bitched and moaned because the guys that threatened said if she came out with the figures that matched the revenue, then he was going down for no reason and he was taking the fall for a billion dollars. And he dismissed it until she broke up with her husband and announced her earnings that matched the revenue from the movie. So, he cringed and called her company, said he was sexually jealous and then took it back and laid into them, He was citing every experience he had with their company over fifteen years, and it was hundreds of pages long. All kinds of harassment and theft and people threatening and forcing and coercing for no reason but to get rich off an idea of his that was experimental and not his real work.

His ideas were greatly complimented by his professors. He had gone back to school and earned a degree after earning film credits and got a bachelor's degree in Entertainment Business and had a scholarship and then moved on to get a Communications MA after the BS he earned was only a year and half program and it was intense as he had to attend lots of hours of class at once and do more than one project or test for many classes in a short time.

After years of battling the cold and savoring an actor's income he left California and earned his degree in Florida before he went and got an MA at Liberty Online and lived for a minute in North Carolina. After he left the BS school in Florida and then resettled in California to earn an MA in Screenwriting and an MBA in Sports and Entrepreneurship.

During this time, he was supposed to have an article base in IMDb, and he was supposed to get an agent because he was offered one, but as soon as he got to Florida, all that got thrown out the window.

And he went to a rip off university and got stuck earning shitty degrees for shitty national universities but earned him a good size diploma and student deficit and GPA of a good point average. One that he doesn't want to ruin. But improve he might.

The Religion

They claim they walk in the dark and live for the darkness. They have seen or done literally nothing in their lives except go to work and try to sell shit out of their purses. Trying to make those donuts. Telling other people to work where they say, never allowing others to explore their own opportunities.

When LK wanted to work vacation and go to school for vacation, she demanded he work at the mall and wouldn't help him with fare to and from the school. And to eat pork and chicken and not only pork but swine and to eat any kind of meat, burned or whatever and drink smoothies every day and pretend that they are practicing vegetarian. And telling everyone that they are, and then saying vegetarians aren't healthy they are anemic, and need more protein and iron in their diets. So, they cook up a couple of hotdogs and tell everybody they're vegetarians.

Fourth of July is a full fucking event. So is Thanksgiving, Halloween, Christmas aint shit, neither is easter but they will go to a party that's for damn sure. They got that purse those three fucking people were fiending for.

Maybe one of them knows about an acreage that's available. She can just put it up and Pat can work on recruiting through his office.

He can create a portfolio except no one will step into that shithole. And it looks like a flower garden with nothing inside. And he was pushing that crack and nothing else. He didn't push pills or pot or coke or meth or ecstasy or bath salts, or even vodka or a rare liquor or a schnapps. This guy was pushing a recruit farm for metaphysics that he doesn't understand how to use it. Looking for trouble. Talking shit about anchoring all kinds of stuff. Let's get in.

They want to control the belief in everyone about whatever religion they are fascinated with obviously. However, they are looking at pictures and hearing rumors. About conspiracy theories and witchcraft and combining it with the pictures they are looking at with metaphysics and New Age teachings.

With these pictures, come maps where they coordinate prayers and channeling to find out information about people they know who are in other places, and then they have someone study the other place that the people dwell in. they meditate on the theme and message of the place and the overwhelming cultural aspects but tune into the cultural energy and the psychics that might be breaking the law or are owned by illegal operations and they study people's psychology through meditating on these people's minds trying with their wills and their vision to tune into their thoughts and intentions, desires you know their heart and purpose but with telepathy and trying to alter that person's reality.

They will also contact that person and reprimand them for not taking part in their ceremonies or for leaving and being unfortunate enough not to learn of their religion. After that, a few months of ridicule until you agree to help them in some way or combat them with anger and violence as a warning, then they will contact those whom you know personally and will ask and talk about you.

Then they will tell you about it and how they now have a secret relationship with these people, acquaintances or what is more likely people whom one was close to, like friends or mates or some blood line member. The other person will confirm and want to brush it off or will feel uncomfortable.

Then the Big K or Pat or whoever will call you on the phone and let you know that they own that person now. And your relationship with them is useless. They will take that shit over. So, one of you leaves. It's not hard. Then it goes on.

The other person contacts you and tells you that they stole your little black book at the request of one of these fuckers. They went into your room, your place and went to your underwear drawer straight up and took the book, copied everything in there and gave it to them. And now you're fucked. And then they will ask you to join their religion.

The smart thing is to ask them what religion is and how does it work. When they explain it to you, you say you don't understand, that they need to explain it further. And you will probably hear everything once and then they will emphasize different forms of metaphysics and teachings each time they communicate, and they also will have this great revelation that they are psychic and will share that. Then there's a break for a short minute.

They will make it immediate as of the next contact, that they are schizophrenic and that they have mental problems. Then they'll confide in you. Then they'll tell you that their actions were not good. Then they will call you again and accuse you of having a mental illness and of hearing voices and of being out of control because your beliefs are out there. And there is no social media or telling people about that shit, or the opposite, but they will say it either way. Get you doubting yourself.

Next is some more big introductions to teachings and teachings about their specific psychic. They will tell you that they get divine messages from celebrities and that angels and spirit guides are protecting them and their message. They will get nervous and maybe talk about one of their operations and a job they might have for you. But not before they will hound you about smoking pot and how unless you are an adept in their religion and you sell crack for them, no one is allowed to smoke pot. They allow youth to smoke pot, but once they become adults, around 22 or so, they introduce the family business and anyone who does not sell crack is not welcome to partake in any sort of marijuana smoking, groups or otherwise. And these are some of the rules as we get going.

And you must follow the metaphysics and you must be able to grip the wind with your mind, without effort, and project your image to speak wisdom and listen intently to as many people in their inner mind as humanly possible. Because one day, the participants are going to not only themselves but their whole family. And the whole camp is going to die.

People like Randy, Arthur, and Russ sign up for this shit. They think it's worth the risk and the thrill to hang out with these dirtbags. They don't say shit about being investigated because they don't care. Russ at least, is a drug dealer and he became one from selling pot and pills and club drugs and who knows what his deal is.

But when he was told that Gale wanted to get to know him, he didn't even care about the secret service, or her, or Shane, or assassination arrest from a psychic, or the bullshit with Nori turning him into the FBI. He didn't care his friends were chilling with Gale now and that Mike was dead from probably a horrible deal or some bullshit he did or said to them and he killed himself, but they didn't help.

They had their minds destroying him with this negative metaphysics, him, and Ant. The Boogie Man. Anyway, you look at it these guys were the street version and connections to the Strasser. And whatever. They were using this metaphysics too the same way. And making everyone go crazy.

The object, Pat asked after he inquired about getting in contact with Russ for no reason, was to control the minds of everyone in the world. To do it by taking their money, taking their loved ones, feeding them drugs, eliminating their hippies and religious folks, cast everyone else to the government through a form of psychosis induced by witchcraft and seances, and then to take over everyone in groups and one by one, by visualizing energy grids and magnetic fields around people, places, and landmarks. They would then anchor spells, energies, focusing dimensions and universes and waves and magic towards giant antennas and landmarks and project their faces through a form of technology they created with their minds using the atmosphere and the space. And they wanted to destroy yogis, masters, and scholars who were inclined to notice their dominance. They feared people and people finding out who they were, yet they remained protected.

And looking at maps, joining in with candles, and creating energy and grids of energy and focusing on the objects and people and places with full knowledge of the normative metaphysics that people are limited by, and that people indulge in privately. They use that as a weapon against them, and cast a spell, that if the person can't withstand their own religion as a psychic, then they deserve to be tormented. And these guys don't stop.

They spoke of breaking into churches to perform not only black magic rituals but Phoenician magic rituals and talked of chanting in the name of the devil and creating pentagram and five directions circles in the church and the woods. And they were preparing to work at the church so they could get keys and break in at night until they bought their own facility. They said they wanted to sacrifice babies to Enlil and his brother Enki, and they were going to kill everyone in the name of the god Moloch.

At the camp, they would teach metaphysics and after everyone paid their membership which was about 3,000.00 USD, they would have to purchase a pair of 90s style Timberlands, not joking, sleep in a bunk bed, and go to classes that they taught and prepare to die, and to ascend to the Pleiades using a Luciferian psychic Merkabah. A Merkabah is a popular New Age concept of building and constructing a large-scale electromagnetic field around one's body, using ancient meditation and also deep breathing and yogic methods, as well as deep imagery and visualization. The meditation and construction of the Merkabah is only workable if the person can access unconditional love and can breathe deeply as well as hear or have access to what is known as a higher self, which is the self from a higher dimension supposedly closer to God.

While the Merkabah course costs a few thousand, many read the books and the information on the internet and try the mediation a little bit. These guys said Christ Consciousness was the devil, so they wanted to create a Luciferian technology different than the concept that the author had created.

The author was this guy who got famous by teaching this method that he said was instructed and constructed by methods he learned both from angels and some Freemasons that came to his house and told him about the Fibonacci Sequence and how it related to the meditation which was supposedly thousands of years old. The truth is that it is a composite of various ancient meditation rolled into one.

And he learned a bunch of stuff from the Freemasons that he put into this book and into meditation. He says the humanity was cut off from its origin mentally and spiritually as well as cosmically through a pole shift, when the poles shifted on earth, and it spun on its axis. This caused us to forget our nature of deep studded interconnectedness with the elements that connect us to the cosmos, and that we live in a world that is based on a negative experience since we only can see the physical form in its certain context. He believes humans have a more integrated and wavelength-based way of seeing things prior to the pole shift, where we restarted and became cave men because we lost our place on earth as it was destroyed in the pole shift. Many people didn't remember anything. So, this physical world is different than the one God created, and the real world has technology created by the mind and things occur differently through the use of will and proper forms of cosmic usage. He says that the technology used on earth is considered external and base on human needs and is therefore Luciferian.

So, as a competitor of modern-day popular religious rhetoric, these guys say that they can create Luciferian technology using their minds and that their cult is better than the Merkabah. They don't need some New Age asshole telling them that the physical world is based on Lucifer. They can use telepathy and teach metaphysics against people as a negative form of magic readily and steadily each day and participate in society openly as a devil worshipper when it suits them. Otherwise, they are members of the church.

They dwell in AA and MA meetings. They think marijuana is evil for their purposes. And that it is used by those who are privileged enough to sell crack. And they don't care about other drugs.

You must smoke crack. And you must try and get more money from your parents. And you must wear the sweatpants and shirts they give you. And you must abandon your family and your loved ones so you can hang out with Shane and Gale and Arlene and Patrick and Big K.

They are looking for prophets a messiah and a link to a UAP they need one of those. A big fucking drone. And some more volunteers. And for the perimeter whenever they buy that property. Patrick got his real estate license too. They don't necessarily need Gale. Or Shane. What does Mitchell do? He supports Gale Shane and Pat and plans parties for them. Smokes crack. Watch his TV like no other. In a house with two rooms and a kitchen, with this room, you know you can't fit anything but a piano and that's it. Like they got. They got it all.

What the fuck is Easter. The day the good Lord died for our sins, and they go and curse the Knights of Columbus and refuse to throw parties there because you know they are Masons now. And Gale is a Rotary. Pat is a Bay Ridge Merchant. And Paul is a Merchant Marine. And Shane is a government stool pigeon. And Les Erin's husband is a Karate teacher. And Jo is a teacher. And Julie is a librarian. And Big K hides out now leering at people like an alligator. This kid rolls by looks exactly like Shane did before his growth spurt and sits on a set of old phone books and yellow pages as he drives a car and stares at Damian out the window and pulls out past him.

These guys are out of their fucking minds, thinking that this shit is cool. And they keep their relationships and communication all vibratory because it breaks the human mind. They want to bite into the human energy system. Control human thought, intention, desire, and action. They want to steer your mind to be preoccupied with their desires and prove that society is supposedly not evil.

They plan on following and talking and laughing to millions of followers in a psychic world that emulates the internet. A dry cleaner's rotary peels people into one direction of control under their authority. And they prefer to have people run for president. Of the democracy in the West.

They make their kids look stunning. Everyone has a new suit and gets their jeans hemmed at the bottom. New shoes and a hair that can comb and look thin. They like thin hair and love to make it die and fall out.

You need to do Amway and try it or some form of pyramid sales that works. You bring the products they will see how it is. They got five buyers lined up all around. You will get started together. And pluck kids out of school and camp and on the street.

The telepathy does not do anything except promote MK Ultra and remote viewing as well as harp on personal activities and acquaint itself to voice to skull technology the UFO victims talk to the people like Damian in their minds through an energy field and project their faces and they are known in Arizona as UFO victims.

The UAP monitors them, takes their data, and watches them from above and they admire it eventually and become UAP and UFO worshippers by utilizing their alien psychic which is monitored by the government as being anti-people antigovernment anti-democratic and anti-republics.

Psychics are kept in sync with a federal monitor. They tend to risk it and lose. The fact that they were arrested by secret service for the usage of their psychics, and it was admitted to openly by the feds, that they were using a psychic and appearing in people's dreams, and it was physically presented as their case against them at the questioning of Shane at Camp Pendleton. And Shane was accused of plotting to frame against the president and of communicating with an illegal form of psychic experimental technology.

They claimed to be an institution that trained and specialized in some psychic self-defense. And they were making the most out of the concept of mind control. They deemed a cause against the all of humanity and the all of government and the corruption of the U. S. government.

They used weird metaphysics, studied all kinds of lore, and made fun of any teaching they knew you studied or might have experimented with; they knew that study. They knew that metaphysics better than you and they didn't at all.

They could not love unconditionally. They intentionally created confusion and utilized a person's sensitivities to visualization or schizophrenia and used it against them.

They purposefully and maliciously used schizophrenia against people. They used the sensory perception against others as well, and recognized when they will be defeated and then retreat without striking.

They are shrewd and make their kids who are never allowed to leave home follow pretending to be good people. They will teach them whatever they will just to get even with people who don't believe in what they do.

Which is a million different pieces of a trillion different religions combined in a specific way that makes no sense whatsoever. And they proclaim they are greater than God and then teach from AA and then teach from Catholic and deny they ever said anything about what you are steaming about. And they will become a perfectionist Buddhist.

But that brings it back to the use and prayer over a voodoo skull, that had red eyes and a black shell, which was a part of some candle worship, that was found in the garbage, not cleaned, was used by other people who more than likely knew the more correct way to use that instrument in some kind of witchcraft, and they used it for years, performing seances and looking at the map and trying to anchor the Pleiadeans into everyone's energy fields and around an energy grid that they created to battle what was known as the Christ Consciousness grid, which was also by the same author of the Merkabah. A guy who claimed to be a descendent of Abraham in 1983 was visited by some angels and Freemasons that taught him the secrets of the universe and the portal to travelling with the body levitating to internal dimension to which one travels physically beyond the speed of light, and builds an engine inside of their body using a projected energy field that will spin in multiple directions and has multiple sheaths in the shape of a six pointed star.

The stars spin through themselves through the human body and travel nine tenths the speed of light and then go beyond it with the conscious will of the meditator. And they will eventually achieve Christ Consciousness. At the end of the mediation, one is to close and end the engines spinning as it creates blinding lights and distracting visualizations and is connected to both the sensations of unconditional love that one develops through the mediation and the breathing mechanisms of one's inner lungs. The Melchizedek's host a workshop, where one story was that a girls eyeball flew across the room during the mediations. But the supposed true story was that she went fully blind in one eye. Poor girl. I really do feel sorry for her.

But that led to the next conspiracy. The originator of the widespread rumor mills that humanity was controlled by a reptilian race that dominated the capitalist and world government and republic system through a Babylonian bloodline and the Anunnaki reptile race of shapeshifters, you heard the story. Of the one where the reptiles shape shift into the government and they were like draining people's adrenochrome and drinking their blood and eating their babies and being worshiped as demons and worshipping the devils that eat people in Bohemian Grove and they sacrifice and kill lots of babies on an altar.

Well, that rumor was principle to David Icke a British author and journalist who was quit the BCC Sports as an announcer and was a soccer player. He wrote a bunch of books about this Babylonian religion that describe a lot of what the elite worshipped. He was describing the

Gilbride and Strasser religion, but they were pissed about it and were talking about battling him and his version of reality in Damian's life and in every one of their followers' lives and whatever. Some more propaganda starting shit about some celebrity writer theorist now. So, what? But they perform this religion. Anyway, that's not exactly where it's going right now. That's that part of things.

Damian went to see David Icke just after Marsha scratched his face up and he was badly depressed. He went to the conference at a big hotel in Seattle and sat through David Icke's presentation. He was a fan of some of his books, and eventually read most of them and seen his videos and believed in his work, but still, he believes in Icke's message of unity, the right of humanity over the system of oppression that binds and wants to blind us. Anyway, Damian is at the conference and sitting in the convention center listening to the talk. He noticed in one of Icke's earlier teachings he brought in a family that was an original ancient Illuminati bloodline that was a predecessor to the Merovingian bloodline. The bloodline was known as the Melchideks.

Damian thought it was similar to the Melchizedek's of the Flower of Life and Merkabah teachings. He had yet to have read about Abraham and Melchizedek in the bible. He read about it in Psalms then referenced it to the New Testament and then the Old. He had a concordance with Marsha, she was a fanatic. And practiced Merkabah with him. And she was reading the book he had of Icke's before he left a few weeks earlier.

So, he had read that the Melchideks were a savage kind of cave people who instituted learning and were rough around the edges but had initially started the world's civilization at the hand of ancient Merovingian bloodlines and the Babylonian Kings which eventually led to the same bloodline to the rulers of every country that ever existed is related to the Merovingians.

That was a bit conspiratorial and quite evil. Damian had trouble looking at the paradox. How the Melchizedek's from the bible which is mentioned by Drunvalo which is the name of the teacher, were also related possibly to these Melchideks and how their name was descendant to one another. So, this became an issue for Icke. That he had this question.

He wanted to know if they were related.

Icke got flustered at the Q & A signing where Damian confronted him. Icke demanded that he realize that "the Melchizedek's had a great teaching and taught very good things." But he was flustered, and his voice rose very loudly as he repeated that sentence again for the second time. And his face turned red. And his security grabbed him and shut the gate between him and the crowd, he was sitting in the front window of a kitchen inside the hotel. He was signing books and Damian and LK confronted him and they were there minding their business, after that and just looked around like it was something out of a sci-fi original. He left and they went their separate ways.

Nori called the Gilbride brothers on the phone and told them all about rumors she heard about David Icke and Drunvalo and they had to convince everyone to turn those teachings into a psychic. One that would cause psychological distress to as many people as certainly possible. And they had so much remorse that a moth could like maybe to notice some if it were a giant fluorescent light bulb with a minimal flicker. They gave a fuck about their kids, and you and others.

And they put little clay people into your body's energy and tied tubes and strings to your ligaments and your limbs and followed them around with their minds and extorted your control through hypnosis, and a conscious method of deteriorating everyone on the planet, with their consent.

They administered mind control in any negative manner and attempted to steal thoughts because they were fuel and seen as energy and could be important to someone else other than them. Either they were destroying your happiness or selling your ideas for few choice bucks, and they were quick to call someone the 'N' word. And a 'mook.'

They listened to the Jerky Boys for years and decades. Patrick had a tape of it before it was commercial and before the movie came out. He had some yellow and red cassettes that he played it on.

He listened to the Beastie Boys and to some gothic 70s Disco Rock R& B shit a lot. Forgetting about trying to get laid with a kid, and a dude that was a kid, DK gave him the benefit of the doubt and regretted that shit. Music for the founders of the cult was mostly doo-wop, but they wound up getting a pretty huge CD collection.

They collected all their old LPs from the 1970s and had some 8 tracks, a bookshelf filled with Koontz and King, and nothing more. They also had a giant-size old-style Box TV with the handle even up until today. They still have those. They have landlines and old-style phones. They collected antiques at the same time every one of their parents showed up on Ellis Island and still had drawers filled with silver and oak and shiny new floors and ancient renaissance couches that they sit on.

They have a temporary denomination in the Christian religion. They will become Catholic again and then switch again to Non-Denominational, Methodist, or anything else. At the time of their dawn, they were into becoming Lutheran, and Old Lady Patricia O'Hanlon was asked to leave the church entirely and leave the premises of the Catholic Church permanently. She was Frank's wife, Pat, and Big K's mom and she was pretending that she wasn't satanic, but she was a fake Buddhist and learned to read self-help books and turn a blind eye to life. She pledged her life to Dementia in a hospital.

They say they are addicted to crack cocaine and rock cocaine. Even with them being a couple of old ladies with decently nice houses and nothing to do but watch some shows every night and drink their favorite shots before bed and then wake up and do it again. Wow.

And they went out of their way, to do find out about Dahn Hak and Drunvalo and David Icke and do the opposite of what those teachers and organizations represented and taught. They were just doing the opposite of what everyone taught. And they were obsessed with listening to remote viewing and trying to follow it around, to various people, and then they were just farting in the wind. Destroying everything. Making sure that people lost hope and felt despair underneath their mind control methods. To know and destroy others.

Obsessed with remote viewing, they tried to pressure LK into something he would regret, by always pushing on his nerves and squeezing his nipples and crushing on his buttons, waiting to get revenge on them, waiting for their serpent to strike them on the ass as any decent pet would with an oppressive owner. They knew how to irritate the world of the streets that didn't believe in them owning their right to privilege over everyone's mental world, personal space, and interaction with their planet and world. The audacity of the ownership and claiming of others' lives through the dominance of personal energy.

Casually sliding through the universe around the worlds of earth, they cast doubt and fear into the minds of those whom they choose to try and dominate with their personal metaphysics. Gathering magical tidbits through the particles of space and along with the use of tubulure projection, they emit sensory visions themselves through the cosmos of the internal earth. Singing their song of drainage and confusing notions, they attempt to crash through the atmospheric shell around a human being whom they designate as a target.

Anyone with any sense knows that to get what they want and use the energy they steal directly from someone's mind for personal use and consumption, as if it were a smoothie or a milkshake with personal vitamins, they long to try and devour the person and eat alongside their third eye, stroking along their optic and vocal nerves attached to the skin and ligaments from within, they shoot tubes and bubbles that they attempt to pipe into the minds of one's mockers, hoping to gain favor with Satan and gain access to the Sons of God, whom they will dwell with when everyone takes their Kool-Aid, studies their form of cult-ed metaphysics and takes their drugs. Within the warped world of 21st Century drug culture that seems like a great deal for someone completely suicidal.

Taking over the authority of their end of the drug trade in 2005, many wondered if they weren't just some psychics talking shit and it looked like they were just selling out of a bag.

A purse.

As long as they can feed off of someone's bubble their personal space and try to get into them in public, using other people, they are prey and easily manipulated to either take excessive action and get into trouble by not paying attention due to rage and frustration as well as confusion, make a mistake and wound up regretful, time wasted and risking their lives, or more than likely their distraction will acquaint with inaction, and people will miss their opportunities and their overlooked leftovers will be reacquainted with possession by these vultures, who deem it necessary to become psychic hinderances and dwell in the space outside windows at night like a vampire from Salem, Massachusetts.

Steaming satanic shit along the surface of their target's shell, slipping in with energy that follows through them and watches them from far away using remote viewing, stapling their spirit of satanic sheets looking like blanket along the human eye, trying to eat in people's membrane and following them while maintaining the indecent integrity of dwelling beneath their eyes, and hiding extended eyes into their membranes of the brain and blood and skin and flesh and ligaments, hiding. They use their mind to hide inside people's ligaments hoping to manipulate them from within, to destroy them from their own realm of scum, and skem and shit layer, bubbles of leftover breath and gas, heart attack ingredients and the recipe for a stroke. When all the blood supposedly rushes to your brain and you get overwhelmed and stressed and almost die, your brain kind of short circuits and stunts and they want to eat in your memories. They tutor people in their minds that to follow others like Damian and LK would be to the benefit of all. But it's not in the greater good and they know it.

It is ironic that even though it was this fabricated mist become energetic reality for anyone caught under the psychic influences of Patrick and Damian, but it wasn't far-fetched that they flew and steam around like shit on the outside of his pants laughing at him and steaming it up in everyone' s nostrils on the TV and recording sets, with and without his presence. They gassed his presence around hoping that his reputation as a NY gang leader, boy scout leader and director of survival and Order of the Arrow RIT with an actual Native American and his time on the sets of Hollywood and in the music, industry would enable them to get by protected and still gas his name in hopes of gaining metaphysical and cosmic understanding.

It wasn't farfetched to believe that some of the movie and music superstars do join in, following Damian around and contributing to his cosmic schizophrenia, too. He met superstars at times, and some were nice, and some were nervy and took too much from him. So, even though they are not founders of the cult, they travel and swarm around him like the federal government on a target, flies on shit, and fungus on a mushroom, they don't fucking slide off unless it's under the skin like a no see um. The work of the devil they instigate, the Christians as they too mock and take part and follow it around like a bubble of gas buried in his fat pockets and empty fleshy tits. His man boobs.

Big K had a big deep and bubbly voice for a man. This enabled his voice to travel far into the ear drums of all who could hear, and all who asked to look at that big mountain of an idiot that ate in the membrane of the planet and try to tell it what to do, and he had a big bald head for no reason and glasses, and he prided himself on shaping his shoulders to look like Uncle Fester. It was his goal to look like Fester, just a bit more sophisticated. Amazing what an 8th grade education will get you when you really apply yourself.

Now, get down and apply some grease and effort to your own Mr. Miyagi. Elbow grease. It can get you places in a company or organization. Wax on, wax off.

Or take the easy way out, write tickets until you find a good voodoo artist, pick through the trash, and put that person to work with some garbage found instruments you break the universe with a little wax and skull magic and a couple of Atlases. How about those tourist maps they have when you check in at the spa or hotel, those can work just fine too. But you might not be able to locate your loved ones with intuitive operatives and remote viewing capabilities.

They were operating on an internal freeway that travelled telepathically through the universe of their choosing and wrapped itself around the target from far away, using the crater and clip that they cling to when the target is near. They establish contact and follow their tag around that they left invisibly onto the flesh and invisible subconscious as an energy around the target's body and they can bubble and project themselves into the target's environment. If they take over the road it can be dangerous so people driving around if they hear them floating, they often try to anchor them and listen to them like they were a spirit or a psychic kind of supernatural ghost. This might keep them from having some kind of fucked up accident.

Drivers will often anchor them, talk their talk, and let them bubble through them and bus drivers especially, because they do think it will protect them like an evil spirit could against those threatening bus drivers and truck drivers. They would swing like a cloud through the space and have tubes and tunnels at intersections and cakes and pledged into the sides of buildings and also cars and through motorcyclists.

The actress was no help because she was supposed to pick up the documentary that Damian was writing about the family. Instead, she cashed in on his other idea and left him hanging with the research and no place to classify the materials. This creates animosity, because while she is playing with the technology like its Virtual Reality. She gives them the power to move and slither like serpents fusing and boiling cists into the hearts and brains of their vehicles whom they use for haunting the target. Humiliating with the face of the Homan drug addicted crack monger. For instance, T had no more teeth from drugs, and was a daily user of anything that was going around. Including Big Cock.

Squirming like a pool of waste as a bubble in the mind of their targeted victims, they coax you to pay them somewhere just below and above 3400.00 USD and they will teach you the art of pretending to sacrifice towards Moloch while hatching the egg around each person and like a serpent surrounding them like a shapeshifting owl, flying like a lizard next to them and shifting from one to another trying to get God's attention, and they will torment their victim and targeted subjected souls.

They were hopeless souls to the crack goddess. Wandering spirits lost to their voices through an energetic vacuum, leaving their mind trapped in a universe where visions of Gale dominate their conscience. Telling you what to feel, what to think, like a fog eroding the landscape in front of crowd, leaving them blind, the Strasser created a CIA programmable psychic that can create good or do great harm, and that is what the application was, with Gale. She swarmed in over the Staten Island harbor and wanted everyone to be absorbed by the military base as they crossed the bridge into her town. They would have their minds reprogrammed and Gale would fight like a witch in the middle of the night to steal some secret psychic power from the military base at the foot of the Verrazzano bridge. She was out there like Teen Titans or the X Men battling in the middle of the night, hoping that her crack cocaine and metaphysics would teach followers to rise above the oppression of the matrix. Not just any matrix, she believed in the Matrix of the mind, like the movies and the books and conspiracies. The lizards leave us in a mind control prison, and she gets to slide nazi levers and clips and staples and glitches into the minds and energy of her victims.

She doesn't know that the trade is not revolving around crack. The fact that they brag about crack all day and are halfway responsible for placating the drug epidemic which does not centralize at least monetarily, around crack cocaine in the 21 st century. It's not in style. That is ridiculous, Damian calls Shane on the phone no texts him and asks him to deliver some crack on a certain day and time. He tells him he has lots of buyers for him and that they will be at the park on the morning of the 23rd and he confirms that they will have a frisbee. That Damian won't be there. But he tells them to meet him and deliver enough for a few people who might want to buy. A bunch of fifty sacks.

The mule Shane confirms the appointment and tells him to keep it between them. He will be at the park outside the White House at a certain time looking for a guy and some people with a frisbee. And to wait there, they know who he is. He says okay.

He keeps his confidence but blows up the cult's phone out of frustration because he wants to move on with his life and he is trying to get to the bottom of their interaction with him mentally, and getting their information classified in some kind of documentary. Hell, even inside a mind-controlled prison, it's still a democracy of sorts. I can just talk shit and nobody's going to give a fuck.

Especially when you tell them that they are out to get everyone and that no one is immune from taking their own cup of poison when they sign up to work with their group, obviously. Yet, these guys don't see the inside of a prison cell unless they have a bug up their ass about talking shit in dreams about the president. They can't arrest the fucker for screaming towards himself about brainwashing the old fucker. And getting even with Keith. The brainwash. The bubble bringer. The nasty magic who all people were interested in projecting and laughing at. Keith and Keith, and in 2000, another Keith was born to the extended relatives.

Who knows who he was, but he started hanging around the Strasberg and going to Flannery parties playing with his own Hess trucks, like LK did so many times before. But LK had his trucks mostly from his mom's side, and the Big K Klan tried to imitate and battle their harmonics and their culture that they instilled into LK, the entire time, trying to do the negative backward and opposite with an influence up against their motivation techniques, of teaching LK to be himself.

And Big K would never teach anyone to be themselves. He always physically taught to follow the crowd and to fall to peer pressure because he says that what your friends and enemies believe about you is more important than what your family thinks about you Family is a place to hide secrets, to lie and to reveal the truth, so that their and his motivations are easier for him to cope with.

Being that he is deceitful, he is honest with his family that he is a liar and is actively lying to them but other than that he will deny it if he is not in the act of confessing it. He will pretend everything is just okay and that there are no issues with anyone or him or his behavior or words or his or their demands.

To deal drugs or suffer intense witchcraft that even the Lord is scared of. Dealing worship of UAP's and channeling of the Pleiadeans, while projecting mass hysteria into the backs and stomachs and arms and shoulders and necks and minds and brains and spines and toes and hearts and they can follow you with their minds because of their voodoo sacrifices that they impress upon the atmosphere to believe that they committed some kind of real sacrifice. They use other people's voodoo utensils for magic, and they don't believe there are any consequences.

They scream that they are schizophrenic, then they will scream that they are psychics and that they are bigger and better than God that they are God and that Jesus bows to them and their power. They go of fits against metaphysics for no reason going on rants out of nowhere about vegetarians and all kinds of meditations. Then go on a rant about how it is better for your health if one integrates vegetarian living and lifestyles.

Then they are up the fence about religion, which God should they worship.

They said that they were studying Zen and Buddha, but they are out the asshole not practicing moderation of their normative spirituality. They are inflicting Catholicism and Lutheranism onto people even though they are contradictory in their ingrained message. Lutherans were there to rebel against the tyranny of the early Catholic church and its resistance against arts and sciences and its version of reading the bible and teaching its lessons.

They had a big problem with the authority of the church. So, teaching both as a worshipping tool, and to switch back and forth between denominations is a little bit silly. Especially when they are turning to anchoring their prophet at any turn into the minds of them of their followers. Using their psychic in their psyche to use energy and electricity and work against the body's physical membrane application and they use their minds to deteriorate the target and their body. Not only their mind by splitting into their membrane and affecting brain waves, but by using their minds to project themselves into the bodies of their targets hoping to control their minds by controlling their bodies.

Having authority over the target's nerve endings and decision-making capabilities, through affecting neurology with an extreme power of astral projection using philosophies of Cosmic energy hoping to get transported into a mother ship, they teach their followers that they will be saved by the aliens when they die. And that they should indulge in preparing for the afterlife by studying their metaphysics and doing their bidding that they dictate to you in the followers' minds and then tell them how to operate their spirituality by studying the books they choose and doing the practice that they recommended to them, which is based on whatever bullshit on which it is based. Sounds like they're talking shit and pretending to know what they are spitting besides their fucking teeth and a bunch of nervous vomit.

So, he would rather eat rats and flies and have a fucking a foghorn blowing in his ear all fucking day than either hang out with Gale or Mitch, Erin, Paul, and Julie or do their drugs with them. They are fucking idiots. Nice suit on Patrick. Does it have the scum of his corruption dripping from the pen leaking in his pocket? Dining over wine and penne with red chicken Patrick explained to Damian LK that he was about embezzlement and corruption when it came to finance.

He brags sitting in a restaurant across from his office, that he is in process of adapting a philosophy of embezzlement and theft in his dealings because he can just do that kind of thing.

While his secretary complains to Damian that there is no way that he is making any money, they pay the rent for the place in the richest part of the borough and it is on a well primed piece of property in Bay Ridge and the rent is outrageous, probably running at least four of five grand a month for the store front there. He makes no money.

Shane complains that the Secret Service was harassing and saying the name Damian Forest Light to him over his vegetarian dinner in a Thai restaurant outside his job as a court officer in lower NYC's Manhattan. Damian partakes in a bowl of white rice and a cup of water. Shane confesses to him that the Secret service was investigating him, and they arrested him and took him into custody.

Damian explains that Gale presented the facts that Shane had slept with Marsha, conceived Jacob along with three other people and left Damian with the child support. Then he explains that Gale said that Shane was a great psychic with big powers that can take over the world. And that they would all be working on taking over the presidency and the government.

Then he told him about the newscasts and the PSA and how the anchors from the newscast had shown up at his boss' night club right after the shift and were hanging out drinking with them and took an album of photos and is a regular at the place.

Then he told him about the cult that Patrick was planning the ultimatums lent by Gale and Patrick, and everyone involved including Arthur Homan and Karen Carty, who are both claiming to be silent partakers of quiet dealing drugs and children as traffickers. Even though they signed on with a group that is operating as drug dealers half a block away from the projects and have some low-level government badges.

These clowns can be found dwindling around Washington D.C. and Philadelphia trying to portray themselves as actual employees of the Department of Veterans and State Police; and pretending to be real Homeland, standing outside the White House.

They are there taking Facebook photos of where they are posted up making deliveries just meters away from the front and side gates, and tourists and all the people here to see the head of the Democratic world and its buildings and landmarks and these guys are selling crack to employees of the Federal Reserve. And they are pretending this does not affect anyone. That is does not take a physical toll on democracy as a whole and the free world as it can exist along with the promise of international intervention, the British Intelligence fostered a philosophy of counterintelligence into the forces that were infiltrating the misuse of eastern based teachings to mind control the rest of humanity without authorization from people's personal authority. Invading people's space and teaching their minds without permission from within. Using people' s images as projections to communicate their ideas as if it were some forms of Artificial Intelligence application meant to make one more psychically aware.

Military was aware of an intelligence application that could counter the effect and reigning authority of the feeding fat circulating as a psychic from the anorexic Strassberg combined with the witchcraft and paid influences of Josephine Hansen Diorio the 800-pound medium to which the Gilbrides and Strasser have been anchoring their Flannery O'Hanlon influence. Using Old lore pagan magic these guys are rebelling against the world. In the early 2000's Patricia O'Hanlon, mother of Big K and

Patrick had been thrown out of the Catholic church. She was approached by elders, and they threw her out of I.H.M. service and she was barred from entering the Catholic church ever again.

There must be so many reasons and no one would be curious about what they heard or what they found out.

Karen her daughter, was a devout Catholic who went to church four times every Sunday and was still selling kids and praying for forgiveness. Hoping that she wouldn't take her lusts out on the students of the campus where she served as Vice President of Student Affairs.

And her daughter lived life out paying the cops in Georgia to let her stay and do whatever end of the business she did.

Probably smoking crack. And not sharing with anybody but her followers and minions.

Arthur Homan just wanted to join so people would like him, and he could pretend to be a criminal. Then at some point, they would just ask him to sell crack or trade for them and he would agree but it probably would never happen. This did not exclude Arty from calling people on the phone and telling them he was a crack dealer and a child smuggler and a thug for the cult.

His parents had moved him to the Stated Island dump where he later worked, and they bought a house literally on the cul de sac directly behind the back gate to the dump itself. Nothing like looking up at the stars and philosophizing about the giant dump hills that look like small mountain molehills. They had bragged that the Staten Island Garbage Facility was the highest mountain on the eastern seaboard, which couldn't be further from the truth.

He smoked pot for the first time at 19 and he was smoking crack before he hit the joint. He was getting drunk with a bunch of people his age for the first time in his life, and two guys he had trained in water safety lifeguarding, and ecology; and they were about 16 years old. He was hanging out with Marty Maher and the twins. He stole a lot from stores and more than that he prayed to black magic gods most of his childhood, for one thing, a blonde wife that he thought was super then hot and back and forth.

He was big and bad because both of the twins had put in propositions to have sex and masturbate with him and his brother at camp. And they were like four years older than him. It wasn't a while before they were sharing prostitutes and passing them to 16-year-olds while high on crack cocaine. Arty had a bender for wisdom and knowledge and had grown up Catholic so he never knew the Lord. He sold his faith in his religion and got nearly kicked out of the church, but if they found out he was clinging to the Strasser and to Flannery for a hobby they would probably get up and throw the book at him. They would throw him out of the church altogether in Rome.

These guys were obsessed with Remote Viewing, and they loved to bother Damian by projecting into his head directly and following him around through a bubble they put around his body. Hearing him moving around hotels and walking in the street as if a million spectators were impressed with him cleaning his nails in public or talking to himself and twiddling his fingers back and forth on his knee while thinking or reading. Everyone gave a fuck.

He was the goddamn messiah, what do you expect? What do you think? That nobody is going to notice him walking in the street? Or staying at some dump? Or living in a fucking hole in the desert? People noticed whether he was schizophrenic or not. And he developed the anti-religion. Damian became like a Skywalker, hiding for days without seeing people and walking through bristles and briars his ankles moving him away from wild animals as he emerges from the hills, walking in town to retrieve water or get something to eat for a few days, or going for a walk.

They were all interested in what he was doing, and they hated him because they were compelled to experiment with their spiritual technology on him. They wanted to remote view into his prime principle walking around and they didn't lighten up. Even when the experiment was over, the actress wanted him to remain a public spectacle, as the projections into him, creating his schizophrenia.

This was also a projection of him through his mind and into the minds of others who then projected his image and information into the minds of others, who were of a high number. They all wanted to know how to be psychic. Especially since it was looked down on or as not real.

Following him in a psychic would accelerate their reality too. The thing is that without his voodoo cloud following him, people wouldn't believe they were psychic and his reality was like a radio into everyone's head and the Strasser and Pat and Flannery were projecting him and his adventures in the desert against them, and in the movies and traveling around and his daily routines into people's minds to gain access and listen to their information and scam them somehow.

They were setting people up to get scammed by projecting Damian into a public psychic. They were hoping to not only get money for the dues for the suicide cult, but they were also to gain access to everyone's books and portfolios by helping reform already existent portfolios. But people like Arthur just want to get famous and work in the trade of those who don't get their credentials from working in education or some independent financial industry, they have to work in NYC Sanitation. And treat it as a religion.

It's what gives them the power to do Voo doo and thus control the world, by destroying people with their magic on purpose. And projecting their bodies into a series of bubbles that have psychic technology and Luciferian influences of matter and psychosis emanating into the earth's atmosphere to the point that everyone is grinding against one another trying not to implode from gaseous schizophrenia.

They have a conniption of there are other people on the road and they don't know how to do anything but nitpick and write tickets to people. And force others to try and work to live in a trailer for the rest of their lives. They believe that Damian was supposed to sacrifice all of his destiny and work there as well. Even though they are fighting and cringing at the thought of private sanitation taking their jobs and the residential contracts in the city. As long as they don't invoke a war between the commercial garbage men and the city garbage men on their contracts with municipal and residential in other states and areas, then there will not be a problem.

The Private Sanitation guys do all the business while the city provides services to residents and public places. There is a war brewing when someone thinks there is money in paying for garbage services and the city does not want to pay. But NYC has rent control, and the landlords would raise a living fucking hell against the city and barrage city hall with bottles since most of them are either Hassidic, very old, or junkies watching their parent's building, and no one is even paying for heat, never mind sanitation. That notion is thrown out the window.

That magic getting them thrown out of the church one by one. Not very cool.

To get into membership with a crew that Big K and Pat were members of, the 17 St. boys, Arthur Homan hypnotized people on purpose in their sleep, to believe that he shot people at the local bar known as Farrell's. And he had barely been there twice for a drink. Or a beer. But the guys from a movie that was creatively accredited only privately to Damian but was publicly the property of a couple of big companies including a comic company and a major children's entertainment company, and several other major studios and affiliates. A project that was stated in the press, had over 2. 6 billion dollars in revenue.

The funny part about it all was, that Shane was dealing that shit outside, but Mike was dealing that shit to Janet Reno's fucking sister and everyone's favorite daytime talk show host of the mid-early 21st Century. And Mike was fucking dead, and nobody seemed to notice when Carolynn Hillman- Harrigan the author and sex therapist, the person who initiated a huge astral projection, Nori's mom. She died and a bunch of the original old ladies that founded the voodoo and prayer worship of ingraining the primary and first and foundation-airy levels of the cult itself, they had died. Noone noticed when they had died. They crossed over and a little pocket of the universe had a lot less meaningless and overall useless static and chatter, destroying some motherfucker's ears.

Ripping someone's inner eye and membranes to a fucking headache from a shaking vibration all over their head. Fucking their ears up and giving them a headache. When they were gone the static left, and the cult lost a little bit of power. Everyone who was old and reflective static, went up and fucking died.

Big K shrunk in size. He had some lung disease and became almost like a lunger except he shrunk in size instead of having flu-like symptoms. He went from a solid 170 with daily weightlifting to a mere 111 pounds and had shrunk in height. He had some kind of permanent emphysema and lost his goy, playful bogeyman voice that he used to bounce through everyone's head. And he projected it mentally and hypnotically, hoping people would like him and take him seriously, and no one noticed that he would.

You could say it was the experimental diets, the Nutrisystem for months on end, the evacuation of several dozen cigarettes and cups of coffee combined per day, in his diet, Modak aka Big K, was smoking fucking crack.

Ordering up deliveries for months, from people and getting rid of the craving to drink, he deemed crack as a negotiable term, to his principles.

He could get rid of an oath or agreement for crack and would brag he just wanted to smoke some. that he was fascinated with it. He could not get enough of it, but he supposedly had never smoked it, it was just a dream and a fantasy to him 24/7 and that was his priority.

And he taught his kids every night about LSD and gangs and smoking grass and yelling at strangers for no reason. And this was his nightly lesson to Lk who literally told him to go fuck himself every night and every day, leaving him on the floor with Charlie horses and punching him in the thigh and arm.

Besides hanging out with Randy who would cheat on his girlfriend just to hang out with Nori and pretend to be down with the cult even though he wanted to kill Big K for taking over his mind and making him into a subliminal media schizophrenic.

Besides talking regularly, lying about ordinances, and clearing people's basic activities including to listening to music with the FBI and pledging allegiance to the Harriman as their slave labor, Nori can be found building black magic circles throughout Northern California hoping to anchor the Chitahuri and possess and take over the mind and energetic spiritual physical shell.

She was trying to possess and take over with a flag, the emotional bowels of the human consciousness with the lizard satanic gargoyle from outer space that eats people's energy fields and occupies and gnaws and chews and molests their chakras with lizard outer space alien especially angry Pleiadean energy.

Whoa. This was so important that everyone needed to follow D. around and tell him his intentions and thoughts, and actions all day long, so that they thought they were in charge because they could hear him in their heads, woah. So, intense and disloyal to God, that they will all probably die, for disobeying God's command. Every government and agency and every street and principle of cosmic meditation rebelled against you because you diswayed the mind from existing in its stillness and version of crooked controlled vibration.

Everywhere that Damian went for a while he had a telepathic demon psychic eating with the people passing him in the street. It was pretending that he was a product of their secret brotherhood, without any of them being initiated. He thought it was a mystery school until John's wife started appearing in visions and she used to ride him in his dreams. In his sleep, he'd wake up with sweat just fucking him. And then he would realize that she was always talking about some mind control and talking and snitching on them and it and crime and then the anchors of CBS showed up and started following people around.

Everyone was looming in his mind around his skull like a tunnel and listening to everything that happened to him and all his thoughts and his ears and his eyes and his inner self and his meditation was tracked so that everyone could get a glimpse of meditation int their minds.

Pretending that he was Siddartha, pretending that he was Demian. The world of the one. When he first thought about changing his name, he changed it to Demian, and then he would rise above whatever devil that was and become Damian.

And in Georgia, Sasquatch all skinny runs out and starts running through a side street grove outside Peach Tree City. The snakes line up outside the movie theater sitting in the street, knowing that going in could prove sudden death. Damian dressed up as a fat zombie with lots of makeup he picked up at the dollar store in Senoia.

The cop pulled him over after midnight as he was walking out, hanging out looking at his computer at the set of The Walking Dead and the cops noticed him he took a piece of fruit one night from the grocer sitting outside, he was hungry and thirsty, and he piled up food bank food behind the bench he sat at for a week at the park there outside the outdoor set of the hit television show, The Walking Dead.

He was walking from Atlanta to wherever and took a bus to and from New England, dealing with the summer weather in both places and didn't particularly like either place, too much. There was too much drama, including all that had taken place, and hanging out at the library people pulled up and dropped off water and monies and left him alone to crash in the lightning storms at the picnic tables But they were nothing compared to the giant fortress with desert camouflage riding through the air outside the air force base in Tucson and it landed outside town, across from the base a couple of miles and it was landed in the middle of the desert. It looked like the Millennium Falcon, and it was filled with doors and giant fortress-style ornaments. It was a unique rounded shape with edges sleekly moving through the sky, like a large plane, a 737-flying low. It landed in the desert and was the same color as the sand.

His ride noticed and so did the few hundred other people sitting at the intersection, there was no way not to notice the thing fly over the street ready to land.

The ships were out there in the desert.

Once in Lake Havasu, what looked like the International Space Station went zooming by while he was taking a piss. It was more than early the morning and the stars, and the heavens were lit up like lightbulbs, with the Milky Way spiraling over the landscape and serving cleverly as a black and white backdrop with hints of deep and bright light and navy blue. The space station or what was on the flight path for the international space station at that time of year and night. When he looked up, he noticed a big glowing white sphere tunneling through the skies over the Colorado River. It was after he had seen someone lifting a drone off at night there and assumed that something bigger was amiss.

Another night camping on the Colorado River, he looked up and saw a line of jets far in the sky, like little, tiny starlight following each other in a straight line. As they approached the river, each one in succession turned off their lights and disappeared at the exact spot they crossed the river line. They then soar down into the deserts of Arizona and Southern California on the border down to the border and turn around to go back towards Edwards or Nellis or Area 51 or Area 23 or Area 34.

Patrick was busy spreading his energetic psychic around as a triangle or rectangle and squared off a giant bubble that reflected other people's minds even if they prayed or believed in God and it was the declaration of spiritual warfare. He projected social security numbers into people's minds.

Patrick and Nori would bond together sexually over the phone, and she was big on having lots of phone sex with her masturbating all over the landline in someone's house. She's pretty big and smelly like a dirty armpit and horny, all she does is call guys on the phone and masturbate.

And Pat all he does is look for people who want to help him masturbate. He sits in an office all day alone, thinking about drinking wine and keeping his head up amongst all the threats from various sources, none of them that bad, besides Damian who was pissed and keeps threatening Pat. The dude shared his social security number on some psychic highway.

Stayed posted up in his mental tunnels sharing his energy and his mind to battle his giant Merkabah shield that surrounded him fifty feet away during meditation, so Pat and they created a field of 500 feet to 500 yards even up to

50000 thousand miles that surrounded Damian when he was not in his meditation and they sent watcher guardians through the astral realm to project into his tunnel that connected to his private mind and it wrapped energy serpents around his brain and confessed his thoughts that he put out there and sat there waiting for him to read about meditation or to meditate to learn about the secrets of mastery and the secrets of the universe but he waited patiently for years, every second to go by and for them to leave so he could practice his meditation without them. And they barely left.

They had guardians set up to monitor his thoughts and share his social insurance number with everyone on the planet through their dreams and their subconscious and piped it into that tunnel to torment him. And he dreamed of brutally killing them all. And wanted their blood and their heads cut off. He wanted them to suffer. He wanted them to be humiliated and to get in there and experience their pain. And he wanted them to feel that pain. And to change from being psychic bullies with their bodies suffering and their spirits knocked off of their balance and taken from eternity, and spit on.

The demons are selling crack to homeless people outside the White House. The same demons floating in everyone's circular mind covered in conditioning, their energy bodies and trying to claw through to instigate conflict to manipulate and further own territory that will lead to their reputation of supposedly owning the streets.

And the senators and Rotary members at Gale's Halloween party line up as one or two buyers enter the building, and one or two crackheads ruin it for all. And everyone was turning a blind eye, all the news editors were crying in their chairs because AP would never approve a story written by Damian. He had done all the research itself and it was just accurate and heinous. It was the shit that no one wanted to look at and everyone wanted to expose.

Everyone was just waiting for a scapegoat organization to take the pilot and eat with the majority of illegal operations and get thrown into the media and the Strasser cult escapes persecution, is a toy, and gets to get away with destroying the American culture. Liberating the subtle coercive form of socialism onto its people, quietly distributing drugs while planning to commit genocide on millions of people.

Courting the decisions of people who chose death over righteousness, instigating a drug war through a dominance of the astral curtain. A dominance of pseudo-spiritual warfare. Their prominent decision was to risk the death penalty with their psychic because they had a hole in the system dealing drugs and hiding underneath the Santa suit to trade kids to mongrels and dealers who would take them from their families.

And no one gave a shit. People in the government turned a blind eye and the people in the press pretended that an editorial would make the most of the difference, except they did have influence.

When the statute of limitations came out against those who commit pedophilia in NY State, the world turned on many, because the case that Damian had against the Boy Scouts, changed when he included some of the potential mistreatment on behalf of some of the workers and staff there, who were mostly volunteers, but there were instances when they made offers or tried to take advantage and it caused a lot of rage.

Especially when everyone who turned 18 after becoming an Eagle Scout was thrown out of the troop at Holy Name Church by Marty Maher who demanded that anyone who was going to help volunteer or instructor in any way had to attend his basement parties and the events where he got drunk and even took off his clothes. And after his friends, the cops didn't say anything to him, everyone just left without being asked. No one thought it was a good idea to show up.

Gale threatened anyone and everyone and told everyone that they had to smoke crack buy her drugs get a real job and have a house or they were not allowed to drink, smoke pot, relax, have a weekend, go out with friends, or whatever without having her destroy the world for them and demand they contribute to the trade. Ruined life.

She shot webs of metaphysics at people in full functional psychics controlled by energy and bubbles around them and sprung the webs right into Damian's energy mind his chest, balls cock, and stomach were preoccupied, and his neck was filled with pain and crippling squeezing on his corner of shoulder and neck and back, and he felt like he was going to snap. Like he was going to maul and murder masses of people, commit a massacre. He was surprised he didn't try to shoot a whole supermarket up or kill everyone in a building. He was going unstable.

Occasionally just barking at people as they walked by and started telling everyone to stop talking in his head, to stop repeating his thoughts and stop having a conversation with his personal dialogue. People didn't listen too well after a while, he just started calling Hello Sunshine and howled at them for sending people on set to talk about their founder and producer and how her assistants on the street had approached him and threatened him and his family, taking over certain ideas and leaving him to starve his way to healthiness sleeping in the street while his ideas simmered in the background even bubbling over and no one as noticing. People were not looking at the scripts that he spent time on. He had a student debt after surviving in the streets for years and was producing his work. And Hello Sunshine had lured him in to take credit for his comic ideas but left him to fall and stumble while persecuting the Strasser and then the Flannery.

After years of Big K threatening LK on the phone, Damian called him up over a bunch of years and screamed his ass off at him, louder than anything, bellowing and starting shit to lure him into an argument. And his health deemed him starting with him subtly, but he didn't step up anymore.

Patrick received warnings and threats and his business was egged and dropped off with shaving cream and toilet paper. He knew what was coming when he bragged about doing the wrong thing and being a wild thing with Marsha. He messed up with the conversations he had and all the lunatic thoughts and intentions, ideas, and his perception of mimicking a CIA mind control program to own status and mental real estate as a false metaphysical master and a yogi. He was a fake sensei. He thought he was wise, made sense, and was hilariously funny. He's a loser. A drug pusher and nothing more than a crack smoker and a drug addict with mental problems. The FBI won't even look at the guy.

He rolls with congressmen and senators and has a party to go to every Sunday, still wearing a suit and holding down a position at the Merchant's Association.

He keeps his kids at home, they have never had a relationship or had their own jobs or their own places, and they are in their mid-twenties. And Big K's kids do the same. And Erin's, Julieanne's, and Paul's. Arty's kids will do more than nothing more than go outside once in a while and not be allowed to leave home. If they do, their sanity will cave in, and their parents will cry that mind control has vanished from the Earth.

Poor kids. They didn't see it coming. When they finally ejaculate, they will probably call an ambulance and demand their girlfriends take the ride with them to the ambulance. As she screws the EMT in the back, they will probably either realize they're fucked up or just move back home. I'm betting on the latter.

What these people desire is simple mediocre energy like power, energy from the human body in an etheric sheath drained from the person to the eater, the psychic, the molten vampire. The loser. Using the mind to scrape the mind out of the body to eat it and drink it. Leave you in an energy prison while drinking your chi and your energy, living off of prana and Ki, knowing nothing how to generate their energy, only how to destroy others with their images and projections into their minds, bodies, eyes, ears, heart and all over their external energy and their spine was almost susceptible to this cult prowling on everyone's energy all day long, every day like night time mongrels who roam the earth and scavenging and never getting enough to eat.

When Damian was on the Twitter platform before him being barred even from X, he was griping and bitching about the cult over and over incessantly Twitter just had enough of it, and he is enduring a lifetime ban on that platform. His mind will never be the same, but he has been enduring psychic warfare for most of his life, which paints him alone most of the time. And with the internet randomly putting him on crazy websites, he has a lot to contend with especially trying to get rich, get his movie career going, and get people to listen and try to stop this movement from getting any bigger.

Never mind these guys were addicted to the newest fads and technologies, and had bragged of direct intervention and interaction with a mass racially based gang agreement that gained a monopoly on anti-racially behavior which gave them authority and power and even immunity in the ghetto, except not all of them were covered under the agreements, and being that the reporter was a member of a giant gang with connections all over the world that did not condone but did allow criminal behavior to a large extent as long as innocent people did not get hurt, they felt that each person was entitled to their path and decision making in life and that if someone chose a path of crime then they would have to designate their priorities and look for a way out of their prison albeit mental or physical due to their own decision making.

They had heralded collectively yet spoke individually about the coming and abstinence of the internet before it was a loud and obnoxious point of screentime within everyone's lives. They know they are being tracked by new technology and are therefore not savvy and showing off how they use the internet, but they are shrewd and when they told everyone that the internet was going to take over the world in 1995, everyone nodded them to death. 'We know.' Or 'Really? Do you think so?' or even' What makes you say that/?" They don't stop. People are pretending they didn't create their religion based on things that Damian and Marsha confessed while they were breaking up about the different religions he was studying, and they didn't realize he was just reading texts based on every religion in the world. From Japanese Shinto, Sumo, and Samurai, to the Tao of China and the Zen of Asia, Buddhism of Thailand and Tibet, he read the Tibetan Book of the Dead, the Egyptian Book of the Dead, the Egyptian Book of the Living, the store of Herman Hesse, Kurt Vonnegut and Og Mandino, the Way of Peaceful Warrior, the Merkabah, the Celestine Prophecy, the gnostic gospels, the agnostic teaching of the 12 step, program, the Road Less Travelled, the books of David Icke, the Zen and Yoga and Christianity of Korean friends and acquaintances, he was participative in the Dahn Hak movement which had hundreds of schools worldwide and was going on out with Newal Donald Washe to proclaim the spirituality of the New Human, when someone at a desert retreat center went on a hike and died due to dehydration and the schools was shut down entirely.

The organization changed its name, and its masters were forced to leave and go back to Asia, and American students became the masters and leaders as workers of the centers left which had changed their name to a new name, Brain, and Body Yoga.

The teachings are extensive. But they didn't know about these learnings, they assumed he took part in a non-integrative philosophy of metaphysics. He happened to master a series of exercises based on restructuring the Dan Tien and the major three chakras in his body, which are in the head, the chest, and Tan Tien, and it is a bit different than the Indian teaching which he read from, which speak about seven major energy centers or chakras in the body, these guys speak about three major energy vortexes in the body that are blocked by human conditioning and the resurrection of matter over spiritual memory of cosmic origin. Very deep stuff.

He also read which is what Big K was jealous of him reading, the Bhagavad Gita which is the wisdom of the Lord from an Indian perspective written 6000 years before the birth of Jesus. The second text entitled the Bhagavatam, written two thousand years after the original, it speaks of the birth of the Buddha as a prophecy and Buddha was born 2000 years before Christ walked the earth. He also read some texts known in India as the Upanishads and also was privileged to read from the Vedas.

When he read the Quran, the Secret Service showed up at his front door and he was later put under investigation by Nori and her friends and enemies at the FBI. And life became complicated. And Nori proclaimed allegiance not only to the cult, as Marsha did, who was so jealous that Damian studies spirituality and looked at more than a traditional Christian teaching, and he grew up Catholic, so she assumed she was still going with a minor because he was a member of the Order of the Arrow. She was a boy scout leader volunteer with no skills outside of Basket weaving and making leather pouches for pocketknives to which she would stab anyone in the back after they turned 21. If they weren't a member of the Order of the Arrow, then their cutoff date was 18 years of age. She chose to ridicule Damian to leave him and a perspective that was a mind control prison, talking to him forever and projecting that he was just a child who was abused and abusive and didn't deserve love. Like he was still a child.

And Nori did the same thing and did like Big ol' K and said the wrong thing about how they feel about children.

Shane and Gale are supposedly not pedophiles and that is as far as it goes as far as anybody knows, except Gale knew as did Patricia O'Hanlon and her sister Arlene, about their nephews and sons attempting to have sex with minors and propositioning Damian LK several times to the point he carried a knife against them and warned them many times through several years that if they did flirting with him again he would want to stab them, and then they left him alone after a long battle for over 18 months.

But Big K tried to get kisses and hugs every day which made him uncomfortable and caused him a severe amount of emotional and physical distress, and his hair fell out starting at about 12 years old, coming out in flocks and stranded and random hair.

They made him inferior all day, kept him distracted, they filled people destined in his life through their own projected timeline with spirits and voices, demons, and people stays long and far away from LK. He could not escape his past, even though Scotland Yard and British Intelligence tracked him down and told him to stay away from his past, that the people there were no good and that they were not friends of his nor family that he could consider worthy of being with and spending time amongst. And dwell with as mates, it would be impossible.

They kept a cloud steaming over his head, they looked at the maps and globes and books on the internet and followed him around and lit candles and said prayers and spoke through the vibrations and spoke to the devil and the gods and spirit warriors and Nephilim and fairies, elves, all kinds of otherworldly entities, the Martian enigma, the New Age channeling corporations and they kept yelling at God to protect him and lead him into their realms and it was deep magic eating his lif out in schizophrenia. He knows because they called him on the phone and told him that that is what they were doing without reservation and hesitation. And they did it religiously, and they did it every night.

And they called him up, yelled at him, threatened him, and spoke down to him and screamed at him and demanded he bring them crack rocks from Gale. And that he sells crack for Gale. And that he participates in the cult or that he would never see his family again, his sisters his brother, his cousins, his son his family that he never had, the friends of his he could reserve and preserve, were all going to go away. He had to stay in the family by dealing drugs and taking on the new drugs that were supposed to be coming in at some point to start the cult. And to do it correctly.

They would get a large number of people addicted to drugs and then they would sell some kids at holidays as a testament to corruption in society and the audacities of a commercialized government. To sing Christmas carols and buy expensive gifts while their families received the cheapest presents on the discount rack.

While they brag about their money, and buy expensive clothes and toys and games and gear for all the kids at the parties and have Easter Bunny and Santa suits and can hose the event down with cash and food, and all kinds of booze and expensive favors and party have brand new clothes and cars and houses, yet they do the illegal stuff as a sort of hobby as a favor to the government so they don't have to share territory and make very little money and just occupy the place with minimal traffic and they get to brag and practice mind control to be anti the government.

To rebel against the authority of government and democracy on the individual level, they sponsor a spiritual socialism, one that haunts and destroys, and eats in the fabric of one's mind and body through projections into their brain and their hearts and the electromagnetic frequency of their bodies and organs.

They practice an intense form of possession; where they intend to possess other people to get them to do as they want and say, and by projecting themselves as energy into the other people's minds and bodies to take hold of them and possess them with sickness to control them. Practicing control over other people will enter their subconscious through their brain as entering as energy and trying to manipulate themselves out of everyone's life as a target, so that other people will accept them, and they can begin to sneak into their lives and try to obtain relationships with those considered vulnerable. Women; and children mostly.

Nori follows those she likes to investigate and Marsha with those who will supply her with the power of being considered a metaphor in the Old Testament, or someone she can rake in a Christian pedophile, some way of warping the Bible or religion in the Christian worlds of interrelationships.

Trying to sleep with a preacher, having sex with a guy because his name was David and he reminded her of King David, Damian Keith reminded her of Jesus, and her boyfriend's prior were kids from the Boy Scout camp and her husband who was her high school sweetheart. And he married a woman named Martha just like Dennis married a woman named Johanna and divorced Joanna. Joanna kept her maiden name after all, and Marsha kept her married name and got really bitter and very angry. Maybe it was because she was listening to Bob Marley with a seven-dollar weave. Smoking crack with Marty Maher and the twins, smoking dope and hating that marijuana, calling it evil dope. Blaming marijuana for the evil their heart in their mindful thoughts and alone time. Scorning those and others at all costs.

Never mind that they pretended to love NBC programming their entire lives with their favorite shows starting at Cheers, Night Court, The Cosby Show, Friends, Seinfeld, and any other comedy the network was set to syndicate including Frasier and any other NBC comedy. This includes affiliate HBO where they pledged allegiance to the Sopranos as major fans and also the Matrix, which they use to outline the world in their minds and use their magic to fill the worlds that they envision to be a part of the Matrix in general, in life, but also to link to other people.

But what stuck out to people was their knowledge of technology but their inability to adapt to its use, and those who know them best know that they are using some form of psychic AI that is seemingly appearing in the physical world as an apparition and that people are drawn to dynamically anchoring everything it asks of them.

Big K and his family not only worship the spaceship and the mind control and the Babylonian gods because LK listened to Bob Marley, ate mushrooms, and read books from David Icke and they pretended to start a new religion. They are also pathological liars and were sold out too many for their role in extending the truth to include things that didn't happen and situations that never existed and they would do this in the recovery center where they would try to recruit people for Amway and for whatever other heinously cult they could imagine.

Two of Big K's friends both died as customers of Amway and those who participated in Mitch Miller singing events, where everyone would sing along to folk singer Mitch Miller. It doesn't end there, all those people wound up suffering heinous and violent deaths, but so did their wives and their kids, all of them. Dead. The couple who made it out of their relationship with Big Keith were also friends with enemies and other friends of his including some of his partners. Big Keith cheated on his wife with secretaries from his job with Marsha and Nori.

Gale pledged allegiance to infecting society with subliminal racism, she went at it and admitted to being a subliminal racist. Which she said was her way or the highway and everyone believed it because she bragged, she owned a house in NYC that was priced at over 100,000 which is nothing in NY, most places go for at least 400,000 at the minimum, but with full renovations, they could sell for $200,000.

Being that this woman lives in a place with three rooms on each floor and one and a half baths and she enjoys walking in the morning, working during the day, taking a shot or two, and watching TV until it's time to go to sleep… no one knows what her would have try to take over the drug trade. Someone who goes to bed at 10 pm every night and wants to control the trade as a dealer would probably need to live more of a protected lifestyle. The only excuse is that they identify with being from the ghetto, living in the projects, and moving up to the rich end of the hood as dealer guardians. Prospects growing up in that trade know that the family is in the league or monitored by the government for use of their psychic in a way that people from the news Scotland Yard, and the government noticed. And it put them under watch. Many believed they were just selling to their friends and trying to get a big shot at being famous, and even risking it in a gamble to run for president in some way.

In 2004, it was far-fetched that they could run a presidency, now in 2024 all of those people in that circular ring, have brought up families of their kids and grandkids, with their kids, all having multiple children, and everyone being given the same ultimatums.

Dealing some cracks, just a few blocks away from one of the most famous project houses in the world is a risky undertaking and everyone is surprised they can outlast others and the undertaker. And pledging allegiance physically to 'the black people' who are discussed at the evening hour discussions at Gale's place to whoever is standing by, and they are to know that Gale has friends and is protected by 'The Black People' in quotes, and she is very good friends with 'The Black People'. She follows her own set of rules on the streets. She gets to brag about her viewpoint and holds energy against others.

She is allowed and supposed to be rude and selfish and instigate a hypnotic form of schizophrenia with a subliminal form of racism to teach humanity to sweat her and buy from her and to give her power over the teachings of the cult and purposes of authority by the group. And she commands the drugs even the ones to be administered to the cult followers, who are scheduled to die. They were scheduled to die on a calendar.

Being fed a poison that they were to know most of them when it was time to die, and the teachers and masters were to acknowledge the event and to only serve their own cups and drink from their own cups that day and to have their own cup filled with Kool-Aid and rat poison and boric acid that would be used to wipe out the cult to recruit for a new membership.

The cult had ties in the sheriff's department, police forces, the low-level government, and Washington D.C. However, the group was put on alert due to PSA working against them and those aware of their projected attempt at mutiny.

The plans of this group and intentions as they stood were left to the whim of those involved dwelling in high places. It was exposed time and again by Damian and the Secret Service with help from the president which did not in any way include Donald Trump's cabinet but did include Obama, Biden, and Bush as well as support from the Clinton administration in the exposure of this very powerful and sophisticated plan, which is all that it was and is. It exists as a plan to take over and it is activated but not readily being enacted upon by the leaders and founders due to intervention from the press Scotland Yard and British Intelligence who have been detrimental in assisting in bringing this group to justice.

These goofy motherfuckers show their faces behind their shame, laughing at their guilt and developing a series of strokes against others, strategizing how to deviate from the punishments that await them, somewhere in eternity. They escape through a broken mirror and notify all of their wickedness, and those who are insulted scurry away, hurt and crucified, destitute to social activity for eons after their minds are scarred with the imprinted destruction of their wicked programming and winded manipulation of events through their intentions and their ability to tune into people's body's and try to manipulate them with their power gained from meditation.

Intentionally misusing teachings and instructions given to novice mystery school explorers and hinted at by religious freaks and scholars, adepts and the truths of the ancients are all a victim to the whim of these people and their way of grabbing and holding the energy that evokes the desire to ruin your life and use their form of drug at their specific time. Those whom they sell to, have to eventually live by certain criteria or they will get approached and taught lessons non-articulately and will face reprimand by the members of the cult when they see it fit to manipulate that event to manufacture circumstances and money.

It seemed like their only money came from either working legitimate jobs, freelancing doing construction, real estate, and related business practices, reporting and finance were the main jobs. There is a religious devotion to working a salary job for the city in particular, they don't mention the county or the federal government at all except if they work there, but there is a standard that besides demanding that someone do drugs and deal drugs when and where they say, they must also either live at home the entire time and never leave ever again, or they have to work one of these legitimate jobs. And this is the Ultimatum.

Epilogue

The beckoning of raising the soul above the status of head of state and chief crime lord and rising through the reputation of investigating the messiah and its connection to a new fleet of UAPs and the desolation of project Bluebeam within the psychic minds of their followers walking and working and dwelling outside and in the street.

The world comes down to sands in an hourglass, as they defend the right to use a public psychic. One that guarantees everyone involved in using it, receives the death penalty for looking through the eyes of Damian and all along for investigating Damian Light for being so deep in the forest, that the basketball players stealing his name thought it was a fake experience, of some spiritual renaissance, and that the world they filled a stadium in, was not filled with hypocrisy.

What they didn't tell them was that the forests around the world have become testing grounds, for new animal habitats and experiential and rarer breeds that have been transported and experimented on and then dropped off to breed within newer environments, that many would deem artificially influenced. This is in turn, due to its extremely low wild animal population, data gathered while civilization creeps in on these wilderness places. Leaving scientists and enthusiasts plenty of room to drop their bred animals off into the wild, in hopes of instigating new culture on the earth, in the form of natural kingdoms and animal villages near town.

So, the question looms in the air like the shitty gypsy resonance left over by Scots thrown out of the Catholic church and now hiding, pretending to be Irish, only to be thrown out of New York City and are now scouring the countryside of the east coast of the USA, looking to buy out lands and are creating new developments in newly developing towns and villages.

Places that were bought out and recently developed with low populations that have newer but still low populations.

They sit there witnessing, like puddles of shit assigned to be Watchers, posing themselves as true Babylonian worshippers, assigned as the necessary Nephilim, to keep tabs on their masters and follower. Those whom they teach and those whom they demand to learn from, are all victims to this selfish technology that they assume is newly engineered and sanctified by an ignorant CIA; who when they find out are using illegal psychic technology they hope will go along with the agenda and the plan or it is time to jump ship. When the cult decides that the followers should die because they used up their credits in metaphysics, they realize now that inflation would cause them to charge more money for rent on the farm.

They were organizing it for prices for such projects in the 1990s when Timberlands were still in style as more than just a work boot or camping accessory. Some winter clothing went a long way until these Gilbridge's as the telemarketers liked to call them, were resentful because they couldn't fit in with kids and teenagers after the 1980s. They lost their ability to be seen as hoodlums, troublemakers, and the center of attention by their neighbors family, and friends and had thus lost their keys to identity. They had to join a gang, do acid ditch school, and teach their kids that it was the right thing to do. It was just so happening for the luck of their kids that everyone realized that this behavior was out of the ordinary and refused to fall for the antics of the Gilbridge family.

Patrick was passing out threats to anyone who didn't fall in line with the family agenda and doing it in the name of Gale and Arlene and the other women of their cult, including his sister Karen. Who had little to do with the overall crime scheme of the family, yet she remained a top priority because of her anger and vulnerability to trying to gain status as a recruiter and a reputation as a crime lord by being head of knowledge and affairs of the community of outlaws now operating in several states and setting up shop in small towns in Delaware, Georgia, New Mexico and other spots in the south and Northeast.

As Karen plays guardian and recruiter, security for the exiled family hoping to make atonement in the church; at one of the Westchester universities and colleges she works at, hoping to guard her family's activities in deep hypnosis of shit cakes piled as psychic tubes and snakes coiled up into the atmosphere and the spatial circumferences near people's heads.

When people pull on this pile of shit tubes after seeing a vision of Karen in their heads for the ten trillionth times, they pull at the space as if they were pulling out their own hair and a whole barrel of shit patties and wet feces, shit napkins and shit cakes fall out of the mental arena, out of the etheric and astral realm leaning one to ask the questions that won may ask when the astral curtain gets up on its own and shits on one as they mind their own business.

People were intrigued about how to stay away from the O'Hanlon's resonating and vibrating into their heads and taking them over. So, instead of being hypnotized the followers in Damian's environment gave his mind over to the spell that the O'Hanlon's had requested, using the passerby in their psyche, in their head, in a form of telepathy. To destroy the limitations and mind of Damian Forest Light, his family created a spell to cast onto him. It was with voodoo and candles and astral projection and maps and all kinds of tokens and singing and chants to the gypsy god of voodoo.

They became spirits and could see other people through the eyes of the ancient Cosmic Energy and see the people in his environments as energy bubbles and then pour their mind into theirs by turning each of them into gas and light and dark energy and shadow to create a psychic and all the ancient teachings were warped into a new psychic.

To keep away from being hypnotized, the passersby would tap into Damian wherever they could tap into him through a subconscious wire and pipe his thoughts and energies back to the Gilbride and O'Hanlon to escape becoming a mind-controlled slave, A slave to the Ohanlon and Strasser Carty who were doing this voodoo and following him around with their minds while doing ceremoniously reptilian ceremony on weekend nights, including on late evening Sunday. Or Friday. Like losers.

Wasting a Friday night where they previously got stoned are now jumping at the ideology of drinking coffee all night and destroying swooping down on their enemies with the caffeine fitted for a vulture.

All over the world the cult had maps pinned on their walls and these people were making things complicated for Damian. They were volunteering to put their minds back to them, in a full circle filled with will and wire and energy and light just to destroy him in his place and where he walked and sat. They laughed and instead of helping the situation and turning in the family, people like passersby and Karen the psychic, she tried to become a part of it. Tried to match up to the rest of the crime lords. And now it was getting the attention of everyone near and far. Who could hear such a clatter? A burglar climbed down that old lady and her chimney stealing her Coca- Cherry- Cola.

The actress who was destroying and controlling the information all the while manipulating Damian Kieth's acting career was the producer at Hello Sunshine, whom everyone knew about. Never mind her childish way of getting a jock in her ass and she was now practicing their astral projection too. So much projection and magic that people would not sign Damian and make money off of him, she could dominate his income and residuals while disguising him as a government puppet and a snitch psychic.

This ability of him to create the illusion of being a deranged psychopath and a homeless person created the perfect analogy for him to practice his psyche operations and study human behavior. But no one was the wiser, except his family thought they didn't believe anything they heard mentally about him through their information channels, they knew it was real and turned out to be real in the end.

. They thought they had him beaten and destroyed his chances of becoming a professional actor, musical writer, and entertainer. They might have shut him down, but it gave him a reputation as a writer and a gonzo journalist, and people admired his work from afar. But no awards?

People wanted to know what the actress was doing with the family and if she was a criminal prostitute like them and was just fucking them and trying to get rich. Was she a superhero like she portrayed herself in the media or was she just a bloodthirsty money hungry disgusting, ridden gold digger?

Was she just handing out ass hole and hand jobs to any ole PA and looking for a quick buck or was she going to do the right thing mechanically for the brand of Damian Light? Reading his mind and destroying his every nerve ending and sensory perception inside the being's mind because he was an island that helped them escape the hypnosis that they invited it, that the Gilbrides offered them as an escape. The mystical mists of Scotland and the O'Hanlon as it remembers the boats it sailed away on once and for all from its' motherland of Scotland.

The mists are now infected with horrors that sprawl across the towns inhabited by the imaginations of New

England horror writers. Those deadly fogs crawl into people's minds and pipe Patrick into Damian's mind and reverse his thoughts and his perceptions into people's minds all around the world, in a big, huge carnival type of astral projection, where Patrick has the last laugh even though Little Keith didn't give his ass up to him for molestation and poppy cock.

The followers gave up their minds for the experience of escaping the simultaneous hypnosis that the actress and the pedophile mind-controlled slaves of the cult poured into them through doll-like tubes where they put messages in bottles and sent them around the world to eat the minds of their superficial followers.

Filling his messiah job with the antics of Patrick's imagination, Lisa, and his family design an intricate schizophrenia through a projected strategy of mind control and hypnosis into his mind. He is not allowed to say no to the job as messiah or to his assignment of helping Aunt Arlene with the family auctions and the entertainment at the Halloween party. Christmas is his time to relax with the family and he was asked to take part in the Easter auction, a party he did not show up to normally.

Though his mind was broadcast to millions of psychic followers none of them were curious enough to look or listen to his work online or stream his message in his videos or documentaries, outside of the small social media following he had.

And for that, he was thankful that some people were interested in his work on some level.

The record companies had promised great things, lots of label representation and commercial radio and movie as well as television gigs, commercials, and advertisements, and lots of supply in the record manufacturing plants. Whole shelf and tabloid and spokesperson endorsements. Lots of plugs and loads of albums.

Production albums, remixes, mixed CDs, various genre mix tapes, special appearances, lots of guests, lost catalogs, encyclopedias, gift boxes, and collector edition sets of music. Never mind whatever else they wanted to evenly put together in the entertainment industry. Ancillary products and the like all across the board. But the actress threatened him out of his family.

No, the music industry was hexed by a witch, and they threw him out. No, but they asked him to turn around and leave without question the night it went under. The night they called the meeting and pulled the plug, Damian was with Paulie in Staten Island at the Rotary club where Gale gets her awards and gains some of her clients.

They threw the fucker out for celebrating and Paulie told him that they were shutting the doors to the music group and the Tower stores were closing. And they had nowhere to go. No one would buy them. Wiz and Goody were gone, the two biggest stores in the five boroughs of NYC and they were also going along with the likes of Virgin and Circuit City.

While in NY radios and music still lived on the underground, everywhere else, the lights turned out at all the dance clubs and the record stores were on Clearance. Blockbuster didn't sell radios and music and Circuit City didn't sell movies and video cameras. They needed something more, and they had to sell out their models due to the influences of digital manufacturing.

While Circuit City genuinely went out during the peak of the recession, the owners at Tower went under because they assumed their books would sink below the profit margin with the influx of digital streaming and downloading which was big at the time. Instead of trying to adapt to the digital marketplace, they assumed that the construction of a web page or based market was out of the question and were unfamiliar with transitioning and mixing the format from digital CD to digital MP3 or WAV file.

They assumed that the companies who adapted the files already were going to succeed and take over the music industry as recording giants just like Tower and Virgin had done since their inception. Everyone was making money off of recording new artists and selling them to new labels and up-and-coming music executives who wanted good talent. The record stores were reviewing artists who were inquiring about selling their CDs and LPs and were always signing new talent to make profits directly without having to rely on income generated from retail sales.

The production of a new artist generating lots of sales would put the label's end of profiteering at their jurisdiction instead of passing it out to a competitor. After a little bit of trust and money and following was established by the team of artists and producers, the retail-based label would sign a major label over to the artist's affairs.

While Paulie told Damian that he had premonitions of working with D. Unknown and knew that he was the real McCoy, even though they had never met, people started flooding into Damian's mind in some sort of schizophrenia where the Gilbride magic was enabling everyone who passed him by to partake in the telepathy that they had assigned for him.

And he combatted it with all sorts of various retaliations from whisking energy and voices and lights back to the people passing by knowing his business and flexing their psychic, to threatening them with his mind or sending their minds and heart energies to the astral or physical cops and law enforcement.

He was having attacks in his mind all day with people reading his thoughts and he was being laughed at as Patrick and Gale practiced Voodoo on him continuously all day long. Always copying his thoughts and repeating his business back to him in a rubber band made of magic. and his thoughts and experiences were miserable. He threw eggs at Patrick's business and threatened to kill everyone at Gale's parties. Shane started writing letters to the Rolling Stone pleading. With them to forgive Damian Keith for his schizophrenia even though he told them what they were all up to.

The people on the street looking through his mind in remote viewing he promised to never stop remote viewing as long as they felt compelled to do so and remain with his asshole with a dick of telepathy and to destroy his barriers to limitations and self-preservation they would make fun of him to initiate his life into a celebrity spirality.

then farther along into a spiritual brotherhood of celebrities but he managed to convince the gangs of the world to kidnap everyone who said his name aloud to themselves for no reason and to torture every one of them and to treat them as an active and avid threat of their organizations.

The psychic grew all over the world until millions of people had themselves and their family and friends tied up and kidnapped. If you talk psychic to him, he is allowed to have you kidnapped and to torture you now. And ask you how you know his name. Why you are a CIA escape artist psychic with a need to know his business. And the government gains authority over the eavesdropping of his business in your mind with your electrode radio eating his pattern of thought and activity and behavior and into your brain and eye and capillary cavity and third eye and how everyone watched him, supposedly while he wired the CIA and the government back into everyone's mind for breaking his Constitutional rights as a US citizen.

Everyone hoping to get famous off of particle worship and astral projections of themselves and their favorite artists and energies and gimmicks and social signals and using it as a combined culture to dominate people's attention and take focus away from their own lives and their inadequacies and materialistic tendencies. As a crutch, people and superstars were dependent on his authority in the spiritual realms and over the domains of common-sense street rank and ingenuity.

They believed he had a million followers in music and his books and therefore he was rich, and they had the right since he was white and from the streets of NYC that they had the right due to not liking whites that he was abused and allowed to entertain them through a psychic for free. And he threatened to blow people on the streets brains out and at the store and started snapping and going mad. The psychics wanted their heads splattered. Always nosy and demanding to satisfy their psychic needs for psychic tabloid story and they wanted his story in their heads fusing with their energy like vampires. But yet he had no followers. and no friends. And no fans anymore. He had no representation other than the actress who manipulated and handled him into insanity.

They were dependent on the messages they were receiving from him and his life. The activities he was committing made people believe that there was an imitation and cosmic or mental entertainment industry. They were faltering in their covenant with God and with life and following after a false messiah using telepathy given to them by the Gilbride angels. Always going forward with two steps and then taking ten steps backwards, relating God to the gods in the telepathic and then astral realms interconnecting people in a psychic New Age wire, a tube that coordinates. Being satisfied with calling voices and psychics as a hail of the Devil, they moved forward blindly attributing all social energy to him as if he needed their sacrifice to a cultural stagnation of sociability and normality. A creed to stay mundane.

He assumed they had become codependent on his energy and they were continuously caught by him and anyone else, as using their psychic awareness as a satisfaction for psychological needs and a supplement for physiological demands. They were assumed to achieve this satisfaction through the simulation of relationship and communication and by supplementing actual interaction with subliminal and subconscious telepathic tendencies and relationship signals and patterns. It is a compulsion and an obsession that deteriorates the mind and brain function.

This causes the hypnosis to wander through the skin and saturate all the pores. And follow suit as the blind rage takes over the pawn and they hunt down the puppet master thirsting to cause pain and granting them until they inflict an influx of torture onto their riddled and old minds, their young plagiarized and used flesh. They got stamps on their asses and their arms, looking at everyone as if they had something wrong with them and they were just doing something right. For enough money, she likes sucking some producer's blood as they strangle his little Jew prick with their tongues and wipe it clean with a Kleenex and walk out making the studios a little bit richer; even though they needed a name, and they gave it to a rookie after that cock proved lame and unprofitable. Sickness devoured those sons of bitches and they never saw the end coming.

Coming up their asses even as the whore blew a fart, she could still feel it riding up in there, making her moan and weave. Now wait, she needed a fix. A fucken fix. And who would provide this? Would it be through energy or horror within a world that sees life through the death of a junkie?

Through the goy vision of a movie star, straddled within the mind as hypnosis sucking the coke out of a cocoa cock, making the most of the Pandora box that they have opened... instead of wasting the cult away, the cult wastes the world away and all day long as they enrapture themselves in the sexual visions of deep fake astral AI-generated images.

What an ultimatum. And what a path to extraordinary success in the world of business enterprise. It only takes a little bit of effort and a wool turtleneck along with a keen Halloween costume to keep things going in the country's business sectors. It is a miracle to pull it all off. Dealing with the Soma, while effortlessly working regular jobs and hoping to deal a better solution to the planet. Doling out drugs to the world, all the while dealing kids to the highest bidder, and selling out seats to a '90s commemoration into the world of a suicidal afterlife and the messianic hopes of seeing a mothership before everyone dies in the land, bought by some banker who collected everyone's dues and lived with his kids in a small house in the rich part of Brooklyn.

Woah, the American Dream is at its pinnacle. And at its most exposed and embarrassing. Going to all odds and ends of the universe hoping to score money on a literal vat of Kool-Aid. Your parents just purchased you a getaway at Club Strasser.

A one-way ticket to outer space.

Having telepathic orgasm-based conversations with one another, the passerby flirted with impending death. Having been willed into impending doom. Plugging him into a cellular mental microphone depleting his chest and infiltrating the ear drums and third eyes of children everywhere. All seeing eyes following his every move telling on him and sharing his personal information to flex personal power over him through a psychic being threatened... as this was a never-ending stress in the angry vibrations of provoking Damian to violence to worship the Devil in his mind... and his heart... and the struggle to overcome these influences of these magical forces and people.

Pretending to defend Christ with the voices of the Devil in his heart. Made him into a brainwashed subject that lurks to destruction at any given cost. He had no mercy on the psychics who wanted the right and freedom to share their social knowledge of Damian and his relation to LK, and the right of the struggling psychic to find a loophole in his thoughts, brought out the desire to maim women and followers and leave them dead in street, bleeding out from their sarcasm. Leaving them dead like Jack the Ripper. That gave him pleasure, even though he was a good guy writer. They should have just sucked his dick and shut the fuck up. Dumb bitches.

Now you can call your friends from the Afterlife and tell them all about how black magic brought you one step closer to the Pleiades on a mothership. May your family rest in peace as they wander brainwashed on earth while you make your way to a whole new concept of paradise. Bon Voyage and Adios muchachos. Send me a postcard. Follow to dot the I's and wipe those lenses cheek. Cyborg trap.

☺ Dane

www.ingramcontent.com/pod-product-compliance
Lightning Source LLC
Chambersburg PA
CBHW050800260726
48660CB00004B/1178